CLEM

CHRIS THOMAS

Iponymous Edition
First edition published in 2018
By iponymous publishing Limited
Swansea United Kingdom SA6 6BP

A CIP record for this book is available from the British Library

Cover photographs © Chris Thomas
Cover design @ GMID Ltd

ISBN 978-1-908773-84-5

www.iponymousmedia.com

I dedicate this book to the memory of my father Clem, and to my daughters Hywelis and Siwan.

CONTENTS

ACKNOWLEDGMENTS

Dad died in September 1996, and this book's genesis came from the realisation that he had died too soon, and before he had the chance to chronicle his rich and varied life that seemed to consist of a never ending series of anecdotes.

As a family, we have sat around the Christmas table and shared many family events where the "CLEM" stories would be trotted out. Finally when I was convalescing at my sister Caroline's home, following my cardiac arrest, she would be amazed at my elephantine memory, as I recalled precise details about our grandparents and early years. So early in 2017, I was strongly encouraged to take on the daunting prospect of being my father's biographer. This book would never have gotten written without the heartfelt support and corroboration of my Mum Ann, sister Caroline, brothers Greg and Mark, and huge encouragement from my daughters, Hywelis and Siwan, and nephew Tom.

I am fortunate in having a literary agent and publisher in Tim Prosser of Iponymous who has provided unstinting support and advice to this novice writer.

One of my oldest friends who shared a study with me in Blundells, and who has made a successful career in sports and rugby writing is Rob Cole who owns Westgate Sports Agency in Cardiff. Rob shared a press box with Clem, and has been my consiglieri during the writing and prepping of this book, providing professional advice and huge encouragement to my efforts.

I have received a warm reception and support wherever I have gone to seek knowledge or clarity from friends and ex-colleagues of Clem. In particular I would like to thank Gareth Edwards for his lovely nostalgic memory of Dad roaming around Gwaen-Cae-Gurwen in the late 1950s, Barry John, Peter Jackson, Simon Kelner,

Mavis Nicholson, Rosemary Crosse and Ann Young in
Dublin, Paul Ackford, Len Roberts, Rob Davies, Geoff
Vaughan in Auckland, and his son Justin, Chris Richards,
his Serene Highness Prince Albert of Monaco, Stephen
Jones, Peter and Elizabeth Stead, Simon Jones my cousin,
Eddie Butler, my aunt Liz Jones , my step brother Mark
Portsmouth, and his uncle Donald Portsmouth, Steve
Hamer, Alban Moga from Bordeaux, Paul and Ace Lewis,
Bill Hughes, Phil John, Bernadette Damitio in Biarritz,
Stephanie Damitio in London, Ann-Sophie Damitio in
Paris and The Mumbles Ale House . Also the PUC
connection, Jonathan Stuart, Dominique Autier, Lionel
Rossigneux, Pierre-Michel Bonnot, Pierre Anglade,
Antoine Boucherie and The Bedford Arms.

PREFACE BY GARETH EDWARDS
THE AMMAN VALLEY'S LOCAL HERO

Sometimes you have to think a few moments to capture the right words with which to accurately sum-up a person. Yet whenever I'm asked to describe Clem Thomas there is one phrase that comes immediately to mind – "Local Hero". When I was growing up in Gwaun-Cae-Gurwen there was little or no sport on TV, even fewer televisions in the village, no iPhones, Tablets or internet to flood the mind with images and information. We lived off myth, legend and word of mouth. And when it came to Clem, the myths and the legends abounded and were larger than almost anyone else. He was the man who had put in the cross-kick for Ken Jones' try that helped Wales beat the All Blacks in Cardiff in 1953. He had gone on a British & Irish Lions tour, had his appendix removed and still helped the test team share one of the greatest of all series'. He was captain of club and country and, so we heard, 'a bit of a handful' on the field. All the kids in the village knew about this great 'demi god' that lived in Brynamman. He was a larger than life character to us and when his car drove along the A4069 to his butchers shop less than two miles away we would all rush to take a look. I remember one day he stopped at the local shop and we all saw him standing there. He was using his Barbarians tie to hold up his trousers! That's the sort of swaggering style and dash you came to expect from a local boy who turned out so very, very well. Not just a Welsh international and British Lion, but a public schoolboy who went on to graduate from

Cambridge University. There was so much success to celebrate in the Thomas household, but it was also success that motivated, inspired and enthralled so many of us in his locality. He kicked down the doors that so many people felt were closed to them, marched through confidently and met the world head-on. All I ever saw of Clem as a player were a few fleeting glimpses of those grey and grainy Pathé News clips in the cinema. His career came to an end just as I began to make the pilgrimage to Cardiff to watch Wales play. But he was obviously some player! I eventually got to know him as my career developed on and off the field. He became a much respected rugby writer at The Observer who we all delighted in spending time with on tours with both Wales and the Lions. There was something quite special about being in the company of players-turned-journalists such as Viv Jenkins, Cliff Morgan and Clem. We knew they had been in our shoes, respected their opinions and loved having a beer with them. When I hung up my boots and began working for the BBC I used to look forward to going on Five Nations trips with Wales. A visit to Paris would often mean a long, leisurely lunch on the banks of the Seine with Clem and his great friend Peter Robbins, the former Oxford University and England back row forward. The wine would flow, the stories never stopped and the sheer conviviality of the occasion always made it an afternoon, and invariable early evening, to cherish. That was Clem – a great host, great player, great writer and someone who lived his life to the full. But, to me and everyone else in the Amman Valley, he was always our 'Local Hero'.

Gareth Edwards

CLEM

1

REMEMBRANCE EVER GREEN

Pan deimlodd fyned ymaith Dduw
Cyfododd gledd I ladd ei frawd;
Mae swn yr ymladd ar ein clyw,
A'i gysgod ar fythynnod tlaw.

When he thought God was gone at last
He put his brother to the sword.
The din of battle fills the ear,
And invades the homes of poor mothers.
Hedd Wyn

Its 4pm Saturday, 19 December 1953. There are five minutes left to play. The score is Wales 8, New Zealand 8, and the 58,000 crowd is roaring at the men in red to deliver the coup de grace. Wales had drawn level with a dubious penalty following long periods of All Black forward and territorial domination, but now Wales are fast moving left on the All Black 25 yard-line, Cliff Morgan chips the ball forward, and the ball goes loose. Suddenly it is scooped up by an accelerating Welsh wing-forward who raises the ball above his head and appears to dummy an inside pass to the supporting Bleddyn Williams. But in a whirl and turn Rudolph Valentino would have been proud of, Clem Thomas spins to his right, and punts an enormous right foot kick infield towards the New Zealand goal posts. For a split second the world freezes. Fifty-eight thousand spectators hold their breath as the ball falls back to earth. It splits the only two players remaining on the Welsh right flank of play. Ron Jarden, the New Zealand wing cannot get near the catch, and can only watch as the Welsh Olympic sprinter, Ken Jones accelerates onto the ball's trajectory. The ball ricochets off its point being an oval it bounces high and heads straight into his welcoming hands, Jones veers elegantly with perfect balance inside Jarden to touch down emphatically between the posts.

Cue bedlam, as Cardiff Arms Park goes berserk, tens of thousands of hats and caps are flung into the air in every direction. The try is converted and Wales win 13-8.

This magical moment became known as the Clem Thomas cross kick. The legend of the historic win and that particular play is reinforced by the stunning reality that it was the last time Wales beat the All Blacks, a statistic that constantly induces head shaking and bouts of national introspection and self-doubt.

Clem Thomas is my Dad and he sadly passed away in September 1996. Whilst this is one of the moments in his life that most Welsh rugby folk are familiar with - and I have no doubt that it was always one of his best rugby exploits - it did not define his career or indeed his life because there was so much more. It only sets him apart as a player of immense competition and uncompromising physicality who went on to win 26 caps for Wales over 11 years from 1949 to 1959.

During this period he captained Wales on nine occasions. He toured with the British Lions to South Africa in 1955, where despite having his appendix removed, he played in the final two tests, a series that was ultimately drawn 2-2.

This book is a journey through the last 70 years of the

twentieth century as experienced by Clem, who used his rugby fame to open up various opportunities for himself. He painted his own rich canvass: whether in journalism as the Chief Rugby Correspondent of *The Observer* newspaper, a Liberal Parliamentary candidate, an entrepreneur from a small farm in Brynamman, a father of four children, or a bon viveur. He encountered many interesting people from different walks of life. Idi Amin, the late Ugandan dictator, looked after the British Lions' playing kit in Kenya in 1955. The self-styled 'Conqueror of the British Empire in Africa and Uganda in Particular' swore that 40 oranges a day gave him 'sex power' and had lots of wives as testament. Amin's infectious laugh and sense of humour kept the tourists in good spirits throughout the tour. Clem's great friend Tony O'Reilly hosted a supper for Nelson Mandela at the Rugby World Cup in 1995, and the legendary 'Father of the Nation' insisted on being introduced to his hero, Clem Thomas. This is his story…

R.C.C. Thomas, christened Richard Clement Charles Thomas was known throughout his life as Clem, an abbreviated version of Clement. To my knowledge my grandparents never referred to him as anything other than Clem, and there is a sad family story at the heart of this. We are currently in the middle of the centenary of the First World War, and the scale of the slaughter that saw 956,703 British Army and Empire personnel killed in action left few British families unaffected. By 1916, British casualties were so great that new draconian conscription laws were enacted by Parliament, with Lord Kitchener given the task of enforcing them.

The village of Brynamman was once known as Gwter Fawr. It earned the name from a large gutter formed into the rock by early coal mining at the start of the 1800s. Brynamman sits at the very top of the Amman Valley on the south-facing side of the Black Mountain, part of the Brecon Beacons National Park. There is a magical road that goes over the mountain to Llangadog, that climbs and climbs until you cross a brow, turn the corner and there, spread out before you is the rich Towy Valley, a gorgeous romantic landscape worthy of any Canaletto or Constable.

Brynamman lies in Carmarthenshire, whose recruiting sergeant was duly obliged to visit my great-grandmother, Margaret Thomas and essentially give her the "Sophie's Choice", the no-win option of having to select one of her two sons, David or Clement to join up under Kitchener's conscription programme.

She chose Clement, the eldest son, which meant David had to remain and run the farm and butchery business.

Born in 1899, Clement enlisted on March 5th, 1917, and was attached to the 14th Battalion, Welch Regiment. The Swansea Pals who had been in France since 1915 were subsequently attached to 114 brigade, 38th Welsh Division, which had famously captured Mametz Wood in July, 1916. By August 1917, the division had captured Pilcken Ridge at Ypres, which is where Clement joined them. During the winter of 1917-18 the division was based near Armentieres, and it was here that Clement was killed by a shell from friendly fire, dying from "accidental injuries", on 28 January 1918.

Naturally, this was a devastating blow to the Thomas family, particularly galling because Clement was killed by a British, and not a German shell. As a fitting memorial "Clement" was added to my Dad's name, and "Clem" became the name by which he was most commonly known following his birth on January 28, 1929, a spooky coincidence that hints maybe the Gods were watching us on this occasion.

The headline in *The Amman Valley Chronicle* and *East Carmarthen News* for 7th February 1918 reads: "BRYNAMMAN SOLDIER KILLED. Private Thomas was a strapping young soldier, and generally liked by his comrades." The article quoted a letter of condolence sent to my great-grandmother by the Platoon Commander:

> "It will, perhaps, be of some consolation to you to know that your son's death was instantaneous and that he suffered no pain at all, although I am sure that this cannot repay you for your great loss. Although I have been in charge of the platoon your son was attached to for a few weeks, I am pleased to say that I always found him a good and obedient soldier, and I should like to express to you the most heartfelt sympathy of his comrades and myself." *H.M. Moorson.*

The War Memorial in Brynamman is situated at Station Road at the bottom of Brynamman hill, and is almost directly opposite Brynamman Rugby Club, a club whose precise origins have been lost in the mists of time, but who nevertheless celebrated a centenary season in 1997, despite local newspapers making no mention of any Brynamman rugby until 1903. If you make the short journey across the road from the War Memorial to the rugby club you will stumble upon an immediate link between my granduncle, Clement, and Clem my father. A colour photograph adorns the left-hand seating area depicting an 18 year old Clem captaining the Welsh Schoolboys against France in 1947. The rugby club became Clem's spiritual home for a period in the mid-1940s, the club having restarted in the aftermath of war when there was a strong resurgence of sport in general. Brynamman was granted official Welsh Rugby Union status in 1921.

Clem was the second child of Dai John and Edna Thomas. Dai John was referred to as DJ all his life and was tasked with running the family butcher business under the watchful eye of Margaret, his mother. Edna came from a family in Port Talbot: her father had been a ship's purser, travelling the world out of Port Talbot and Cardiff docks,

16

and she worked at the Queen's Hotel in Cardiff during the 1920s - a thoroughly modern Millie with ambition and drive. Clem was born in Cardiff, four years after the birth of his older sister, Margaret. Family legend has it that Edna did not approve of the midwifery arrangements in the Amman Valley. There were complications with Clem's birth and he was born with a club foot, which might explain why he was born in Cardiff, and not Brynamman or Ammanford.

DJ and Edna returned promptly to live and work in Brynamman. Their hard work paid dividends and in the 1920s DJ bought 'Bryn Farm' located at the very top of Bryn Road where the black tarmac strip disappears into the Black Mountain, and the end of the world begins. At that time DJ had opened up a new butcher's shop in Cwmgors, near Gwaun-Cae-Gurwen, where the four members of the burgeoning Thomas family sought happy prosperity in difficult times. The local coal industry was in decline and mining communities were suffering the brunt of the Great Depression. The devastating situation in the early 1930s, with many mines closed or idle due to trade depression, created great hardship for vast numbers of unemployed. Many simply left the district, with a mass exodus of young people to London or Birmingham and Rugby. Clem would follow this migration himself in the 1950s when he took himself off to Coventry, albeit to play for the leading club in England at that time, Coventry Rugby Football Club, whilst working for the brake manufacturer, Mintex.

In 1929, despite the difficult trading conditions, the young family decided to branch out and open a butcher's shop in Cardiff. Edna had family in the city and knew the area well. A tragedy had a major bearing on the decision. In 1932 three years after Clem's birth his sister Catherine Margaret sadly passed away. The five-year-old complained of stomach pains and quickly died of Peritonitis. Edna was obviously grief-stricken and a product of her devastation

was to reject her new born baby, Clem. She refused to
have anything to do with him and a wet nurse, Marie
Joseph from Cwmgors, was employed to look after him.
DJ took the unhappy but pragmatic decision to remain at
the farm whilst Edna managed the new shop in Cardiff.
The move allowed her the opportunity to seek solace and
support from her family in Cardiff. Amazingly, this state of
affairs lasted a good five years, before Edna finally
returned home to the family retreat at Bryn Farm. Clem
was by that stage attending Cwmgors Junior School and
his unruly behaviour had become an issue of concern. The
reunited mother and son experienced major teething
problems. The root cause seemed to be Clem's total
rejection of any authority or discipline. My grandmother
would often tell me that Clem was prone to rampaging up
and down Station Rd like a wild dervish, hurling rocks at
windows, ignoring any admonishment and getting into
daily fights and scrapes. It was decided to curtail his
behaviour by sending him to Bryntirion Preparatory
School in Bridgend, where his contemporaries included the
future Tory Chancellor, Sir Geoffrey Howe and Bill
Edwards, later Secretary of Glamorgan County Cricket
Club.

Bill became a lifelong friend of Clem, operating his
legendary, ramshackle sport shop 100 yards from St
Helen's rugby and cricket ground. The close friendship
was tested to the limits in the late 1950's when Clem set
fire, supposedly accidently, to Bill's stock of fireworks and
burned down the shopfront. Bill was a legendary character
in and around the greater Swansea area, a very funny man,
with enormous energy and enthusiasm which he brought
to bear in his own unique style of customer service. He
discovered that I was due to go to Antigua for my
honeymoon in 1994 and I was summoned "for a quiet
word". I embarked on my honeymoon with an enormous
brown parcel which I duly delivered, as instructed, to the
then West Indian cricket captain Richie Richardson in St

John's. It contained the West Indian caps for the Test series. Later that night at dinner, in one of the most exclusive hotels in Antigua, I was astonished to find the butter came from Evan Davies, a famous butter manufacturer from Mumbles, courtesy of Bill's banana boat trading. The next day, we helped erect the practice nets which Bill had belatedly dispatched, also delivered via his banana boat special.

My earliest memories of Brynamman and my grandparents are intrinsically woven into the daily rhythm of life at Brynamman House, Station Rd. In the 1960s, being the first-born of Clem's four children, I would be summarily sent each school holiday to stay with Nana puff-puff and Daddad. The name Nana puff-puff originated due to her disciplined approach to potty training. I would be put on a potty in the bedroom, at a time which always seemed to coincide with the passing of a steam train at the cutting at the bottom of the garden. I delivered Nana puff-puff in an efficient, Pavlovian manner, and bestowed a tradition which my siblings were then obliged to follow. Unfortunately for my two younger brothers, Mark and Greg, the railway cutting was ripped up in the mid-1960s, and my grandmother lost her puff-puff legend.

Brynamman in the 1960's was a rich canvas, a sunlit world of warmth and joy. Even now I can recall the rich, visceral smell of the slaughter house, a mix of cow shit and blood, the Aga-infused warmth of Nana's kitchen and a constant and inexhaustible supply of Welsh cakes, chocolate eclairs, creamy, yellow scrambled eggs, sweetbreads fried in butter, puddings and cakes, everything a young lad like me could ever want.

The working week had a regular rhythm to it; we went to Llandeilo on Mondays, and sometimes Carmarthen (the auctioneers would stagger the auction times to allow the cattle dealers time to travel from auction to auction). Tuesday occupied pride of place in mid-week as my grandparents' grand day out. We generally attended two marts in St Clears and Whitland, with St Clears primarily selling lambs, and a larger cattle-stock ring in Whitland. The day punctually began at 6am in the Slaughter house up on Bryn road where my father would arrive to weigh out and load the delivery lorry that took the lamb and pig carcasses plus the forequarters and hinds of beef to the DJ Thomas butcher shop customers, between Brynamman and Swansea. By 9.30, we would congregate in the kitchen where breakfast was waiting. Then, piling into my Grandfather's Oxford Cambridge, with the plush red leather, squeaky seats, we would set off for St Clears.

With the journey underway we would invariably stop at a couple of pubs. I vaguely remember Auntie Millisent who ran The Dynevor Arms in Penybanc, en route to Llandeilo, because of the fascinating beer skittles room, and then onto The Fox and Hounds in Bancyfelin on the A40 between Carmarthen and St Clears. This is the home of the two Llanelli and Wales players, Jamie and Jonathan Davies, the first an outstanding silver Olympic medal winning sevens specialist, his brother a British Lion test series winner in Australia. In West Wales, rugby genetics possess a holistic presence wherever you go.

Clem would travel independently ahead of our more leisurely caravan, and once Nana puff-puff had met up with Dan Evans' wife - Dan was a cattle dealing friend of DJ in Capel Dewi - she would disembark to go Christ knows where, whilst myself, Dad, and DJ would get to St Clears in time for them to get into the Butchers Arms for a couple of swift ones (normally Bells whisky or Teachers). I would leave them to their refreshments and seek out Bryn, our animal transporter driver, who I used to spend the bulk of the days with, marking each pen of lambs, pigs, bullocks, or cows sold by DJ Thomas & Sons Ltd. I used to take great pleasure in noting the weight, number, and price on an auction tally card. Indeed, my records became so accurate, that over time my grandmother, who was responsible for the books, started to rely on them ahead of the official auctioneer notices!

At the end of the auction, Bryn and I would load the double decker cattle wagon with the daily take, identified either by one straight line of purple marker pen down the forehead (for lambs and pigs), or a triple clip by scissors removing 3 lines of hair from the top of the left hind leg of the cattle and calves. In the 1960s the markets processed hundreds of animals every day, and establishing the owner's identification was crucial, this was Clem's personal signature in the markets of Wales. We would drive the load back to Brynamman, unloading the animals into the holding pens to await slaughter over the coming days. That allowed Nana and Daddad to take their time leisurely wending their way home to Brynamman.

One of my earliest memories is the occasion my Dad was unable to persuade DJ to leave the Butchers Arms. I recall our car drawn up haphazardly outside the pub, and venturing timidly into the dense cigarette and pipe fug. I witnessed the both of them having a blazing row. DJ was holding court, surrounded by a group of farmers, dressed in long brown cattle coats, holding gnarled sticks in one hand and glasses in the other. The centuries old drovers' culture encapsulated for a brief moment in St Clears. The predominant tipple was whisky or rum with milk. Modern antacids had yet to be invented, and these old boys had to rely on other stratagems to manage their acid reflux tendencies. Dad was unable to prise DJ away from the bar and left the pub in a real temper. I remember him stood outside the door fuming, he turned to me and said:

"Right, get back in there and tell your Grandfather

you have to get to Whitland. Tell him you've promised Bryn you'd help load some calves. Make sure and tell him it's you that wants to go, and whatever you do, don't mention me."

I duly did as instructed and DJ left the bar like a lamb. DJ was not a big man, but powerfully built like a scrum half, and was double jointed at the hip - his suppleness meant he got away with murder in the 1960s, prior to the introduction of the breathalyser. Indeed, his cousin Tyddir had got away with involuntary manslaughter in the 1930s, when, after a lock-in at the Glanamman Arms, he gave a lift to three police officers who constituted the entire labour force of Amman Valley constabulary. They decided at midnight to drive the cattle wagon to Glanamman hospital in the hope of scrounging a cup of tea from the pretty nurses on duty. Tragically, on the return journey, Tyddir drove the wagon off the road, smashing down the railway embankment. The entire Amman Valley police force was wiped out at one fell swoop.

When my Dad moved the family to live in Swansea the phone would often ring at 11.00pm at night. The call would inevitably be from either Carmarthen or Llandeilo police station. The desk sergeant would always gravely inform my Dad that they were holding DJ in custody due to his state of sobriety. DJ was a colourful, powerful character who was as well known for his cattle dealing as for being the father of one of Wales's most recent rugby captains and legends. The officer on duty always expressed concern about DJ's fitness to drive himself anywhere, inevitably followed by an earnest and frank discussion about the state of Welsh Rugby. The desk sergeant would then ask my Dad to come and collect his Father from the cells. Upon arrival my dad would often be informed by the police that DJ had miserably failed a series of physical tests and was being charged with drunk-driving. But as soon as DJ caught sight of Clem he would instantly sober up. Clem used to instruct him to stand on one leg and raise first his right foot to his mouth and kiss it, swiftly followed suit by the left foot. My Dad would then turn to the officers on duty and say, "Good luck proving it in court."

However, around 1968, the phone rang late one evening and Dad left the house ashen faced. Carmarthen police informed my Dad that DJ had forced a police car off the road and assaulted two officers. Upon arrival at Carmarthen, Dad found the police prosecuting solicitor, Roger Thomas, in attendance. "This is very serious tonight Clem. There can be no more fucking around kissing feet…" I later learned that DJ had been weaving all over the road, and not only through drink - diabetes was beginning to blind him. The pursuing police had been forced off road and into a ditch, closely followed by DJ. Both officers tried to extricate him from the car, but he stubbornly refused to let go of the steering wheel. Once they had managed to prise his fingers from the wheel, DJ went berserk wildly lashing out at the arresting officers. DJ landed some mean blows, he was a hard man. Being the owner of a slaughter house, he was used to keeping order by means beyond Harvard management techniques. Dad told me that a slaughter man once pulled a knife on DJ and quick as a flash, he grabbed a sharpening steel and felled his aggressor with a mighty blow between the eyes. The reality of running a slaughter house in West Wales during the Great Depression was far from rosy.

My Dad had no other option than to try and broker a deal with the police to avoid serious charges being brought. After a great deal of debate he finally managed to persuade them to drop all charges in return for a cast iron guarantee that DJ would never drive a car again and all financial damages would be paid in full. DJ subsequently acquired a designated driver, John Gwynn, a distant cousin who became both chauffeur and minder to the end of his days.

The one major life experience that I shared with my Dad was the shock of being despatched at the tender age of 8 to a so called preparatory school. Bryntirion in Bridgend for Dad, Abermad in Aberystwyth for me, followed for us both by a public school, Blundells in Tiverton. In general, I believe that in the eras we both went to these schools we benefited from the emphasis placed on sporting traditions and achievements, because it was at Bryntirion that Clem first began to display his freakish ability to master the various skills required to play rugby football at the very highest level.

It was far from easy for my Dad. He had to battle the deformity of a club foot, with one leg shorter than the other. A consultation with Dr Nathan Rocyn Jones, later to become President of the Welsh Rugby Union, and its Hon. Surgeon, resulted in the leg being kept in splints and callipers for over a year, supported by built up shoes. So successful was the treatment that, always games mad, he captained the school at soccer and was vice-captain at rugby. My Dad always credited his sports master at Bryntirion for this early success, who encouraged him, inducted the discipline of regular training sessions, and devised special exercise regimes to build up the wasted muscles.

Clem was despatched to Blundells at the age of thirteen. The public school, in Tiverton, Devon, was founded in 1604. Blundells was a solid, long established school, with strong ties via scholarships to both Oxford and Cambridge Universities. The school also had close links with the military training establishment at Sandhurst and the Royal Naval College in Dartmouth. Church was attended every day, Combined Cadet Force twice a week, and games were compulsory.

Dad was billeted in Francis House where his housemaster was Bundy Thomas, with whom he always enjoyed a good rapport; I remember visiting Blundells on the occasion of the 1970 Soccer World Cup final, and enjoying Bundy's hospitality as Brazil ravaged Italy.

The benefit of attending public school was the quality of the sports infrastructure, the amount of time dedicated to sport, and the coaching expertise most schoolmasters brought to bear. Under the quality coaching at Blundells, Clem's rugby playing talent began to rapidly blossom. Graham Parker (OBE), his coach - a former double Cambridge blue and English international from Gloucester - instilled the phrase 'blood on the boot' and this became a regular refrain of Clem's when later playing for Wales. Dad patented it as his standard battle cry and used it throughout his career, signaling him as a harbinger of hurt toward all opposition. It was under Parker's influence that Clem merged the great driving force and discipline which at that time characterised English forward play with his native rugby football cunning and often extreme aggression in the tackle.

In the 1980s I was in Edinburgh walking with Dad down the Golden Mile on the morning of a Scotland v Wales match, when we bumped into an old foe from the 1950s, a burly South African called Chico Henderson who played for the Scots in the back row. Both adversaries recalled a previous encounter where, with only fifteen minutes played, the Welsh forwards led by Clem embarked on a furious foot-rush. Dad caught Chic on the small of the back, and he was in so much pain he was forced to leave the field. Thirty years later and they bump into each other, for the first time since on the Golden Mile.

Quick as a flash Clem cracked, "How's the back Chic?"

"Well, you know it's getting a little bit better everyday thanks," retorted Chic, before they both dissolved into guffaws.

Clem's disciplined approach to dealing with his physical disability was deeply ingrained at prep school thanks to the dedication and commitment of the games master, Mr Thomas. Dad was a wild child on arrival at Blundells but was soon transformed into a muscular, public school, toff-type character. He spoke Welsh with the slaughter men during the school holidays but delivered an outrageous plummy, syrupy drawl when in the company of English speakers. This often confused a lot of people and many an individual became the victim of their own prejudice.

Clem was one of the hardest men ever to play for Wales; when he competed he did it for keeps with no quarter asked for and none given. In my opinion, the reason he blew all away in front of him as a schoolboy was entirely due to his tough upbringing on the farm in Brynamman and the early rejection by his mother during his formative years. That's not to negate the love and affection he received from the myriad of aunties and uncles in Brynamman. Welsh families, on average, are prone to be bottomless pits of in-laws and a deep well of tough-love is always on offer, whether wanted or not. A young Clem had mastered a serious physical deformity and developed a taut muscularity working on the farm and in the slaughter house that not many public schoolboys could emulate. Dad always pushed himself to explore where the limits lay and he discovered there aren't any if you go at a challenge with self-belief and extraordinary ferocity.

Blundells brought Clem his first international honour and the opportunity of being the first ever English-based Public Schoolboy to win a Welsh Secondary Schools cap, when he was selected to play against Yorkshire Schools. Other Welsh stars of the future also played that day, most notably Carwyn James, C.L. 'Cowboy' Davies, Malcolm Thomas, and Sid Judd. It was later reported that, "R.C.C. Thomas, of Blundells (Clem), was the outstanding forward of the match". By the age of 18, Clem had played four times for Wales, a happy portent for the future. He also captained the team against France Schoolboys at the Stade Colombes in Paris in 1947.

In his last season at Blundells (1946-47), he was the captain of rugby and enjoyed an unbeaten season at home, a feat that was not to be repeated until 1975 when I was the Blundells captain. We emulated my Dad's team and went unbeaten whilst playing on 'Big Field'. I have a postcard of my Dad's with an Ipswich postmark dated 7th Nov 1946. It is addressed to "The Captain of the Football XV, Blundells School" and reads, "As a former captain of the XV (1896) I offer a suggestion for your match v Sherborne on Sat. Bottle up the stand-off half and prevent him feeding the wings; be sure and "go low"! Downside failed in this respect last week. Am hoping for your success. The best of luck." *C.C. Castley 7.XI.46.*"

The only match Dad managed to watch when I was captaining Blundells was the last home game of the season played on a Wednesday against an enormous group of Ulster boys from Campbell College, Belfast. At this time my father was the Chief Rugby Correspondent of *The Observer* newspaper and his commitments made it difficult for him to get to the depths of Devon on any given Saturday afternoon. Campbell College had destroyed Sherborne in their first game, and we were considered an easy touch since we had played badly at Sherborne early in the season. But we had improved, and were a fast, well drilled team. I anchored the pack from the second row and we had a classy young scrum half in Andrew Wyeth, who later played for England schoolboys, Bristol and Clifton. The Irish team was very strong upfront; we saw little of the ball and were forced to defend for almost the entirety of the game. But winning two quick rucks in each half was the deciding factor. Both rucks resulting in Wyeth making scintillating breaks which bagged us two converted tries.

12-0 was a notable win and we returned to 'Old House' for tea jubilant and euphoric. Our adversaries, Campbell College, had an impeccable record in Irish schools' rugby. My housemaster of Old House, Ted Crowe, who was also the first XV coach, used to share a study with Clem at Blundell's in the 1940s. Ted returned to Blundells after acquiring his degree at Cambridge and became another in the long line of first-rate public school masters and rugby coaches. Dad also reckoned him to be one of the most talented cricket players he had ever seen. Ted had invited his old friend Danny Hearn, the rugby master at Haileybury, who had suffered a broken neck in 1967 playing for Home Counties and Midlands against the All Blacks. A mistimed tackle on his opposite centre, Ian Macrae, resulted in his head hitting the thighbone and the injury meant he was unable to ever walk again. With true grit he refused to be cowed, and although confined to a wheelchair, continued to coach rugby, even taking his teams on overseas tours. Hearn always maintained that given his time again he would always play rugby: describing it as a marvelous team game, requiring selflessness, courage and determination.

Clem always had a very sceptical attitude towards injury. He would constantly repeat the mantra that he knew "the limits of his own body", and he believed in the ability to self-heal, almost willing the injury away. To counter the risks and effects of injury, especially soft tissue ones, he had devised his own training protocols that demanded far higher levels of fitness than was the norm. When he played for Swansea in the late 1950's he would train with the Swansea team and complete the team session. Then when other players were taking their showers, he would launch into a one and a half-hour sprint session. Gradually, young Swansea players like Morrie Evans, Dudley Thomas, and Chopper Morris would join him, and to this day they swear by those extra work disciplines that allowed them to flourish into top quality players.

To my knowledge there is only one player who played in competitive matches for Swansea RFC in teams containing Clem and myself. Morrie Evans started his career with the Whites in the 1958-59 season, scoring 12 tries in 26 games, and within 12 months had established himself with a further 11 tries. Only Dewi Bebb outscored him with 14 tries. Morrie would go on to play fifteen seasons with the first team, and a further five for the Swansea Athletic side. I played with him upon my return from playing out in Clermont-Ferrand, on an end of season Swansea tour to Jersey in 1977.

Morrie was one of the best wing-forwards never to play for Wales. In the mid-1960s he moved positions from wing to wing-forward where he would use his pace and natural aggression to create mayhem amongst opposition halfbacks. He was uber-physical, bordering on sociopathic at times, but loved the game, had great footballing skills, and was the Grandmaster of the 'you-start-it-I'll-finish-it' mentality. During a line-out, if the ball was thrown above your head, and you were marking Morrie, you knew what was coming next. The first sound would be crunching cartilage, quickly followed by a couple of yelps as you ran across field. By the time you got to the next breakdown, the sponge and bucket man would be onto the pitch administering either iced water or the last rites. And that is exactly what happened to the poor Jersey No. 8 who made the fatal error of competing against me on the first throw. I didn't lose another line-out all game.

On Saturday, 20th February 1954, the famous touring team, the Barbarians played and lost to the 4th All Blacks, captained by Bob Stuart. Seven weeks previously, Clem was part of the successful Welsh team that beat them 13-8. That afternoon, the "Baa-Baas" were the last match of the tour and they went down 19-5 in front of a 50,000 sell-out crowd at Cardiff Arms Park. The crowd greatly enjoyed the spectacle, belted out *Auld Lang Syne* at a deafening decibel, and hoisted Bob Scott (Auckland) and Tiny White (Poverty Bay) shoulder-high to be carried off the field of play.

The post-game dinner was held at the Esplanade

Hotel in Porthcawl. That evening the cellar nightclub was jammed to capacity with Kiwis and Baa-Baas, cigarette and cigar smoke creating a dense fog. The sweating throng of players, released and relaxed, were truly going for it. Clem was with a table of friends, that included the Welsh scrum half, and one and only playboy, Rex Willis, along with his Cardiff team mate Cliff Morgan. Dad retired to the bar to get a round in and witnessed a barrel chested, overtly muscular man with a broken nose shouting at his companion. Events became quite heated and the man shoved the poor women off her stool. Clem quickly stepped forward to break her fall and helped her back onto the stool.

> "What the hell are you playing at?" he asked incredulously, in his best Cambridge accent.
> "Mind your own fucking business mush…now fuck off with you!" was the colourful reply.
> "HOW DARE YOU USE LANGUAGE LIKE THAT!" shouted Clem, the hubbub in the bar dropping in volume; you could almost hear a pin drop.
> "What are you going to do about it then mush?"
> "If you've got the guts pal, I'll see you outside. I'll teach you some manners and how to behave with a lady…"

Rex Willis practically sprinted through the throng, knocking Kiwis and drinks aside with the intent of trying to put the genie back in the bottle.

> "Rex will be my second, and we'll sort this out like men in the Esplanade car park." Dad announced grandly, before Rex could get a word in.

The crowd emptied into the car park to bear witness and formed an orderly circle around the two prospective combatants. Rex dutifully folded Clem's pristine Barbarians blazer across his forearm like an exotic Spanish wine waiter and announced that it would be a fist fight, Marquess of Queensberry rules and all that, submission or knockout.

The two fighters circled each other rather unsteadily in the half-light of the car park. The majority of the crowd was comprised mainly of Kiwis and Baa-Baas and their natural inclination was to cheer for Clem. No-one seemed to have the first idea who the other fellow was. *Whack*! Dad absorbed a lightning fast shot delivered with worrying precision, and felt the blood, from an open wound run down his face. It was quickly followed by more punches, all finding their mark. "It was at this point, that I realised I was in trouble," Dad recalled laconically many years later.

Clem feinted to the left and delivered a powerful right-hand to his opponent's nose. Blood splattered into the crowd, staining both fighters' white shirts. Dad recalls that, sensing the upper hand, he accelerated his attack: connecting another three hard shots but feeling as if he might have broken his hand in the process, "it was like punching granite!"

His assailant opened up his body and caught Dad's ear as he narrowly missed another head shot. Clem transferred his weight and moved forward landing another perfect right-hand to his opponents broken nose and he crumpled to the floor...end of fight. Rex Willis told me this story, many times over the years; it was one of his favourite "Clem stories". Dad's opponent that day turned out to be the amateur heavyweight champion, Jackie Braddock (Manchester). When Dad hosted a Sunday lunch for the All Black Ron Jarden in the early 1970s he gave an amusing and colourful rendition of the events of that evening that more than corroborates Rex's version.

So where did Clem's incredible competitiveness, his legendary temper, and his underlying physicality come from? Years later, as he mused the sharp decline and fall of

Welsh rugby as a global force during the 1980s he honestly thought that standards of living in the northern hemisphere had moved away from hard, manual, out-in-all weathers lifestyles and jobs, to a more sedentary and cushy culture. Dad often speculated that youngsters were more interested in a soft pub culture and lacked a layer or two of hardness. This hardness was still evident amongst the rugby playing populations of New Zealand, South Africa, and Australia. He regarded those countries as being frontiers where the migrants had accepted a different way of life and had yet to succumb to the urbanisation prevalent in the UK. New Zealanders and Springboks accepted a more physical approach to the game, and played with a crueler intensity than was the case at Twickenham or Cardiff Arms Park.

A few years ago I had the distinct privilege of sitting next to the legendary Colin Meads at an official All Black luncheon at Café Royal in Piccadilly. The New Zealand Rugby Union had woken up to the fund-raising potential of putting on events in places like London, and on this occasion, it was a pantheon of current and former All Blacks. Colin Meads, the 'Pinetree' and icon of New Zealand rugby, remembered Dad with affection, not just because of his rugby exploits and journalism, but because Dad had once visited his farm in King Country and talked farming. Meads judged this to be of far greater worth and relevance than any rugby ties ever could be!

The farm in Brynamman where Clem spent his formative years is a defiant speck on the side of the Bryn; where the rough tundra of The Brecon Beacons begins and the wind howls like a banshee the full complement of 365 days a year. The few remaining trees and hawthorn bushes are shaped in the direction of the prevailing wind, stooped and old, and the ground never seems to fully dry out. Clem learned to ride a horse, shoot his 4-bore shotgun, and fish in the mountain streams with line and by tickling trout.

Farming and Agriculture shaped the man. Clem's rugby master at Blundells, Graham Parker OBE, always credited the tough upbringing as a reservoir of strength. He was a legendary school master of a type you only come across in English public schools. Mr Parker played full-back for England against Ireland and Scotland in 1938, contributing 15 points to the 36-14 win over the Irish, kicking 6 conversions and a penalty. But he was best known as a cricketer, scoring 2,956 first class runs for Gloucestershire from 1932-51 at an average of 21.89 and 57 wickets. His stand-out season was in 1937 when he made 662 runs at an average of 44.13. He joined the military in 1938 and did not return to cricket until 1947. During this time, he served as a major in the Royal Army Service Corps, seeing action in both North Africa and Italy which earned him a military MBE. This was later upgraded to an OBE following his command of the Combined Cadet Force at Blundells where he taught for twenty-two years.

Clem thought the world of Graham Parker, who he said many times gave him the encouragement and confidence to develop his game, and who pulled the right strings to get Clem into St John's College, Cambridge. Even in those days it was quite a feat, particularly for a boy from Brynamman, although being captain of both Blundells and the Welsh Schoolboys International team helped the process somewhat. Dad "went up to St John's" in the fall of 1947 to read Agriculture. It is still a mystery to this very day as to how he survived academia for three years. Survive it he duly did and emerged with no degree, but one Cambridge Blue (1949) earned nine months after his first Welsh cap against France in Paris.

The only stories that Dad liked to recount from those halcyon days involved rugby, cricket, rowing, and above all else, his close friendship with the iconic Richard Burton. His brother Graham Burton shared rooms in Cambridge with Dad. Both students would descend on the Old Vic whenever Richard was treading the boards. They would take in the matinee and invariably followed a mammoth session on the beer with Richard in the Old Pit in the bowels of the theatre. The festivities would often spill messily into The Waterloo Bar on Webber Street opposite. According to Dad this was the reason the Old Vic Costume department had so much rusty old armour. Richard forever got caught short during the longer soliloquies.

My great friend Paul Lewis, who sponsors The Ospreys through his access equipment company (Lyte Industries), often tells me how his father, Tommy, an 8th Army veteran from Sandfields, Port Talbot, remembers seeing Dad, Richard Burton, and Elizabeth Taylor, propping up the bar at Aberavon Rugby Club in the 1950s. Elizabeth Taylor was resplendent in furs and jewellery and caused quite a stir amongst the committee men. Legend has it that the trio drank into the early hours and were still at the bar when the manager returned for work the next morning.

One apocryphal story Dad loved to recall was the occasion Richard Burton played Henry V, and they were all backstage after the lavishly attended first night. *The Western Mail* theatre critic was despatched from Cardiff to watch over and report on Wales' golden boy. Burton's friends and retinue were squeezed into his tiny dressing room, celebrating a tour de force, when the critic, red-faced and perspiring in the smoke-clogged jam, waved at Burton from afar. He shouted that he had to dash for the last train from Paddington. Burton beat a path through the throng and grabbed him by the arm, topping up his glass with an enormous scotch.

"Tell me what you thought of the play," asked

Burton fixing him with a keen gaze.

The critic hesitated and finally blurted, "Well you know that part in the play when you utter the unforgettable lines, 'Once more, unto the breach, dear friends, once more; or close the wall up with our English dead!', well... I didn't feel much like following." And with that parting shot, he ran off into the London night.

My Mum, Ann, tells the story of how Burton came up with the best put-down line ever at a party that Clem dragged him along to in the Uplands in Swansea. Burton had just released *The Robe* and *The Desert Rats,* and his profile was on the verge of turning him into the huge, international mega-star he later became. That evening a particularly obnoxious, arrogant Swansea woman, with a cut-glass Oxford accent spent the best part of an hour making rude and disparaging remarks to everyone's embarrassment. In particular, she kept making fun of his pock-marked face, commenting on how clever the Hollywood lighting and make-up departments must be. Finally, Burton snapped and in his crispest, deepest mellifluous voice retorted with authoritative finality, "Do be quiet you horrid woman. I've met your type and breed before..." She was never seen in polite Swansea society again.

After going "up" to St John's College, Cambridge, Clem missed out on a Blue in his first two years. Dad always blamed a friend for the failure to appear sooner in the Varsity Match. Hugh Lloyd-Davies was from Ammanford, his father a conductor on the local Rees & Williams Buses. Alan Watkins, *The Observer* political journalist, often described Lloyd-Davies as having two vices: sexual intercourse, to which he was inordinately attached, and snobbery, which is altogether rarer in South West Wales.

On the morning of the Varsity match (1947), Lloyd-Davies failed to arrive at the appointed meeting-place for the journey to Twickenham. Clem, who was travelling with the team even though he had not been selected, went to Trinity Hall with another friend to search for the Cambridge University full-back. They found him fast asleep, the result of his heavy drinking the night before. After rousing him, they bathed and dressed him and managed to convey him to the ground with the minimum of fuss. Lloyd-Davies proceeded to win the match for Cambridge, 6-0. Naturally his teammates were ecstatic, but Lloyd-Davies soured the occasion by telling Eric Bole, the Cambridge captain, that they would have won by a greater margin if his compatriot, Clem Thomas, had been playing and that if Clem was good enough for Swansea he was good enough for "this fucking shower of shit." An entirely just, but perhaps less tactful observation, to which the university captain, an evangelical Christian, did not take kindly and never entirely forgave.

Lloyd-Davies returned in 1948, but refused to train with his teammates and was replaced by Barry Holmes, an Argentinian who was later picked to play for England. Before he could do any more damage to Dad's fledgling rugby career, he got sent down for cheeking a proctor in Welsh. Lloyd-Davies went on to play for Swansea, London Welsh and then the Harlequins where he ran up eye-watering bills that were eventually paid by Sir Wavell Wakefield, the club's President, a Conservative MP and an England international of the late 1920's.

The irascible Lloyd-Davies, finding himself short of money, washed up at Barrow Rugby League Club. Resplendent in a bowler hat, striped trousers, and carrying a rolled umbrella, he kicked three practice goals without changing his dress shoes and was promptly signed for a fee of £1,000. The first Cambridge Blue to become a professional. He also claimed to have seduced the chairman's wife (Miss Barrow, circa 1951) and only managed to turn up for one training session for his new club. Tiring of Barrow he decamped to Paris, becoming the most expensive signing in the history of rugby league at the time. Unfortunately, he only lasted the one match. Back in the UK, events took a turn for the worse, and he was imprisoned for nine months at Liverpool City Quarter Sessions for obtaining a diamond ring and a pair of gold cuff links by false pretenses from a Liverpool jewellery firm. Upon pleading guilty the Recorder lectured him, "A man of your standing and education knew perfectly well that such an offence could not be passed over without some punishment."

Lloyd-Davies was alleged to have told the Liverpool jeweller that he was a barrister, which he obviously was not. He had made out a cheque for £94, the value of the ring and cufflinks. The cheque was later returned marked 'RD'. Lloyd-Davies pawned the ring for £10 and the cuff links for £2 10s 0d. His defence council affirmed that he was thoroughly ashamed of himself and every penny had been repaid in full. In mitigation, Lloyd-Davies was having a course of treatment not unconnected with drink.

Unfortunately, his savage sentence did not act as any deterrent. He went to prison again for stealing an overcoat from the library of Gray's Inn. Upon his release Lloyd-Davies returned to Tycroes, where he did odd labouring jobs before returning to London. There were various sightings of the mercurial Welshman, on one occasion in the company of Jack Doyle, "The Gorgeous Gael", former boxer and Hollywood actor. *The Jungle Telegraph* intermittently reported that he was passing himself off as a colonel; had gone completely bald; was sleeping rough; and was a gardener with Islington Council. Legend has it that he sadly passed away in 1986.

Clem continued his rugby education at Cambridge, the team later touring Paris and southwest France. Dad could never understand why, upon arriving at the various town fixtures, he was pressganged by his French opposition into nightly mammoth drinking sessions. Finally, arriving at Toulouse, and nursing a 5 day hangover from hell, a teammate confessed to sending telegrams to their French hosts alerting them that Cambridge University had in their party the infamous Clem Thomas, who no man had ever bested in drinking. The French naturally took this to be a challenge and embarked on a mission to drink him under the table.

It was during this tour and a subsequent visit to Tarbes in 1950 that Clem noted the deliberate tactic employed in French rugby to cross kick from the wide out wing position. This would alter the direction of attacking play and keep the ball in-field. It was the same tactic he would use many years later that gave Wales that key victory over the All Blacks.

In hindsight, Post-Vichy France may not have been the best of places to let loose a bunch of Cambridge University undergraduates, many of whom had fought in the Second World War. One particular incident led to the French authorities making a formal complaint to the British Embassy in Paris. The rowdy undergraduates hijacked a tram travelling through the centre of Clermont-Ferrand in the Auvergne, putting French citizens' wellbeing at great risk. The team returned to Cambridge University with a trophy: a cut glass chandelier stolen from the foyer of the Grand Hotel in Clermont; a law suit and glut of angry letters trailing in their wake.

In 1948 Clem toured Sweden with the Woodpeckers, a touring team mainly comprised of Oxbridge players. Dad had met a Swedish girl at a university social event some time before. She was strikingly good-looking and after chatting her up she gave him her card with strict instructions to call on her if ever in Stockholm. The team were billeted at the Swedish equivalent of the YMCA, and subject to a strict curfew. Undeterred, they embarked on nightly escapes over the rooftops in search of Scandinavian nightlife. After a few nights of riotous behaviour, my Dad plucked up the courage to phone the number on the card. His Swedish girlfriend swiftly confirmed dinner, and asked Dad to bring a friend along. So my godfather, Geoff Vaughan, later to become an accomplished doctor in Auckland, was pressganged into service.

Clem and Geoff were slightly startled when they handed the card to a taxi driver and he promptly saluted them both. The penny began to drop when their driver stopped outside the Swedish equivalent of Buckingham Palace. After gesticulating at the guard house, Dad and Geoff approached with some trepidation. The guardsman also smartly saluted and instructed them to follow him into the Royal Palace. They walked about a mile through courtyard after courtyard, until arriving at a tower, where they took a lift to the top floor. Dad's girlfriend, Margaretha was there to welcome them and it quickly became evident that she was the old King Gustav V's niece. That night, they dined with the King in his private apartment. Amazingly, the royal entourage duly turned up at the various matches they played on tour, and Dad was presented a wood carving of the King, which I still have in my possession to this day.

Gustav was a keen hunter and sportsman. He presided over the 1912 Olympic Games and was a close friend of the Baron de Coubertin, an international rugby referee. Notably, King Gustav V represented Sweden (under the alias of Mr G) as a competitive tennis player who played well into his eighties. He was elected into the International Tennis Hall of Fame in 1980. During World War II, he interceded to obtain better treatment of one of France's tennis mousquetaires, Jean Borotra who was a Davis Cup colleague of another close French friend of Clem in later years, the great Marcel Bernard, the French tennis champion. Marcel Bernard was a great character, and I remember him staying with us over the Wales v France 5 Nations weekends in the 1970s.

Marcel was one of France's great tennis players and administrators with a career spanning his winning the French Open doubles and mixed double championships in 1936 with Jean Borotra, one of the original 'musketeers' from that era, and Lolette Payot. He went on to clinch the greatest prize, a singles win at Roland Garros (1946), defeating Jaroslav Drobny in the final in 5 sets. That same year he also won the doubles crown with Yvon Petra. Marcel played Davis Cup for France for 21 years, and in 1946 was ranked 5th in the world. He eventually became President of the French Tennis Federation (1968), and today the Open mixed doubled cup is called the 'Coupe Marcel Bernard'. His name is also commemorated at Roland Garros by the walk-way 'Allee Marcel Bernard.' Marcel was one hundred per cent Parisian-chic and classy, dressed like a mannequin from a catwalk, sparkling, friendly eyes, and always looking for the next joke or quip. He was intelligent and articulate beyond the reach of ordinary men, and enjoyed a close friendship with the Haedens, Damitio, and Chatrier families of whom I will expose more later in the book.

Whilst at Cambridge Clem kept himself fit in the summer terms playing for the St John's College cricket team. At Blundells he had won his first X1 colours as an erratic, aggressively fast bowler, a role I was also destined to follow some thirty years later. It is well documented that Clem was seriously quick, a schoolboy contemporary who played against him, David Sheppard (the Right Reverend Lord Sheppard of Liverpool) mentioned in his autobiography that when he went up to Cambridge in 1947 the fastest bowler he faced was Clem Thomas, who was always keen to bowl at him in the nets (*Parson's Pitch* 1974). Sheppard played cricket for Cambridge University, Sussex, and England, topping the English batting averages in 1952 scoring 2,262 runs at an average of 64.62. Interestingly, the two men had already faced off against each other two years previous before going to Cambridge as freshmen. In June

1947 Sherborne had squeaked out a narrow win over Blundells. Blundells made 202 for 8 declared, which Sherborne responded to with 204-9, winning by 1 elusive wicket. David Sheppard made 56. But the previous year Clem had terrorised the Sherborne batting, bowling them out for 139 and taking 5 wickets for 25 runs, contributing to a famous Blundells victory.

The best story about Reverend Sheppard came from his Ashes tour in 1962, when he kept dropping easy catches, which clearly exasperated Fred Trueman, who accused Sheppard of only keeping his hands together when he was at prayer.

Dad loved the world of cricket and always retained close links. During the 1960s and early '70s, two Cambridge University Cricket Blues played for Glamorgan CCC. Ossie Wheatley was a fast-medium opening bowler and Tony Lewis was a massively talented ball player who also played rugby for Neath and Gloucester. 'Uncle Tony' was the last man to captain England on his Test debut in 1972 and captained Glamorgan to its second Championship in 1969. I have fond memories of them both staying with us whenever Glamorgan played at St Helen's.

On Saturday, 31st August 1968 at around 5pm, a very ordinary game of county cricket at St Helen's, took somewhat of a turn for the unexpected. The West Indian, Gary Sobers, already unhappy at the negative tactics used by his team mates sauntered out to the crease. John Arlott, the cricket commentator, once wrote of Sobers that when he was on the kill it was all but impossible to bowl to him, and that he was one of the most thrilling of all batsmen to watch. Sobers and his partner John Parkin accelerated the scoring to allow an early evening declaration, and had put on 40 in just an hour.

Tony Lewis sensed it was time to set a trap for Sobers and put Malcolm Nash on to bowl his experimental slow left-armers. His first three deliveries were each imperiously hit for six with a minimum of backlift. Lewis told Nash he could revert to 'whacking it in the blockhole'. But Nash said he had it under control. Lewis later wrote, "Malcolm had entered the dangerous area where pride moves in, but on rubber legs". So again Nash set off on his six step run-up, and again Sobers smashed the ball over backward square leg and over the mid-wicket boundary.

Fifth ball of the over, Sobers smashed a mistimed shot to the long-off boundary, but the ball's trajectory forced Roger Davies (an Old Blundellian!) to back pedal furiously whilst leaping in the air to take the catch. Davies fell back over the boundary rope, clutching the ball. There was some confusion and a lot of deliberation amongst the crowd. Sobers started to trudge off towards the pavilion, but the umpires, Eddie Philipson and John Langridge calmly debated the affair. Then Philipson correctly signalled another six.

The crowd exploded and a shiver of electric anticipation rippled through the ground - *six sixes! Is it possible? Never been done before...anywhere in the history of cricket!* Tony Lewis sent all his fielders to the boundary, stacking Sobers' leg side. Eiffion Jones, the Glamorgan wicket-keeper could not resist the wind up and indulged in a bit of mild sledging, "Bet you can't hit this one for six..." In runs Nash.

I remember sitting with my pals Mark Portsmouth and Jeremy Swain just behind the long-off boundary. Dad had pitched up and was in the players' pavilion above the bar. The world held its breathe...Nash bowls a quicker ball which Sobers anticipates and hits through the line in a flash...THWACK! In a heartbeat, the ball was over the boundary past long-on; "All the way to Swansea!" shouted Wilf Wooller in his TV commentary.

> Sobers commented later, "I caught it right in the middle of the bat and not only did it clear the short boundary, it went over the stand as well,

running down the hill towards Swansea town centre."

After stumps that evening, there started quite a party in Swansea Rugby Clubhouse (The rugger and cricket share a spiritual home at St Helens). I was a kid at the time so found it relatively easy to tag along with the players, officials and hangers-on. Clem and Ossie were organising the evening festivities and doing their utmost to contain a celebratory Gary Sobers. Sobers suddenly sat bolt upright remembering he had a problem that needed fixing.

Dad patted him on the shoulder and said, "leave it to me," and disappeared behind the bar to use the phone. Within two minutes he was back. "Right, it's all fixed up," and turning to me, "Christopher will travel in the car with you and show you where to leave it. Get yourselves over the road and we'll all meet there."

Sobers' prized Cadillac had developed a fault and I was tasked with accompanying the great man to Ace's Garage in Newton, which happily sat opposite the Rock and Fountain pub which was gearing up for a night of celebration in his honour. My great claim to fame is Gary Sobers drove me home on the evening of him hitting an historic six sixes. How cool was that for a sports mad eleven-year-old? Dad was a regular Mr Fixit.

The Rock and Fountain was the go-to place in swinging 60s Swansea, situated in Mumbles and owned by an old family of venerable wine and spirits importers, the Munday's. The pub then was run by Tim Munday, who was a great friend of Clem and his circle.

I can still recall receiving a very odd phone call from my Mum on March 3rd 1974 telling me that there was nothing to worry about. I didn't have the foggiest what she was talking about. I later learned that Turkish Airlines 981, a McDonnell Douglas DC-10 flying from Orly airport in Paris to London, crashed in Ermenoville Forest with the loss of 346 lives, at that time the deadliest plane crash in history. Dad had been booked on that flight, returning from the France v England 5 Nations rugby international. All his travel was handled by *The Observer*, for whom he had become the Chief Rugby Correspondent, and because BEA was on strike, he had been found a seat on the Turkish Airline flight. Fortunately for him and all of us, Dad was a bit of a bon viveur, as we shall discover, and his close buddy and partner in crime, Peter Robbins, ex England wing forward and rugby writer for *The Financial Times* phoned Dad in Paris on the Sunday morning and persuaded him to stay on for lunch, which I'm glad to say he did. It was a typical brush with death that Clem became a master of over the years. On that particular occasion, he narrowly avoided joining his uncle in a graveyard in Pas-de-Calais. The headstone in remembrance of Clement Thomas at Aire Communal Cemetery in northern France simply says:

'REMEMBRANCE EVER GREEN'

2

THE END OF THE WORLD

Aros mae'r mynydelau mawr,
Rhuo trostynt mae y gwynt;
Clywir eto gyda'r wawr
Gan bugeiliaid megis cynt

The mighty hills unchanging stand,
Tireless the winds across them blow;
The shepherds' song across the land
Sounds with the dawn as long ago
John Ceiriog Hughes

Clem discovered the lucrative black arts of entrepreneurship during his Easter holiday break in 1944. He had arrived back in Brynamman from Blundells, looking forward to being indulged by the exceptional cooking skills of his mother, with lashings of everything rationed now freely available on a farm with an abattoir. All the things he had gone without were now in abundant supply: cream, butter, eggs, cakes, cheese, plenty of meat, and even the luxury of roast joints on a Sunday. The Thomas family has always been inordinately fond of their food, and Clem was no exception.

Brynamman had changed during Clem's absence. The sleepy village was now buzzing, practically teeming, with an army of khaki-clad American soldiers.

The mandarins in Whitehall and the army top brass had been wrestling with the thorny issue of where to hide the largest invasion force in the history of warfare. The Nazis still had a nationwide network of spies whose task was to report troop build ups, and an enormous amount of effort was expended trying to obfuscate and deceive the build up to Operation Overlord, the D-Day landings. So where do you hide an armoured or infantry division or two, each typically consisting of a force of 15,000 men? The solution was to billet them on an escarpment between Brynamman and Cwmllynfell. Far away from prying eyes The Black Mountain is generally considered to be one of the wildest regions of Wales and is associated with numerous myths such as the Arthurian legend of the Lady of the Lake.

Clem quickly discovered that the American soldiers had access to most things. But the men of the 28th Infantry division craved one treat that they could not get in their canvass encampments across the Black Mountain: ice-cream. The one staple still heavily rationed even to the US troops who had access to chewing gum, silk stockings, cigarettes, candy bars, and canned fruit, was refined white sugar.

Dad had free access over the mountain to the American camp by horseback, and had already tried to engage the yanks in a bit of barter. But he quickly realised that what they wanted more than anything was ice-cream. In 1939, when the outbreak of war became inevitable, my grandmother Edna went into manic-panic mode and purchased the entire sugar stocks available in the grocer shops throughout the Amman Valley and beyond. She invented hoarding. I can remember that as a young boy the front room, the largest in the house, had been transformed into an Aladdin's cave of gastronomic delights. There was case upon case of canned peaches in syrup, red salmon, shrimps, sardines, corned beef, pastes, crates of Double

Diamond and Mackeson, and sides of salted belly fat for my grandfather's bacon breakfast. Edna was addicted to hoarding and it remained a matter of habit from 1939 throughout her entire life.

In the late 1940s DJ had bought a large house at the bottom of Brynamman hill called, appropriately for a three-storey 8-bedroomed Victorian mansion: Brynamman House. Inside, my grandmother Edna ruled the Thomas household, her seat of power being the kitchen with an enormous Rayburn aga and a massively built oak kitchen table around which the extended Thomas family, including the one-eyed John Gwynne, DJ's driver, would enjoy huge breakfasts of fried eggs with golden yolks and home-cured bacon before setting out to their daily adventures in the cattle markets of Carmarthenshire. If she needed anything from the abattoir she would wind-up the old, chipped Bakelite telephone as old as Alexander Bell himself, and instruct DJ to bring his 'Teddy' (his affectionate nickname for her) a pack of chops or, more often, sweetbreads or lambs' liver, back home. She kept four enormous tabby cats who gorged themselves on the bountiful leftovers, and a docile, spoiled golden Labrador called Carl. It was always an open house in the 1960s with the world coming and going. Wizened farmers in flat caps always wearing their long, tan, ankle-length drover coats would call in to collect a cheque or more likely, cash for a deal done previously in the week by DJ or Clem to acquire livestock direct from the farm, thereby cutting out the auctioneer premium. Edna specialised in making dramatically strong, sweet cups of tea that could give you insomnia for a fortnight. The colour was a deep, shiny brown and the texture was so thick with sugar, you could stand a teaspoon upright in it. This was dispensed with her Welsh cakes, which melted in your mouth due to the light, buttery, sugary, crumbly texture of the patty, or a chocolate éclair stuffed with sweet Chantilly cream or even a massive wedged slice of golden, strawberry jam sponge. All fancies were religiously homemade on the precious aga under the beady scrutiny of the cats, with the Bakelite phone constantly ringing in the background.

Her sugar mountain was legendary and with access to plenty of fresh cream Dad hit upon the idea of making home-made ice-cream. He co-opted the use of his mother's industrial-sized freezer cabinet, normally used for meat and game and set himself up as an ice-cream magnate. Dad would mix the cream, milk and sugar, heat it up to stir and dissolve the sugar grains, and then put it in the freezer where he would have to stir the mix every thirty minutes as it froze. Demand from the Americans skyrocketed to such an extent it became an industrial enterprise. Such was the appetite from the Americans that they would despatch a jeep to the farm to make hourly pick-ups. They even went so far as to station members of their catering corps at the farm to focus on making the ice-cream, supplying industrial-sized metal mixing bowls to increase output.

My grandmother was delighted as she now had unfettered access to the Americans' luxury goods and they were more than ready to barter to ensure a constant and uninterrupted flow of ice-cream. Edna realised she had the upper hand: if she turned off the supply the Americans would have had a riot amongst the ranks. She used the leverage to amass US nylon which was in great demand throughout the UK. Edna became known throughout Wales and farther afield as the nylon stocking queen of the Amman Valley.

The 28th Infantry Division is the oldest and most decorated division in the US Army and some of the units can trace their lineage way back to Benjamin Franklin's original battalion. The first deployments to South Wales from Louisiana were made in October 1943, with an eventual force of 14,032 men spread from Porthcawl to Pembroke Dock. They were known as 'The Keystones' as Pennsylvania was known as the 'Keystone State' due to its red Keystone insignia and the divisional historical records. The friendliness and hospitality of the people of Wales put the 28th troops very much at home in their six months spent there.

After landing in Normandy on July 22, the Division experienced some of the most intense and brutal engagements of the war, acquiring the nickname the "Bloody Bucket" division by German forces due to the red insignia. It bore the brunt of the Ardennes Offensive in December 1944 launched by the 5th Panzer Army led by General der Panzertruppe Hasso von Manteuffel. The division arrived in Wales with 14,032 men of which 9,600 died, with a further 884 missing in action.

Clem's only other wartime action, apart from infantry manoeuvres on Dartmoor with the Blundells Combined Cadet Force concerned the small matter of making a claim over a crashed Luftwaffe Heinkel that got shot down following a raid over Swansea docks in 1941. The plane crashed somewhere between Brynamman and Cwmtwrch, and with his friend, Bryn Llewelyn, who later owned the coal washery in Ystalyfera, Dad cannibalised what was left of the wreckage.

At the war's end Clem was only sixteen years old, and any stories about him knowing the great Rocky Marciano in those years are simply not true. The future heavyweight boxing champion of the world, the only heavyweight champion to have retired with a perfect record, having won all 49 of his fights (43 by knock-out), was a member of C company, 348th Eng. Combat Battalion, consisting of five companies of about 750 men that participated in the invasion of Normandy Omaha beach east. Although Rocky Marciano was a truck driver billeted on Mumbles Pier, sleeping on a straw-filled palliasse mattresses. He was also billeted at Scurlage on Gower and at the US Forces military hospital that is now Morriston Hospital, where I was born. Legend has it that his boxing career started in Swansea, after a brawl with an Australian soldier in the

Adelphi pub, Wind St. The 20-year-old Marciano said he had been arrested by the 'snowdrops' - the US Military police who wore white painted helmets - and they put him to boxing on military boxing cards rather than court martial him. It was at such an event, held at RAF St Athan air base in the Vale of Glamorgan, that Rocky Marciano went toe-to-toe with Dr Jack Mathews, the great Wales and British Lion centre three-quarter, famed for his bone crunching tackling, who boxed for the Welsh National School of Medicine team at Cardiff University. Jack remembered that "it was a four- round contest and no winner was declared." Jack played with Clem in Paris against France in 1949 when Clem won his first cap for Wales.

My grandfather, DJ had been a very keen boxing fan, and undoubtedly fought as a young man. I remember him waking me up in the middle of the night to listen to the Howard Winstone fights in the late 1960s notably against his nemesis, Vicente Saldivar from Mexico City. In the mid-1940s he promoted the Swansea-based British and Commonwealth welterweight champion boxer, Cliff Curvis, who at that time fought his very first professional fight at Brynamman swimming baths, no less!

But the truth was that Brynamman began to go through hard times in the 1930s, despite DJ's fortunes improving as he expanded his customer-base of butcher shops in the densely populated areas in and around Swansea. Unemployment became a major problem in Brynamman. Crowds of people would flock to the abattoir to scrounge an off-cut, piece of offal or sheep's head to take home for dinner.

DJ always ensured the abattoir was open to all. Thursday always drew the largest crowds as that was the day when Bertie the slaughterman focused on killing the cattle. One lazy Thursday, it was business as usual as the last of the morning's slaughtered bullocks were winched away to cool and set, and the last beast of the day was shepherded into the old, wooden-fenced slaughter area. There was a ring set in cement on the floor to tether the livestock to. The animal that Bertie had held back till last was an old black bull, bought in Carmarthen cattle market earlier that week. The protocol to humanely slaughter a bull in those days was as follows: Bertie takes a length of rope which has already been fastened through the ring in the bull's nose. This is done in the holding pen. The rope is then threaded through the ring cemented in the slaughterhouse floor. The rope is pulled and fastened, which forces the bull to lower its head and the swinging pole-axe finishes the job by stunning the beast and allowing the slaughterman to cut the carotid artery, which bleeds the animal humanely.

Over time Bertie had become enamoured by the crowds and fancied himself a bit of a showman. He had quite a gallery of spectators that day as he threaded the rope through the ring in the bull's nose. And then he made one ghastly mistake. Bertie could not resist the opportunity to show off a bit, so he ignored the ring on the floor, and tied the rope around his own midriff in order to swing the pole-axe. But he had to coax the bull to lower its head. He swung the heavy sharp pointed pole-axe expertly as he had done countless thousands of times before, aiming at a point between the bull's eyes to stun it, and DUNK! Bertie's foot slipped in a pool of wet blood and the pole-axe glanced painfully off the bull's eye-socket bone.

Total bedlam and pandemonium ensued, the bull simply went berserk. Bertie was dragged like a rag doll around the slaughterhouse. The angry velocity generated by an outraged, wounded black bull weighing over 1500 pounds, capable of running at 15 miles per hour is quite a sight to behold. The bull lowered its horns and smashed through the old, rotting fence inside the abattoir and headed for the open sky-lit despatch area, dragging Bertie with it. The bull turned right onto Bryn Rd, hurtled down it for 500 yards, and then took a left onto Brynamman hill, the main road that connects upper Brynamman to lower Brynamman. Down the hill hurtled the bull, dragging the screaming Bertie who was fighting to stay alive. There, sombrely progressing up the hill towards the runaway bull and Bertie was a full funeral cortege led by two black horses in their black and silver mourning tack topped by black plumes. The driver of the cortege was forced to pull to his right. Then his two horses bolted in panic as they confronted the charging bull accelerating down the hill, slipping on the greasy tarmac. The cortege was rolled onto its side with the coffin unceremoniously spilling into the narrow stream that ran parallel to the road. The mourners had hardly expected a burial at sea!

The bull charged on, reached the bottom of the hill, and fled over the bridge that divides Carmarthenshire from Glamorgan. The beast fled towards Gwaen-Cae-Gurwen still dragging the badly mauled and bloodied Bertie. Eventually the police caught up with the poor animal and mercifully carried out a coup de grace with a revolver. Poor old Bertie spent four months recovering from his wounds and injuries in hospital, and from that day onward, was forever known as 'Bertie the Bull.'

Another slaughterman whose real name Dad never knew had a day job as the conductor on the South Wales Transport bus from Brynamman to Swansea. The conductor had known Dad since he used to hop off the bus at Cwmgors School at the age of six, usually without paying. He apparently gloried in the pseudonym of 'Dai-Kill-a-Pig' because on his route from Swansea to Brynamman he would stop the bus at his home to kill any number of backyard pigs which every miner had in those days. He would then make sure the temperature of the pig bath was exactly right for scalding and dehairing. Then continue the journey. On the return trip he would stop to disembowel the pig and the next day he would cut it up; if you wanted a nice piece of spare rib, Dai-Kill-A-Pig was your man.

In 1951 Dad jumped on the bus to travel to Swansea to play the Springboks. Knowing Dad's fateful destination and Swansea RFC's miserable playing record that season, Dai-Kill-a-Pig conducted an in memoriam service for Clem all the way to Swansea. If anyone's confidence deserved to be shattered then Clem's ought to have been beyond repair. In fact it only strengthened his resolve. Dai-Kill-a-Pig's parting words rang in Clem's ears, "Duw, Duw...If you hold them to forty points you'll have done bloody marvellous".

That afternoon a crowd of 40,000 saw one of the most exciting matches ever played at St Helen's. With only seven minutes to go the mighty Springbok side, which lost only one match out of thirty-one fixtures, against London Counties, were fighting for their lives. But then Aaron 'Okey' Geffin the famed Jewish goal-kicking prop landed a penalty from inside his own half. Okey had perfected his goal-kicking skills at a prisoner of war camp in Poland during the Second World War and created a then world record in the Springboks' first post-war Test by landing five penalty goals against New Zealand in 1949.

Jack hearts sank as the kick imperiously floated over the uprights and sank further in the last minute when Chum Ochse wriggled over in the corner and South Africa won by 11 points to 3. The wing ended the tour as South Africa's highest scorer with fifteen tries. Four years later, when Dad was playing with the British Lions in South Africa, the great bald-headed wing-forward Basie Von Wyk told Clem that the Swansea match was one of the hardest games he had ever played in and that he was relieved to get off the field in one piece. He claimed he had never been tackled so hard and so consistently in his life.

The following week, Clem was travelling on the same bus and Dai-Kill-a-Pig, who had been to the match and who was a law unto himself as far as bus inspectors were concerned, was still choked with the emotion of it all and conferred upon Clem a free bus season ticket for life. Dad recalled many years later that he felt as if he had won his first cap; he was very proud of that moment.

The British government introduced food rationing in January 1940. The scheme was designed to ensure fair shares for all at a time of national shortage. The Ministry of Food was responsible for overseeing rationing. Every man, woman and child was given a ration book with coupons which were required before the restricted quantity of goods could be purchased. Each adult was rationed per week, with the rationed amounts being 4 ozs of bacon or ham, 2 ozs of cheese, 1 shell egg, 3 pints of milk and meat to the value of 1 shilling and 2d. This provided many who were living off the land an opportunity to make large profits by diverting produce on an occasional basis to what became known as the black market. My grandfather was no different, and took an active role in maintaining a regular distribution channel from the Amman and Towy valleys into the large population centres around Swansea. Making a living from a small hill farm with a village abattoir and one butcher shop was a precarious existence, and in those days he simply went along with the opportunity that he helped create, which was to fulfill the strong demand for meat and cheese from the epicentre of the nearest major conurbation, the retail butchers at Swansea Market.

There were severe sanctions and penalties for being convicted of black marketeering in World War II. The Ministry of Food acted like a Soviet secret police operation, investigating complaints against those suspected of being involved in the black market and prosecuting to obtain £500 fines with a possible 2 years in prison a further draconian deterrent. The government also required offenders to pay three times the value of what they had been caught selling on top of the fine. However, many took the risk because their customers had no incentive to inform the government via its network of informants and inspectors. Black marketeers were often the only way the public could acquire what they really wanted, whether it be luxury perfume, nylons, or a rack of lamb. The government fought a never-ending battle with those involved in the black market and despite appointing over 900 inspectors to enforce the law were never able to overcome the insurgency - human nature always prevails.

Its 1994, and I am at a house sale in Llangadog, just over the mountain from Brynamman, for an auction of contents conducted by Brychan the Auction, a legendary auctioneer from Carmarthen. It is a sunny day in mid-June, and whilst we bid for the various bric-a-brac, the dealers sweep up all the old, quality Georgian, Victorian and Edwardian furniture. The old Welsh Dressers are in particular demand, all now destined for the auction rooms of New York and Chicago.

The epicentre of the black market ring operated by my grandfather was The Red Lion pub in the centre of Llangadog, not to be confused with The Black Lion pub, an old coach house, only ten yards away and directly opposite the Butcher's Arms. It is entirely possible to embark on a pub crawl in Llangadog where you only have to walk ten yards in any direction! During a lull in the auction, Dad told the story of the black market ring that had been run out of The Red Lion during the war. The farmers from the Towy Valley would bring their produce to be sold to the pub where it was stored in an old Anderson shelter buried in the garden to avoid the prying eyes of the Ministry of Food inspectors and their informants. Then once a week, regular as clockwork the black market produce would be closely packed into a hearse and would wind its way over the mountain and down the Amman Valley to Swansea Market. The hearse, groaning under the weight of beef, lamb, pork, bacon, fresh eggs and cream was also eligible for extra petrol coupons so the transport was always readily available and didn't affect the bottom line any. The journey from the end of the world to the needy urban classes in Swansea was lucrative indeed.

My grandfather owned one of the few motor cars in Brynamman during the 1930s. Owning a car in those days was a rare thing indeed. But after the war the economy switched to civilian demand, and the old British car manufacturers began introducing a stream of new models from 1948 onwards. My grandfather had learned about wear and tear on a motor car as his business expanded and he spent most of the week travelling along the pitted country roads of West Wales, which were sometimes no more than dirt tracks. DJ needed to change his car every two years, a need that became a habit even after his retirement. Of course, the one to benefit was Clem, especially on weekends, and in 1949 he learned he'd been selected to play in his first Swansea v Llanelli match. The Jacks v Turks is the very essence of what a local derby is all about; distilled its mutual hatred – pure, boiling, parochial rivalry on a grand scale.

Dad wanted to get to the legendary Stradey Park early, to be fully and mentally prepared for his first experience of the derby. The home of the Scarlets was practically in the centre of the town and had witnessed some blood and guts encounters between both near neighbours. The fierce rivalry was always prone to get very heated indeed and was the fixture both sets of fans most eagerly awaited each season.

Clem took the keys of DJ's brand-new Morris Oxford and headed for Llanelli. As he was motoring through Pontardulais near Hendy, he passed the old Teilo tinplate works where he noticed two strong, knarly looking men hitching a ride. Dad slowed down and recognised them as the two Llanelli wing-forwards he was due to play against that afternoon. Aled Jones and Peter Stone were both Welsh trialists. Stone won his first and only cap later that season against France in Paris, partnering Clem in the back row. Dad stopped and offered them a lift. The wing-forwards hopped in, complimenting him on the fancy new car and muttering about "fucking jacks" - as Llanelli natives are prone to call anyone from Swansea.

Jones and Stone had just come off shift, and Dad had only driven 800 yards when they ordered him to stop at the next pub. "Come on boyo..." they said as they dragged Dad into the bar and ordered four pints of beer. Each pint was methodically drained in slow, steady succession. Less than a minute later it was, "right let's get to the ground and give this kid a good thrashing!" And off they went. This, according to Dad completely discombobulated him for more than a few moments. Being a Cambridge undergraduate he was more than used to a tipple or two but he looked on in awe as both men sank their pints in boat-race fashion, prior to an elite rugby fixture no less. Even with the beer swilling around in their bellies, Dad said they were awesome opponents on the pitch, a real handful. He learned to respect the capacity of hard, industrial steel workers to perform under tough circumstances. It was, he said, a moment when I felt like a boy playing against real grown-ups. Of course, the specific gravity of the beer in those days was only around 1027-1030, with a pint of mild costing 1 shilling. The men had come off a 10 hour shift, working in the extreme temperatures generated by the furnaces, and were dehydrated, the solution to which was a shedload of liquid refreshment.

Dad must have taken the lesson to heart because he used alcohol to fortify his spirits and those of his colleagues when he became captain of Wales. Clem would instruct the Welsh rub-a-dub man who brought on the bucket and sponge, and half-time oranges, to also bring on a hip flask of sweet Sherry, a nip of which he swore by to get you revved up for the second half.

Whilst at Cambridge University Clem had finally

decided that his home club would be Swansea RFC. He had hoped to play for the 'All Whites' at the Easter holiday break in 1947, when he was still at school and captain of the Welsh Secondary Schools team. But Swansea would not accommodate him for their games over the Easter weekend against the Harlequins and the Barbarians. So he played for the 'All Blacks' of Neath instead, and only joined Swansea during 1948. His choice of club was important as it paved the way for his future development as a player; he was attracted by the world-class record and reputation the Whites had amassed, the quality of the stadium at St Helen's with its sand-based pitch that was wide and never muddied, and the quality of the fixture list equalled by only Cardiff. The Whites had a plethora of matches against the top English clubs, including Harlequins, Coventry, Leicester and Bristol plus the annual games against Watsonians on Christmas day and the Barbarians at Easter.

Swansea in the late 1940s was the first Welsh club to have beaten each of the Southern Hemisphere international touring teams of Australia (1908), South Africa (1912), and famously New Zealand in 1935 with two schoolboy half-backs from Gowerton Grammar School, Haydn Tanner and Willie Davies. The All Blacks first ever defeat by a club side. The White's captain, Claude Davey, a bulldozing centre scored twice that memorable day.

If Arsenal v Tottenham is North London's most passionate local derby then the Jacks versus the Turks is rugby's equivalent in West Wales. The atmosphere generated by the build-up among the fans always guarantees that come game time there is more spice than the Bangkok street food market. The rivalry is full of blood and thunder, with incidents on the pitch going back decades. Clem once famously wrote that the rivalry is explained by the fact that Loughor Bridge is the point at which the cavalry turns back. Once you cross that distant outpost you're on the reservation, and arrows are sure to fly.

Before my friends from West Wales become upset, Dad in fact had a very soft spot for Llanelli RFC. He formed close childhood friendships with guys like Carwyn James who played in the Welsh schools team with him, and Johnny McLean President of Llanelli RFC (he was Clem's fag at Blundells, and played fly-half for Swansea) and they remained life-long friends. It was Clem who got Carwyn into Fleet Street rugby journalism, introducing him to *The Guardian* after *The Observer* objected to him writing for two broadsheets (before the merger of the two entities in 1992).

Clem suggested to John Samuel, Sports Editor of *The Guardian*, that Carwyn should write regularly on a contractual basis, thus reducing his own income as its Welsh Rugby Correspondent. The Cardiff Branch of the National Union of Journalists opposed Carwyn's necessary membership application and it was the Llanelli Branch who accepted him, since without it he could not work for a closed shop newspaper. Prejudice, no less than coal, is a Welsh product that lies in seams but is never as difficult to mine.

For many years Dad called into Cefneithin to keep a watchful eye on Carwyn James. During Carwyn's finest moment - his coaching of the Test Series winning British Lions team over the All Blacks in New Zealand, the only successful Lions tour to New Zealand - Clem was part of an unofficial brains trust that supported Carwyn. It met in the coffee shops and late bars of the hotels they lived in, and Carwyn would bounce his ideas off Clem and senior players like John Dawes, McBride, and Gibson. I know for a fact that Dad insisted you could never beat the All Blacks without matching them upfront, a basic premise of all international rugby. But Carwyn agreed, and selected a squad of hard scrummaging, athletic forwards, and employed tactics like 'Stop Sid' - bringing Derek Quinnell in to replace Peter Dixon on the blind side in order to physically look after the All Black scrum-half Sid Going who had wreaked havoc in the 2nd Test match.

Clem wrote:

> Carwyn was a close personal friend of mine. He came to see me about a week before leaving on tour to ask my opinions on various matters, and suddenly asked me how I thought his Lions team would do. Having been in New Zealand and Australia with the Welsh team in 1969, and knowing that a third of the team was made up of the same Welshmen, I was unable to offer him much encouragement. Subsequently when I pitched up in Wellington halfway through the tour, where he was having dinner in the team hotel with a delightful half-Maori girl, he gleefully gave me a hard time for a minute or two over the results so far. I immediately sensed a quiet confidence in him, as if he held a royal flush and, as the ace coach holding the 'king', Barry John, he certainly did. Carwyn was a very complex man and a wise man who, after matches liked a quiet corner. He was certainly the greatest rugby intellectual I ever knew and, after his untimely death in 1983, I sorely missed those fascinating post-mortems we held in the BBC Club after every international at Cardiff.
>
> We were lifelong friends, and I was his captain when he played for the Welsh Schools in 1947, and again when he won his two caps against Australia and France in 1958, first as a centre and then in his real position of fly-half. Yet strangely, in those early years, he showed none of his remarkable qualities as a rugby thinker, but then perhaps he was a little too shy and diffident in those days. He was unfortunate that his playing

career coincided with Cliff Morgan's.

Carwyn also coined the now infamous phrase, "Get your retaliation in first", which was originally intended to combat the illegal line-out play of the All Blacks but which, in the end, was to cover a much wider field! This, together with Willie John's slogan in 1974 of "Take no Prisoners", was to become another part of Lions folklore. Two other important elements of Carwyn's strategies for the tour were the use of the counter-attack and the way in which he targeted as a danger the All Black powerhouse, Sid Going, more noted for his strong breaks and linking with his forwards than for his passing to his backs. Hence Derek Quinnell was selected to look after him.

Despite his great friendship with Carwyn, Clem did not go and play for Llanelli. Brynamman is equidistant from Ammanford, a sphere of Stradey Park influence, and Pontardawe, a mining village plumb centre in the Swansea Valley, whose roads and railways ran south west to Swansea Town. This was the era of Dylan Thomas, post war, with Swansea in full reconstruction mode. Swansea was, "an ugly, lovely town...crawling, sprawling...by the side of a long and splendid curving shore." Clem must have felt, "This sea-town was my world," when recruited by the Swansea RFC committeemen who promised the world and great opportunity to both him and his father, DJ.

Swansea rugby club evolved from being the epicentre of a cluster of villages: Morriston, Uplands, Dunvant, Mumbles, Bonymaen, Trebanos, Waunarlwydd, and Gowerton, as well as the vast number of Swansea Valley teams, all of whom contributed their very best players to appear and feature at the magnificent oval at St Helen's. The ground is practically situated on the beach a jewel in Dylan's "splendid, curving shore." There is a unique conjunction of playing first class rugby and cricket at St Helen's and the club's full moniker is Swansea Cricket and Football Club, SCFC. In Swansea there has always been a great sense of pride in the institution amongst the liberal and middle classes, as well as the working class who played rugby football. *"Once a White, always a White..."* This was generally a life-long commitment and was characterised by an unquenchable spirit and a burning conviction that there has always been a superior style of open, flowing, inventive rugby played in Swansea, which at its best is unsurpassed in the world. There is a confidence that, on their day, the 'All-Whites' have been able to take on any team from anywhere and prove more than a match. It was this romantic notion of rising to the occasion that appealed to Clem throughout his time spent playing at the club. And against the two great rugby powers from the Southern Hemisphere, South Africa in 1951, and New Zealand in 1953, Swansea more than lived up to these ideals.

I can speak with some authority on matters regarding Swansea rugby, as we are three generations to represent the 'All-Whites'; my grandfather on my mother's side, Bruce Barter, Dad, and my two brothers, Greg and Mark, and of course, me. I believe we are the only family to have 3 brothers play for Swansea first team. My Grand-uncle was Roy Jones who played wing for Wales and captained Swansea in 1929, whilst my uncle Ian Jones, a handsome, muscular, Brecon educated ex-Royal Marine played in the centre with Dad in the late 1950s. He married Bruce Barter's youngest daughter, Elizabeth.

By the 1940s SCFC had become the principal community for the liberal classes of Swansea to share their interest and love in the two main sports other than association football, which was considered the preserve of the manual, working class in the great conurbations of England. The irony in all this social history analysis is that Wales' two major conurbations were Cardiff and Swansea, and to this day both remain primarily soccer cities despite rugby being the national sport.

Swansea rugby club is located in west Swansea, next to the University on the seafront, a very bourgeois, residential area by Singleton Park with the golden sands of Swansea Bay in front. The men who ran the club were from the liberal professions: teachers, solicitors, barristers and judges, estate agents, steel stockholders, and local entrepreneurs. In the late 1940s when men like Judge Rowe Harding, Bruce Barter and Roy Jones were beginning to wield influence, recruitment became a serious issue. They instigated a series of trial matches at the start of each season to which hopeful recruits would come to make an impression before the assembled committee and Chairman of the selectors.

One aspect that Dad always appreciated within the freemasonry of being an All-White was the banter and cutting South Walian humour. This sardonic wit was nowhere more pointed than in Swansea. No matter who you were, or where you came from, there was always some comedian to cut you down to size and back to earth with a withering one-liner or barbed quip. When I went on my very first tour with Swansea to Jersey in 1977, I went out before breakfast and found an up-to-date edition of the French sports daily, *L'Equipe*. The two years previous I had played at Stade Clermontois in Clermont-Ferrand and at Begles-Bordeaux. Returning to the team hotel, I was quietly reading my paper when an expletive went off from the old pro's table, as Peter Thomas, loose-head prop and hooker and natural funny-man shouted, "Fuck me! Look at Educated Archie in the corner. He's reading a yellow fucking French paper!" From that moment forward I have forever been known as 'Educated Archie' in Swansea rugby club amongst my peer group, although it is often abbreviated to just 'Educated' or even 'Arch'. Whenever we thought the opposition had broken our line-out codes, we would just shout some thesaurus-like extension of 'Educated Archie.' I hadn't a clue who Educated Archie was… but it was considered such an apt name for me that it stuck like chewing gum to the sole of a shoe. I've since learned that it was a BBC comedy show broadcast in the 1950s featuring ventriloquist Peter Brough and his doll Archie Andrews. The show introduced comedians who became well known including Tony Hancock, Benny Hill, and Bruce Forsyth as Archie's tutors.

These mischievous, light-hearted, and good-natured observations about players (especially opponents) and fellow-spectators were typical. Underlying it all, like some melodic ground bass, is that note of laconic satire and realism that always keeps Swansea feet firmly on the ground, never allowing Jacks the opportunity to become too levitated in their raptures during the good times. One of the healthiest instincts of the club throughout its history has been its capacity to shrug off defeat and disappointment and start again with renewed hope. The jinx of inconsistency or under-performance has never been allowed to cast too long a shadow; behind the passing grey clouds, bright sunshine is invariably at the ready to light up Swansea Bay.

Swansea Cricket and Football Club was to become a key institution that nurtured and developed the young Brynamman-based Cambridge freshman. Simply put, not only did it become the club from which he launched his outstanding legendary career, but it was where he met his first wife, Ann, and met many of his closest friends and colleagues, including his father-in-law Bruce Barter and future brother-in-law Ian Jones.

It's 1950, and Glamorgan are playing a match at St Helen's. Dad is high up on the top of the sports pavilion, in the players' viewing area, watching the day's play gently unfold through the afternoon session. Beneath him is a stunning looking blonde girl, quite collected and confident in manner, and he recognised her from his occasional playing commitments with Swansea RFC. In fact, most of the younger players in the club knew her because her father was the selector and committee member, Bruce Barter, a fine centre three-quarter for Swansea throughout eight seasons in the 1920s. Bruce, my grandfather, had also played tennis for Wales. In those days the Saturday ritual followed by my grandfather was to take his wife, Grace, and two daughters, Ann and Elizabeth, to town for shopping, and then return to Langland corner, where they lived, for lunch. Then it was all hands-on-deck to get to St Helen's by 2pm for a spot of light socialising ahead of kick off, 2.30pm prompt.

After the match, the women would often help in the St Helen's pavilion serving teas to the visiting team. In those days everybody in the club mucked in and did various duties always on a voluntary basis. And if this was the ritual in the early 1950's then I can vouch that it had not changed much well into the 1970's.

So began the courtship of my Mum, Ann, a fine athlete on her own account, who became Junior Welsh tennis champion in 1949 in both the doubles and singles. Her father, Bruce had been a fine tennis player, playing for Swansea tennis club at St Helens in the 1920's when nets and courts would be set up at the Mumbles end of the ground. At his death, Bruce was President elect of the Welsh Lawn Tennis Association. He famously started the junior tennis tournament in Langland Bay in 1937, establishing it as one of the most sought-after entries in the UK, won on one occasion by the great JPR Williams, the legendary attacking Welsh fullback.

Mum would go on to play at junior Wimbledon where she eventually lost to Shirley Brasher (née Bloomer), the future wife of the acclaimed athlete Chris Brasher, co-founder of the London Marathon. It was Chris who later in life would mentor Clem's first efforts at rugby journalism on *The Observer* sports desk. Mum later went on to read a degree at London University in domestic Science, and captained the London University tennis team. Despite having two strict, very Victorian-minded parents, Mum was a full-time party girl in those days. Smoking kaleidoscopic-coloured Sobranie cigarettes, and ever appreciative of a gin, ice and tonic, Mum would often be at the hub of après-match festivities and celebrations. Of course, the home games evenings at St Helen's were raucous but were a mere aperitif. By around 8pm or a little after there would be a cavalry-like charge to the cars to race around the panoramic, curved, Swansea Bay. The destination was the bars of Mumbles and Langland, the Osborne Hotel being a particular favourite for its Saturday night big band and dancing. The players, invariably led by Clem, who drove a soft top sports coupe' he had purloined from an old lady in Cambridge, jockeyed for position as they madly dashed down to Mumbles, often engaging each other in battle as soda siphons were spent trying to soak the next car! Can you imagine a Welsh international Osprey player today daring to imitate the legends of Saturday evening from yesteryear?

Mum finally got her man, and Dad got his girl, when they were married on 31st March 1954 at All Saints Church in Mumbles. My Mum has memories of the day, with the crowds in Mumbles three or four deep along the Mumbles road opposite the ramp down to the village itself. It was of its time a celebrity wedding, as Clem's reputation of being the finest wing-forward in the British Isles developed. The only glitch to the wedding plans - and its quite a glitch - was the January 1954 outbreak of foot and mouth disease that meant the postponement of the Wales v Scotland home match scheduled for St Helen's in Swansea. It was in fact the last international ever played at Swansea, eventually played on Saturday 10th April.

Mum remembers her honeymoon in Torquay consisting of a series of daily training sessions as Dad tried to maintain his fitness levels. Mum's patience had already been tested to the full by a series of pranks initiated by Welsh rugby's playboy of the early 1950s, Rex Willis, the

Welsh scrum-half. By the time they had reached Bridgend on their way to Torquay, their car began emitting a disgusting stench that Dad thought may have come from a skunk or something as he had never smelled anything before so disgusting. Mum became mutinous as she desperately fought back the need to vomit, and eventually Dad swung off the road onto a verge. To his horror he saw attached to the now fully heated exhaust pipe, a large Arbroath smokie - a kipper in any other language.

Clem enjoyed a very close relationship with his father-in-law, Bruce Barter. Bruce had led a chequered life. As a schoolboy at Ellesmere College he gained a reputation as a top schoolboy centre three-quarter. The last Swansea international player to make such an impact at Ellesmere was the late Mark Keyworth, a playing colleague of mine with whom I played many games. Mark Keyworth was a hard, hammer of a player who gave a vital tough edge to the England 1980 Grand Slam team captained by the esteemed Bill Beaumont, President of World Rugby. *The Ellesmerian* (Magazine) noted in December 1918 that:

> [Barter,] who showed promise at the beginning of the season, unluckily made a slow recovery from flu and was unfit for a long time. He had a useful kick and was fairly fast but inclined to keep the ball too long. After scoring two tries each against Denstone and Liverpool College, Ellesmere beat Birmingham University, a varsity side, 3-0; As time was getting short, excitement ran high - it reached the climax when Barter receiving from Jones, raced clear through the Varsity backs and scored a brilliant try."

The school magazine in December 1919 however, had commented:

> The weakest part of the team was undoubtedly at

three-quarter even though Barter was one of the
best threes we ever had...A three-quarter who
combined pace and skill effectively. Very good in
both attack and defence, and proved a tower of
strength to his side."

Bruce went on to score six tries against Ruthin School
on Wednesday, October 15th 1919, but left Ellesmere
early during 1920 due to a career-ending heart attack;
suffered by his father Frank Bodinham Barter. Tragedy
had struck earlier in Bruce's life when he lost his mother at
childbirth, and his Dad remarried his wife's sister to bring
up Bruce and his three sisters, Milly, Laura, and Joyce. The
family came to Swansea sometime in the 1890s, with Frank
starting a fishmonger business based on Swansea High
Street. He bought a large home in The Uplands, known as
Kelston House.

Bruce's athleticism had been passed down to him
from his grandfather, Joseph William Barter, born in 1849.
He married Caroline Bodinham in Ross-on-Wye, and
proceeded to father nine children. Frank was the second
born. They lived in a house that subsequently became the
bus station in Monmouth before the great diaspora of the
Barter family. Joseph was a born traveller, an instinctive
Victorian of the age of Empire who sought adventure,
fortune, and knowledge from the North American
continent. He crossed the Atlantic three times in just over
twenty years, the first time on his own, and the second and
third with his burgeoning family. Edgar, Frank, Arthur,
Gertrude, and Herbert were born in Monmouth. But
Albert, Ethel, Mable, and Manly were all born in North
America, along the trek between Minnesota and Manitoba
in Canada - which was to become Joseph's final home.

On his first expedition across the Great Lakes of the
North, he befriended local Indian tribesmen, and played
lacrosse with them. My Aunt Elizabeth has a trophy he
won at one of these tournaments, and my grandfather

Bruce would tell me the tales of his grandad's Red Indian friends. One chief went so far as to demonstrate his respect for Joseph by insisting on conducting a blood brother ritual where he drew a razor-sharp hunting blade across the palms of the two men, allowing the spurting blood to co-mingle. If you go to Manitoba and check out the electoral roll, there are an awful lot of 'Barters' for an oil and cattle town in the middle of Canada. .

The Canadian Pacific Railway reached the area in 1881, and Manitoba began to grow into an important commercial and agricultural centre. One can understand the reasons why Joseph took his family there in the 1890s, as between 1896 and 1914 settlers from all over the world poured into Western Canada in response to the offer of free 'homestead' land. Agriculture and ranching became key components of the local economy, shaping the future of Manitoba for years to come.

Frank Barter was taken seriously ill with a heart attack in 1920 at the young age of 45, leaving four children, of which at seventeen years old, Bruce the eldest was suddenly expected to take up the reins of the family business. A challenge and a destiny he accepted throughout his life, although he had once dreamed of becoming a doctor, an ambition, alas, he would now never fulfill. Being the kind of man he was, diligent, forthright, and intensely practical and kind, Bruce picked up the mantle and wrapped the role of head of the family around himself. He sought to make the most of his situation. He simply got on with his life.

Bruce was a founding member of the Swansea Uplands Rugby Club, attending the meeting of players of the pre-World War I Swansea Grammar School on their return from military service in 1919 at The Uplands Hotel. This is how they came to name the new club, Swansea Uplands which originally played its games in Singleton Park, The Recreation Ground and even St Helens.

By 1921 Bruce had been snapped up by Swansea

RFC, a difficult year both on and off the pitch for Swansea, as the Depression deepened, with 94 tinplate mills idle, and unemployment worsening by the day. Bruce became a stalwart of the club, but his best performances were from 1924 onward when the club recovered its playing reputation, an opinion reinforced when in 1925 Leicester were "outclassed at St Helen's" as Swansea put them to the sword. As ever with Whites versus Tigers matches, it was the play of the backs which caught the imagination of the supporters. "All four Swansea tries were capitally engineered", *The Leader* reported, whilst *The Post* declared that "Barter was the life and soul of the Swansea side. It seemed that the player brought the crowd to its feet...as he sold a dummy to run over for a dazzling try". The St Helen's crowd was ecstatic. The boys were back.

The sport of rugby union football was rigorously amateur in those days. There was little tactical planning in the team's training sessions, and Swansea was typical of most rugby teams at the time. They were imbued with the Corinthian spirit: too much preparation smacked of professionalism, which was considered unfair, and frowned upon. The whole ethos of the game was built around the natural abilities of talented athletes to combine with colleagues and through teamwork take advantage of the opportunities to compete as they arose on the field of play. It was this display of individual talent and athleticism that bred the adoration of young men who had such flair and talent. By 1925, Bruce Barter was fulfilling that need for Swansea supporters.

The South Wales Evening Post covered a fixture against local rivals Neath and reported that, "Barter...realising that a superhuman effort was needed...zigzagged his way through the Neath defence...beating three or four men...and sent Sid Philips over for a try." As far as the newspaper was concerned, Flash Gordon and Bulldog Drummond had nothing on the Swansea centre. Although unlike the heroes of the emerging world of Hollywood,

Barter did not have a script to follow, nor planned entertainments to star in. Theirs was a stage of numberless options, of the need to take decisions in a fraction of a second in the face of men trying to smash you in your tracks.

Bruce was renowned as the team comic. Despite being tee-total he was the life and soul of every post-match party. He was a fine musician, particularly with the violin and piano, and on away trips he would often take his ukulele along, dressing up in imitation of Harold Lloyd, one of the most popular and influential film comedians of the silent film era. Lloyd is perhaps best remembered for his daredevil physical feats, particularly hanging from the hands of a clock high above the street in *Safety Last* (1923), considered one of the most enduring images in all of cinema.

My grandfather continued his fine form into 1926 and 1927, featuring prominently in the touring games against The Maoris and The Waratahs, and continued to feature in Welsh trial matches. However, that Welsh cap continued to elude him, almost certainly due to his tearing of an Achilles tendon which was "just like a violin string snapping", as he described it to me.

By 1930 he had become a committee man, and proceeded over the next 48 years to fill every post and responsibility at the club, from Chairman of Selectors to Fixtures Secretary. At his untimely death in 1978 he was President of Swansea RFC, an honour he took very seriously. I remember him being in charge of the microphone at home games in the 1960's and I would be given the task of testing it before each game by blowing down the microphone to elicit a loud crackling. But I was strictly forbidden to actually ever say anything.

In marrying Ann, Clem was unwittingly creating a rugby dynasty that became his hinterland for the rest of his life; but his relationship with my grandfather went further than their mutual passion for rugby. By the late 1950s, Dad had joined DJ in expanding the wholesale meat business, and had started a contracts business. They supplied wholesale frozen meat to cash and carry warehouses, schools, hospitals, and even British Steel.

Bruce meanwhile, had been forced by the Luftwaffe to switch his fish business away from a retail fishmonger shop to a more lucrative wholesale operation based in Swansea Docks. After the illness of his father in 1919, Bruce had taken on the fish business in Swansea High Street but realised moving into wholesale was the way to go. Bruce was a refined, well-known entrepreneur; Jack Sullivan told me the story of how as a boy he had the job of running the telegrams at 5am every morning from Swansea Post Office in Wind St, to the auctioneers on the docks. They would be eagerly waiting for news of the market prices already established earlier up in Aberdeen and Hull fish markets. This would help them set the price parameters for the daily fresh fish auction set for 6.am in Swansea. The fishing trawlers unloaded their catch in the South Dock Basin where a new ice factory had been built in 1901. Jack Sullivan's special arrangement with grandpa involved him stopping by the office on his way to the docks. Grandpa was able to quickly peruse each telegram ahead of the auctioneers and never paid more than he had to for his fish.

In 1919, Consolidated Fisheries Ltd of Grimsby established a base at Swansea, complete with dry dock facilities, engineering, repair shops, and ships' stores, all located within the South Dock Basin area. Consolidated Fisheries operated a fleet of around 40 deep-sea fishing vessels from Swansea - including many of the 'Castle' trawlers – right up until 1957, when the company finally closed down its operations.

The decline of the fishing industry in Swansea is clearly illustrated by the following figures for fish landings at the port; in 1930 - 15,000 tons, 1952 - 3,669 tons, and by 1970 a mere 279 tons. As a boy in the mid-1960s, I remember going down to the daily auctions with my grandpa, and was always struck by the fact that in the fish market, the fish were sold by the stone, and that when I went with my other grandfather DJ to the cattle auctions, the price was almost always set in guineas.

Bruce had suffered a massive blow to his burgeoning business in February 1941. The German Luftwaffe launched a three-day blitz on Swansea Town (19th – 21st Feb). The Germans were aiming for strategic targets in the docks, where large oil bunkers and facilities were based. Unfortunately, the bombers mistimed their bombing runs, and dropped their bomb loads onto the centre of Swansea, densely populated and the heart of the commercial world at the time. The town centre was decimated with 30,000 incendiaries and 800 high explosive bombs across three nights of relentless attack. A total of 230 people were killed and 397 injured. In total, 575 business premises were burnt out, 282 houses demolished, and a further 11,084 damaged.

One Swansea fireman said, "There was only rubble. I couldn't find anyone. The town was flat." And that was the end of Frank Barter & Sons Ltd Fishmongers in High Street, blown to smithereens by the Luftwaffe, and sadly for Bruce, not insured. He suffered a double blow on that fatal night, as not only did he lose his business, but also his house in the Uplands which was extensively and permanently damaged by the bombing. As Dylan Thomas, who was in the town over those nights and witnessed the almost total destruction of all the Victorian and Edwardian buildings that gave Swansea its unique character exclaimed, "Our Swansea is dead!"

Bruce was a member of the home-guard at that time, and had responsibility for one of the few ack-ack guns that were the sum total of Swansea's fragile defence against air attack. He was told that his home had been hit and he rushed back to the Uplands from the Docks area where he was based. Neighbours had taken the two young girls, Ann and Elizabeth, into a nearby shelter, but there was no sign of Grace, my grandma. She had gone off to the cinema earlier that evening, but at 3am in the morning as Swansea burned, there was no sign of her. Fearing another wave of bombs, Bruce took a snap decision to get the children out of the bombing and somewhere to safety. He piled them into the back of his Rover, threw a blanket over the two of them, instructing them sternly to keep their heads down, and hurtled his way down towards the Mumbles road.

Bruce took the girls to Langland corner where his brother-in-law, Roy Jones (capped for Wales v France in 1928), lived and provided safe haven. A worried Bruce drove straight back to Uplands, and eventually met up with Grace who had sat out the air-raid in the bomb shelter near the Albert Hall.

Unfortunately, Bruce lost his business and his home over those three days. It left the family with very little, but he focused on the wholesale side of the fish business, falling back on 20 years of business relationships, and admirably traded his way back to prosperity.

Throughout the 1950s Bruce and Clem forged a series of business partnerships where they were able to jointly submit bids for both meat and fish supply contracts and add additional products to their bid propositions. Looking back, they must have been an impressive double act: an unstoppable blend of Clem's aggression and salesmanship, and Bruce's steady, sure temperament and steadfast values.

Clem's roots were now firmly entrenched in Swansea. His life had previously shifted from Brynamman to Cambridge, with a short stint in Coventry. On leaving Cambridge University he had taken a job with an engineering supplies company from Cardiff, one of the partners of which was GV Wynne-Jones, the legendary sports broadcaster who commentated on virtually all the Welsh matches that Clem played in. The business involved selling engineering and mining equipment, including safety equipment, to the steel and coal mining industries in South Wales. Clem was primarily taken on to sell to the mining operators, both the National Coal Board and to private coal mines.

In 1951, GV Wynne-Jones had created a real stir when he published his book, *Sports Commentary* in which he accused the Welsh Rugby Union of 'shamateurism' and got himself barred from Cardiff Arms Park, thereby preventing him from broadcasting the Wales v Ireland match. As well as his allegations concerning 'shamateurism' among rugby union players, he didn't endear himself with the WRU hierarchy by caustically questioning their distribution of tickets for important games. He was simply setting the scene for Clem who years later, stayed fiercely close to the Welsh cause, but who also unleashed a torrent of criticism at the moribund, out of date institution.

3

TWO HEART ATTACKS, A DEAD COW AND A VARSITY MATCH

"You are about to awake when you dream that you are dreaming... During the next two days James Bond was permanently in this state without regaining consciousness. He watched the procession of his dreams go by without any effort to disturb their sequence, although many of them were terrifying and all were painful. He knew that he was in a bed and that he was lying on his back and could not move and in one of his twilight moments he thought there were people round him, but he made no effort to open his eyes and re-enter the world... He felt safer in the darkness and he hugged it to him."

Ian Fleming, Casino Royale

Its semi-finals day in the Schweppes Welsh Cup, Saturday April 7th 1990, and I am driving Clem up the M4 to Cardiff Arms Park. Only weeks earlier he had endured a brush with death, suffering a serious heart attack in the press box at Parc des Princes where he luckily had access to the first class emergency services available at the large sports stadia in the centre of Paris. This is the comeback story of the day, of the month, of the year, even. By the early 1990s Clem had cemented his position as the doyenne of the rugby press box, having written for *The Observer* for over thirty years, first under the ownership of Lord Astor, and then in 1990 by The Lonrho Group Plc, controlled by "Tiny" Rowland.

Unbeknown to us both, as I drove his sumptuous Renault 2.5 V6 Turbo up the M4 on the day he finally felt well enough to resume his press box responsibilities, it was our destiny to be on course for a rendezvous with death, a second time, and to be saved by a king!

In Paris, the morning before the France v England match at Parc des Princes, Clem had gone to watch the England 'B' team play their French counterparts in the Stade Jean-Bouin, a small club ground adjacent to the Parc des Princes in the western suburb of Paris and the home of Stade Français. It was freezing cold and Clem had forgotten his overcoat, and in his own words "got chilled to the fecking bone," a factor which no doubt contributed to a small artery in his heart closing 45 minutes prior to kick-off.

I can speak with some authority about collapsing with a heart attack in a rugby stadium. Unfortunately, I have first-hand experience of enduring such a traumatic event. I can highly recommend that, god forgive you suffer such an attack, a modern sports venue is the best place to be. I recall climbing the steps of the Liberty Stadium in May 2015 to take my seat in the directors' box courtesy of my great friend, former colleague at Deloitte's and business associate, Rob Davies. It was the last game of the regular Pro12 competition, and the Ospreys, Swansea's Regional rugby team, were playing for a spot in the impending play-offs. I turned to step into the directors' seating area and suddenly crumpled into a heap. I was suffering a cardiac arrest; a similar affliction had struck Fabrice Muamba, the Bolton Wanderers player in an F.A. Cup tie in 2012 against Tottenham Hotspur at White Hart Lane. Similar to Fabrice, I thank my lucky stars that I was fortunate to have the cardiac arrest in a sports stadium.

The Liberty Stadium, named after the Property Group created by Rob Davies and Mike James (former Swansea rugby club player and chairman) is a modern 20,000 seater bowl, home of the Ospreys and Swansea City Football Club. During match days there are a prescribed number of St John's Ambulance carers and Paramedics in attendance and an ambulance on standby. If you are going to keel over, then the Liberty is as good a place as any and probably a damn sight better than most. I fell at the feet of the Stadium manager, Andrew Davies and within spitting distance of Barry Lewis, a St John's Ambulance carer. I was within a few rows of both the Ospreys and Swans medical staff, all of whom rushed to my assistance. Barry and a colleague immediately began delivering vigorous CPR, the correct action in any cardiac arrest. They sprang seamlessly into action as if it were a daily occurrence. If not for their swift intervention I would have undoubtedly died on the spot or been left with severe brain damage. Andrew Davies radioed for assistance and the paramedics arrived with the defibrillator pads; it took them 7-8 attempts to revive my heartbeat. I was down without heart function for almost 30 minutes. The St John's team did a fantastic job keeping the oxygen moving to my brain. And how can I ever thank them enough?

I was put on a stretcher, carried down in the lift, and put into the ambulance in attendance. A quick journey 5 miles up the road took me to the Intensive Trauma Unit in Morriston Hospital, where I was put on life support and plugged into every machine imaginable. The trauma of the experience has left a few scars, but you just have to try and get on with your life. Clem did much the same back in 1990 by insisting on a prompt return to his press duties.

I have no personal memory of what happened to me on that fateful Friday or even the week preceding. I could have murdered someone and would not have been able to furnish an alibi. I have since spoken with friends and family and managed to piece together assemblance of events. I had stayed up late to watch the Tory drubbing of Labour in the General Election and then headed up the M4 to Groesfaen. I had arranged to lunch with one of my oldest friends, Rob Cole who captained Blundells the year before me, played for Penarth and today runs the Westgate Sports Media Agency. Rob is one of Wales' foremost rugby writers, his father was the former Editor-in-Chief of *The Western Mail* and as Chief Executive ran all the regional press in the Thomson group from London. Later, I went to Cardiff station to collect my youngest daughter, Siwan, from the London/Paddington train and we drove home to Sketty. I then recall picking up my G.P. Dr Dave Hughes from Langland, a portent perhaps of events to transpire, and we drove to the Liberty. Dave testifies that I was in tickety-boo form and certainly did not appear to be a man about to suffer a cardiac arrest.

Dave Hughes is a fine doctor, who was a houseman at The Heath (University of Wales Hospital) in the early 1980s. He once attended to my grandmother Edna following a botched pacemaker procedure at Singleton Hospital in Swansea. Legend has it that Edna was driven by ambulance from Swansea to Cardiff and Clem decided to follow by car but lost contact even though it was only travelling at 20mph, a speed Clem infrequently travelled at.

At the Liberty stadium, Dave shot off to meet some doctor friends and I went to the directors' lounge. I had a drink with Rob Davies and Chris Richards, deputy Chairman of the Ospreys. Many moons ago, Chris joined Deloitte, Haskins & Sells, a chartered accountancy firm the same day as me. He was an outstanding 110 meter hurdles athlete and I persuaded him to give rugby a go. In no time at all he was playing for the Swansea first team due to his fine athleticism and scorching pace. Chris once won a bizarre competition at the old Swansea Morfa Athletics Stadium. He was crowned the fastest winger in Welsh rugby, holding off Elgan Rees of Neath in the final of the

100m challenge.

I remember waving to Jonathan Davies up in the Liberty press gallery and him giving me the thumbs up in expectation of an Osprey victory. Then I promptly collapsed, the blame for which I in no way attach to Jiffy!

The swift action and expert attention of the Liberty medical staff are the reasons I was able to survive the initial cardiac arrest. They gave me an opportunity to live, but once the doors of the ambulance closed, my real fight for life began.

I spent 55 days fighting for my life in the ITU where I suffered two bouts of double-pneumonia, an induced tracheotomy, and spent the first 8 days in a coma, ninety per cent dependent on life support. The surgeon informed my sister Caroline, that if I suffered another cardiac arrest, they would not try to bring me back. The darkest days were the realization that I was not capable of enduring the intensive C PAP oxygen therapy. I found it both exhausting and physically debilitating. I got through it thanks to the professionalism and care of my nurse Ed, who coached and mentored me through this toughest of periods. Ed told me the only person who could get me through the exit door, was me. Caroline also drummed this message home with some much needed tough love. I put my game face on and vowed to do everything asked of me and more by the medical professionals.

88 days later, I was finally discharged and have been attempting to pick things up ever since. The writing of this book is part of the process.

Back in 1990 Clem found himself in the back of an ambulance bouncing along the Boulevard Victor Hugo en route to l'Hôpital Américain de Paris. Legends that have passed away at The American hospital include Aristotle Onassis, the actor Jean Gabin and Hollywood siren Bette Davis. We were all relieved that Clem didn't see fit to join that inauspicious list. I received the news late Saturday afternoon, and with my sister Caroline, organised to fly over to Paris the very next morning. My stepmother Joyce, an eminent doctor, had informed us Dad was pretty poorly and we should brace ourselves.

Upon arrival at Charles-de-Gaulle Airport we were whisked away to Neuilly-sur-Seine on the west side of Paris by my old friend Jacques Damitio. I've known Jacques since the 1960s; his father had been a star athlete, competing in both the long and high jumps at the 1948 London Olympics, and was a close friend of Dad's. In Jacques' inimitable fashion, foot gunned to the floor, we charged through the relatively light Sunday lunchtime traffic and screeched to a halt in front of an Edwardian fin de siecle brasserie.

"No visitors until 2.30," he said, hopping out of the car, "And I'm hungry, let's eat." Jacques proceeded to consume a massive grilled andouillette, whilst Caroline and I fiddled nervously with whatever we had ordered. This was definitely not the moment to enjoy a lunch in Paris. We were both worried sick about our father's health.

Finally, we arrived at Clem's room expecting the worse. There he was, sitting up in bed, surrounded by French friends and his wife Joyce. Dad was holding court in a jovial loud voice. As we entered he burst into one of his trademark laughs, a deep and posh sounding, "HO-HO-HO-HO!!" He was twice as large as life and in fine mettle.

I couldn't help but notice that he had an enormous tray of food perched in front of him, that only the French, with true love in their hearts would have dared offer up to a cardiac patient. The tray was practically groaning under the weight of charcuterie, oysters, Brandade de Morue, Coq au vin, a wealth of cheeses and rich chocolate mousse. Clem's life-long friend, Pierre Combin, a renowned Parisian restaurateur who established *Le Gaulois, La Route de Beaujolais* and the *St Vincent* had arrived a few moments earlier on a mission of mercy to, "ensure Clem got his strength back quickly." Caroline's jaw practically hit the floor as she took in the situation. "Christ," she exclaimed in her best matronly fashion, "He'll have another bloody heart attack if he eats that lot!" The joke promulgated by his press colleagues, Ian Robertson and Nigel Starmer-Smith, was he chose to have a heart attack because he couldn't cope with an English win in Paris! England had won the match 26-7.

Dad flew back to Swansea a few days later. He was quite poorly for many weeks, but by the end of March had regained sufficient fitness and energy to want to get back to his rugby journalism. Clem admitted that he had let the cigarettes get the better of him. He had a terrifying addiction to the demon nicotine. I can always remember him chain-smoking and had to endure a tobacco dense fug in his car every trip from Swansea to Brynamman on the way to the abattoir. Later in life, when he had the inescapable pressure of copy deadlines after rugby matches, I would be despatched to buy 40 Benson & Hedges or Silk Cut, and Dad would smoke his way through the lot as he worked up the articles. In the 1960's it was always Senior Service or Gold Leaf, and it seemed to me at the time that the whole world smoked. Nana puff-puff smoked Peter Stuyvesant, as did my other grandmother, Grace. Dad once told me that he only started smoking on the British Lions tour to South Africa in 1955. The tourists were the recipients of unending hospitality and generosity from their Springbok hosts and cigarettes were in abundant supply. Of course, in the 1950's every film star and starlet was constantly drawing on a cigarette, and it became almost de rigueur across society. Dad said to me before his second heart attack which sadly proved fatal that it had been cigarettes that were to blame for his heart disease. He had always considered himself exempt from any major physical frailty after years of taking good health for granted, as do so many of us. Dad would often point to his father's high-fat, high-sugar diet and industrial intake of nicotine that outdid anything he ever did – and DJ lived to the ripe old age of 80.

We glided into the car park, for the Schweppes Welsh Cup in the bowels of Wales' sporting cathedral, Cardiff Arms Park. Dad wanted to park the car near the exclusive press box elevator. He was still recovering from the heart attack and was often short of breath. We had not anticipated another brush with death so soon. Certainly for Clem, 1990 would turn out to be a year of living dangerously. We both crammed ourselves into the tiny press elevator - more of a sardine tin than anything. Dad was 6ft 1in, and I'm 6ft 4in, our weights are a closely guarded state secret and can only be revealed 50 years hence. But if I had to hazard a guess I'd imagine our combined weight to be around the 36 to 38 stone mark, give or take. Regardless, it was well within the specified safety limit announcing the sardine tin would accommodate no more than five people. That was pushing it some, with both of us squeezed in there was no room for anyone else.

The press box at Cardiff Arms Park was located at the top of the North Stand, which for the purpose of the Schweppes semi-finals double header remained closed to the public. The supporters filled the South Stand and terraces. The lift proceeded to journey upwards, but suddenly juddered to a screeching halt. An awkward stoney silence ensued whilst I pressed the up button, again and again, but to no avail. With absolutely no movement I began pressing the down button, we remained stuck. I threw caution to the wind and pressed the alarm. We heard the ever so faint chime of an electric bell that sounded better suited to a child's bicycle than a public lift.

It was now apparent to me that we were stuck for all eternity somewhere in the North Stand, enveloped by reinforced concrete. It felt like a tomb with no-one likely to be outside in the public waiting areas. The Cardiff Arms Park had become our Soviet-style mausoleum. I decided on extreme measures and began hollering and bashing our steel coffin. Clem screamed in frustration, "For Christ's sake Christopher…stop panicking!" I calmly interjected that I was merely attempting to make some noise in the hope that someone might hear. Suddenly there was a mighty roar, informing us that the first match had kicked off. Then the elevator light flickered and died, leaving us in total darkness. After a moment of silence, "Keep banging!" was Dad's shouted advice. Time seemed to drag forever and then I felt an acrid, burning smell accost my sinuses. It was the kind of smell you often associate with a Scalextric Set, or electrical wire on fire. "There's something burning" stated Dad, "This is ridiculous…we could die in here."

I redoubled my efforts and kicked the shit out of that lift, but it became increasingly difficult to breathe. I started to worry about Dad's health what with the lack of oxygen and acrid fumes. "Who's there?" someone hollered from somewhere distant. "It's Clem," I screamed in desperation. Then I suddenly recognised the voice, it was Barry John, the legendary ex-fly-half of Wales. "Get the fire brigade, quickly Barry, be quick!" There was a deadening silence as the smoke intensified. An age seemed to pass, all of eternity and then quite suddenly the sardine can jolted. We dropped like a stone back to the car park entrance. When we hit daylight, coughing and spluttering, we could barely see each other, so dense was the smoke. The fire brigade were all rigged out in suits and oxygen bottles. We reeled about, gagging for the lack of air. The overwhelming emotion I remember was relief. "Quick," said Dad, by now the game was 20 minutes into the first half. We took up our positions in the North Stand and were subsequently joined by all the rugby journalists, evacuated from the press box due to the huge plumes of black smoke that funnelled up the lift shaft. The entire electrical system had caught fire and raged throughout both matches as the fire service fought to bring it under control.

Whenever I meet Barry John, a delightful, articulate and bright man, I always hail him as, "The man who saved my life…and Clem's…but he had to think about the second one!!" The last comment isn't entirely fair as Dad and Barry were always great friends. Dad was one of the journalists on the 1971 British Lions tour to New Zealand who encouraged his coronation, and the common parlance of 'King' as a term of respect. Dad always rated him as the greatest fly-half he ever saw and he was our saviour too!

Clem once said to Barry, "BJ, I would only have had to play you once, and after my first tackle had crushed you, you'd be finished for the rest of the game." To which Barry retorted, "Clem, you wouldn't have even stepped on my shadow…" Clem chuckled at this, and for years that became his favourite Barry John story. He loved Barry's audacity and calm confidence in his ability, however Clem's self-deprecation only extended to such gifted people as Barry.

Barry cemented his reputation as one of the sport's greatest players with his pivotal role in the British Lions winning tour over the All Blacks. He recently told me: "Clem flew into New Zealand in 1971 for the last two test matches. I remember going down to the dining room in the St George's Hotel in Wellington, and as I was mobbed by dozens of Lions supporters, I was amazed to see Clem and my father-in-law, Sir Alan Talfyn-Davies, having dinner together. I go over, and Clem asked if we could have a few words, so he took me aside and said, "Barry, you've no idea how big your name is right now in the UK." I replied that I had never felt any pressure to perform, until that moment, so thanks for putting the frighteners on me! Clem said that wasn't his intent, but that I could not duck the press or public reaction to my playing exploits forever. The following evening, after we'd beaten the All Blacks in the 3rd test match that included a ten-point contribution from myself including a try under the posts, Clem laughingly said to me that following my brilliant display that day, I'd now made the matter even worse!!! Now everyone wanted a part of me."

Barry often tells an amusing story about travelling with Dad: "I remember standing impatiently in line with him at Edinburgh airport returning to Cardiff. Some enormous, fat guy was being difficult at check-in. Five, then ten minutes elapsed. We were tired and hungover. Suddenly Clem erupted and stormed determinedly up the side of the lengthening queue to the front where this fat guy was still moaning and complaining, "Listen you fat lump of lard", intoned Clem in his best Cambridge University baritone voice which had more than a hint of menace. "Either move now to let us folk check-in promptly, or I'll remove you from this terminal myself you fat selfish lump!" The crowd waiting cheered, as most now recognised Clem - "Well said Clem, move the fat git!" yelled someone behind me and then the whole crowd started braying. It was classic Clem stuff…a strong, aggressive and timely intervention. Clem was forever the populist!"

Barry John was Welsh rugby's equivalent to Bob Dylan in that he was nonconformist, with a unique talent which allowed him to take his sport to a new level. A creative genius of such prodigious talent and achievement who never sought the fame, acclaim, or responsibility that came with winning a test series against the All Blacks in New Zealand. Unlike the classical Welsh fly-halves, Barry John didn't have a low centre of gravity that encouraged the 'jink' or the outrageous side-step of a Dai Watkins or Phil Bennet. Barry John glided where others scrambled, ran with his lithe bearing, ball out-front always in two hands, where a mere twitch would send defenders plunging past him as they grasped thin air. He was genius on a rugby pitch. And he played for the fun of it all, perhaps making him Wales' greatest sportsman. He wove poetry into his game, and confirmed Carwyn James' assertion that rugby football is an art, of which he was the master, and of course, the king.

Having been saved by the king, in retrospect I do not think we took the incident as seriously as we perhaps should have. 'DEATH IN THE AFTERNOON AT CARDIFF ARMS PARK' almost certainly became the headline. It was simply luck that Barry John had turned up late, and mistakenly gone to the other side of the ground. That was why he was walking up the stairs alongside the lift having first tried to call it himself. Sometimes close calls become actual events, and actions can have serious consequences.

In 1944 in Francis House at Blundells, Clem was forever mucking about with his great mate Grenville Charrington. They were the scourge of the prep room. Charrington was a fanatical boy soldier in the CCF and had returned after half-term break with a First World War Webley IV pistol, an 11.6mm calibre weapon. Whilst extremely reliable in the mud of Flanders, it was notoriously difficult to shoot with any accuracy. An awful lot of practice was required since it jumped on firing.

The challenge for young Charrington was that now he had procured, by fair means or foul, a dodgy weapon ammunition was sorely needed. Blundells, like every public school with a CCF, the firing ranges were for .22 competition rifles or the British Army stalwart the .303 Lee-Enfield bolt-action magazine-fed, repeating rifle. It has been the British Army's standard rifle from its official adoption in 1895 until 1957. Originally a redesign of the Lee-Metford (1888) it featured a ten-round box magazine which was loaded with the .303 British cartridge manually from the top, either one round at a time or by means of five-round chargers. The Lee-Enfield was the standard issue weapon to rifle companies of the British Army and other Commonwealth nations in both the First and Second World Wars. A total of over 17 million were manufactured in that period and it was the weapon the

CCF trained the next generation of soldiers with. When both Clem and I were in the CCF at Blundells, this was the weapon we were taught to strip, clean and fire on the rifle range.

Dad remembers Charrington working at his desk in the prep room one evening having purloined about a dozen rounds of .303 cartridges. They were 7mm and far too slim for the hand pistol. Charrington, like a mad professor had managed to acquire a soldering iron from the physics lab. He was engrossed in soldering rims onto the live .303 cartridges in the hope they would prove to be a workable fit for the Webley. "Utter madness," commented Dad, who was the only one remaining after every boy bolted out of the room. His reward would be to accompany Charrington and get an opportunity to fire the revolver; no doubt, a pretty cool thing at a public school in the middle of World War II.

Clem was probably one of the few boys who knew and understood how to handle a gun. From the age of eleven he learned how to fire a small-bore shot-gun, and was the proud owner of a .410 bore farm gun. Dad perfected his aim shooting rabbits, pigeons, and crows around the farm on the Brecon Beacons. He liked to boast of his shooting exploits and claimed they were an entrepreneurial way of making pocket money, selling rabbits and pigeons to a hungry constituency always ready with a few pennies for game for the table. I can testify that the .410 bore shotgun throws the least weight and is easy to handle, perfect for young shooters. It became very popular after 1900 for small game animals such as squirrels and rabbits, where the small diameter patterns of a full choke are less problematic than with birds.

Francis House is on the Blundells road where the school buildings finish, with three large playing fields further west leading onto the Uplowman Woods, a good three to four miles from the school - the perfect territory to try out Charrington's antique revolver. It was summarily decided that Sunday afternoon was the optimum occasion, with no masters present or expected. That day, four boys sneaked across the playing fields. They walked for the best part of an hour away from the school, and any known dwellings. Finally, in the thick of the forest, they fired the Webley pistol. Charrington took the first two shots, squeezing off each round as the other three took refuge behind an old oak tree. The pistol was impossible to control with any semblance of accuracy. The recoil and kick were so aggressive that the boys who tried missed large trees from a range of barely 10 yards. But it must be said the Webley's reputation was holding up despite the Heath Robinson ammunition bravely engineered by Charrington.

After an hour of disappointing marksmanship, the boys decided to call it a day and trudged off back to school. They cut across Lowman River, and finding themselves in a meadow surrounded by a wide ditch, spotted a cow. The poor beast was minding its own business happily grazing. Charrington had a mad gleam in his eyes as he snorted, "I've got one bullet left lads." He raised his arm determinedly, aiming down the barrel, his hand steady and gently squeezed the trigger. BOOM! The cow instantly collapsed, stone cold dead. The bullet passed clean through its skull. It rolled onto its back, hooves in the air, nerves jerking muscular spasms and simply was no more. There was utter shock and disbelief between the gang of four. No-one had expected Charrington to hit his target, least of all Charrington. None of the boys had an accurate idea as to the penalty for shooting a cow in wartime. But all were in agreement that punishment would be pretty punitive and extremely cautionary as an example to other offenders. Rustication and expulsion were almost inevitable. The lads fled back to school after having covered the cow's carcass with leaves and twigs. Charrington and Clem hatched a cunning plan.

That evening, a little after midnight our gang of four

enlisted five dormitory colleagues, swearing them to secrecy. My future stepfather Hugh Portsmouth was included in the cabal. They snuck out and raided the Francis House allotments garden shed, liberating eight shovels. They returned to the scene of the crime and dug out a deep, long trench. The skill for which had been learned in the CFF conducting military exercises on Dartmoor. The carcass was unceremoniously dragged into its muddy grave. The ground refilled, the sod replaced, and the boys were back in bed by 4am, a job well done. Dad would say that to this very day the farmer never knew what happened to that damn cow!

Grenville Francis Nicholas Charrington left Blundells to join the Suffolk Regiment in the British Army. He got posted to the Far East where he saw action in the Malayan Emergency (1948-1960), a guerrilla war fought between Commonwealth armed forces and the Malayan National Liberation Army (MNLA), the military arm of the Malayan Communist Party led by Chin Peng. The rubber plantations and tin-mining industries had pushed for the use of the term 'emergency' since their losses would not have been covered by Lloyd's insurers if it had been termed a 'war', which it undoubtedly was. The irony was the MNLA had been secretly trained by the British during World War II as the principal resistance against the Japanese occupation.

One day in May, 1951, whilst reading *The Times*, Clem came across a citation for a Military Cross awarded for exceptional gallantry to a Lt Grenville Charrington, "for relentless pursuit of Malayan bandits through dense jungle with a total disregard for his own personal safety." Dad said at the time how he felt awfully sorry for those poor bandits.

Amazingly the preoccupation with firearms in the Charrington family continued through the generations. Lt Charrington's son Richard attended Blundells a few years behind me and was also in Old House. He had already at the age of 13 lost a finger from his left hand to a gun powder explosion and was totally gun crazy. He also totally corroborates the story of the dead cow and it has since become one of the legendary wartime tales of Francis House.

Throughout his life, Dad suffered from bad sinusitis, a condition that was diagnosed in late 1946. This led to his ear, nose, and throat consultant recommending a period of stay in a dry, clean air environment, away from the freezing fog, rain, and chill of a British winter. Clem was despatched to St Moritz, Switzerland in the spring of 1947, to utilise a course of inhalation treatments considered at that time to be extremely beneficial to painful, ongoing sinus infection. Many years later a Swansea CFC doctor, an ENT consultant diagnosed a crushed septum as the cause of all his woes. This was straightened during another procedure to treat a terrible split lip incurred playing France in 1954.

Unfortunately, Clem had to withdraw from the Welsh schools side that played England in 1947; finding himself instead at 10,000 feet altitude in the European playboys' winter paradise of St Moritz. After a few days spent all alone lodging in a boarding house and enduring a series of treatments at the local sanatorium, the days began to drag and he became quite restless. Clem hit on a solution to his boredom and took up skiing. He took to the snow as a duck to water. As luck would have it St Moritz was selected to host the V Olympic Winter Games (1948). The resort had been selected ahead of its only rival, Lake Placid (USA), because it was located in Switzerland which had remained neutral throughout the war.

When Clem took to the downhill pistes, he was coached by a Swiss local with close ties to the Swiss Ski Federation. He found himself learning on one of the most challenging courses in the Alps. The runs that he was told to focus on by his coach were at Piz Nair, the location a year later for the main Olympic downhill event. This was where the Swiss squad were ensconced hard at work on their training. After six weeks of practise, Clem was flying under the stern, patrician instruction of his Swiss coach. Dad said he spoke absolutely no word of English, but fanned his hands and arms about to convey the correct positions he wanted Clem to adopt.

Every year the British Ski Club organised a lowlander race for those skiers who came from countries where low altitudes prevail and skiing is uncommon, as in the UK. That year's lowlander race was held in St Moritz where the hopefuls for the British team were also in training. Clem got some valuable assistance from his coach who persuaded the Swiss team to lend Clem a set of the latest downhill skis so he could compete in the race. The skis had longer runs and more flexible poles than those used in other Alpine events.

Henri Oreiller (France) won gold in 2mins 55 seconds at the Olympics held a year later. But that particular year, Dad won the event! Clem didn't match Henri but he went fast enough to win. Dad credited his stunning performance to natural athleticism, balance, and balls. He gloated a good forty years after the event, "I just put my head down and pushed hard. Very bloody hard...How I didn't crash and fall is still a mystery I can't fathom. But what I do know is I went down that ridiculously steep bastard of a mountain fast, bloody fast."

Dad was approached that evening by representatives and skiers from the British ski party and invited to join their pre-Olympic training camp. Dad gracefully declined, explaining that he had been accepted at St John's, Cambridge, and intended to take up his place in September. He also excused himself on the grounds that his first love was rugby union football, and that he doubted he could stay injury free if he took up downhill skiing full-time.

I believe that the skiing incident best illustrates Dad's

enormous capacity to compete at full tilt, regardless of the sport - when he puts it all on the line - and goes all in, as the Americans like to say. Clem always had a propensity to identify a challenge or a dare, and he seldom, if ever, backed down from a challenge. Especially if it was some new task that he had to master or if his opponent was someone he simply had to beat at all costs. Dad hated losing, but was never a bad loser, and if he won he would simply have a little chuckle to himself, as if he knew he was going to win all along.

The only place where he threw total disregard for his own safety out the window was in a motor car he was quite lethal. Every son can empathise with another guy by sharing similar experiences of their fathers' changing cars as the years and decades pass. My earliest memories are of a Cambridge (of course) blue Sunbeam Alpine. But as my siblings grew in number, the cars became more family oriented: an Oxford Cambridge, Austin1800, and in the mid-1960s a Vanden Plas Princess 4-litre R. It was Dad's pride and joy at that time and bought for the purpose of ferrying the family - all six of us - on holiday. I remember driving through France to a camp site of permanent caravans in Frejus, adjacent to St Raphael, on the shore of the Mediterranean. The R in the car's name meant Rolls-Royce, and it was the first time Rolls-Royce had sullied one of its engines by dropping it into a mass-market car.

The Vanden was aimed at the snob market for those who could not afford a proper "Roller." Sales never really took off, probably because the car resembled nothing more than a swollen Oxford-Cambridge. It was the classic British motor of its time: a lot of posh for the dosh. I recall sweeping majestically down the autoroute through Lyon with the speedometer pushing 120mph. The car seemingly cemented to a running rail on the straight French roads. Even to this day, I am still thrilled at the prospect of travelling long distances at high speed across the European continent. Unfortunately, that particular excursion ended rather badly for my younger brothers, Gregory and Mark. Both became badly infected with a rather nasty, hacking, whooping cough. They got so ill that Mum had no option other than to take them home. Mum flew them out of Nice Airport to be met by my grandfather, Bruce. The upshot was that Dad took his time on the return journey, shadowing la route de Napoleon through the French Alps via Grenoble with a two day stop off in Paris. We stayed with Philippe Chatrier, who was then the President of the French Lawn Tennis Federation and later President of the World Tennis Federation.

I remember Caroline and I visiting the Eiffel Tower for the first time, and rolling royally down the Champs Elysees in the back of our Rolls-Royce powered Vanden Plas. I also remember us dining with Nora Beloff, the future wife of Clifford Makins, the sports editor of *The Observer* newspaper. It was Clifford that promoted Clem to Chief Rugby correspondent, after primarily covering Welsh rugby from 1960.

Nora was a massive personality and made a huge impression on us. She was an outstanding journalist and worked in Paris after the second World War for Reuters, *The Economist* and *The Observer*, and went on to become the political correspondent, and later an international roving reporter, for *The Observer*, covering the world, particularly Washington, as well as Moscow and Belgrade.

Nora was the first female political correspondent of a British newspaper and belonged to a generation in which women needed to be brighter and more fearless than male rivals for plum jobs. Her obvious qualifications did not always make her friends amongst her male colleagues, whose arguments she tended to dismiss as "nonsense!" And some of her many distinguished political and diplomatic contacts flinched when she came on the telephone to bend their ears. She was incapable of allowing a sloppy thought to slip past without challenge.

She often wrote critical pieces about the Labour

Party, and Labour Prime Minister Harold Wilson went to extraordinary lengths to try and get her dismissed from *The Observer*, all to no avail. Nora was mercilessly lampooned in the satirical magazine *Private Eye* as "Nora Ballsoff", and sued for libel after Auberon Waugh jested that she was frequently found in bed with Wilson and other members of the cabinet but nothing improper had occurred. Her esteemed council Peter Carter-Ruck, himself a regular Eye target as "Carter-Fuck", in a stroke of genius called as witness the old and frail writer (author of *The Charge of the Light Brigade*) Cecil Blanche Woodham-Smith, walking with a Zimmer frame and laboriously carried into the witness box. In quavering tones she described the shock she had felt at the vile attack on her impeccably respectable friend. Nora won damages of £3,000 but lost a separate case against *Private Eye* over the magazine's publication of a memorandum she had circulated within *The Observer* about the former Tory home secretary, Reginald Maudling. The costs, estimated at £10,000, were awarded against her.

If ever the term "they don't make them like that anymore" applied to anyone then it applied in abundance to Nora Beloff. Her former editor Donald Trelford, with whom she had fallen out, wrote that Nora "had one of the most distinguished careers any woman has had in British journalism". Until her husband, Clifford, sadly became ill in the late 1980s, they were regular visitors to our family home in Swansea, mainly for rugby and cricket events.

Following the Vanden Plas, I recall Dad going full metal jacket and buying an MG BT. He would practically have to squeeze himself into it every morning. That car could truly shift, and how he didn't kill himself is a total mystery to me. The distance from Langland to Cardiff is approximately 47 miles and following each international match, Dad always wanted to get home to Swansea. He preferred to be close to home so he could stay out of trouble, relatively at least.

After one particular match, Clem, his brother-in-law

Ian Jones, the renowned artist Andrew Vicari, and Bob Lloyd-Griffiths - Dad's best friend and future High Sheriff of West Glamorgan - decided on a small wager. A road race ensued with the first car back to the Rock & Fountain public house in Newton taking the spoils. VVROOOM! Off they roared, leaving a trail of burnt rubber adorning the car park of Cardiff's Athletic Club. They sped headlong down the A48 until they got to Port Talbot where Vicari, breaking too hard, spun his car and landed sideways in an electricity sub-station...WHIZZZZZ... BANG GEDUNG!!! Suddenly the whole of Port Talbot was plunged into total darkness as the electricity supply system quite suddenly disintegrated. Luckily for Vicari, Clem pulled up in time to witness the total destruction. He had got caught short some time before and pulled over to empty his bladder. Vicari arose Lazarus like from the wreckage and hopped into Dad's car. "Push on Clem and be quick...We simply have to beat Ian and Bob." Dad was incredulous but did as instructed and they fled from the scene. Vicari informed him that the car actually belonged to his brother's friend from Neath and he'd borrowed it. "They can pick up what's left in the morning and sort it all out. I'm off to London first thing..." Dad had a good laugh about that.

Ian Jones once made the mistake of lending Clem his Porsche 911. Dad needed to get to London in a hurry. London is approximately 200 miles from Swansea and Clem got there in two hours flat. Ian said he never in a million years wanted to repeat such a hair-raising experience. In the late 1970s Dad started to buy Japanese, and went through a series of Toyota Celica's that were perfect machines for the type of motoring he had to do: hundreds of miles around farm roads in the week, and 200 plus long-distance journeys to rugby grounds across England at weekends. Then he opted for a BMW 5 series for a good few years, before discovering the executive Renault2.5v6, he really appreciated the smooth ride and suspension. Dad's last car came about as part of a business investment he made in a Swansea car dealership and was a Nissan Maxima QX. Unbelievably, 24 hours had not elapsed since his passing and people were already cold calling my step-mum Joyce, wanting to buy the damn car!

Dad was very fond of telling the story of one of his gastronomically excessive weekends attending a French Championship final held in Bordeaux (28th May, 1967). Dad took along his great friend and fierce rival Peter Robbins, the England back row forward, whom he always referred to as "the man with the Beaujolais belt". They were booked to be back on a Monday evening, but that year's final featured Begles, the premier club from one of Bordeaux's communist suburbs. Begles sadly lost to Montauban, 3-11. I say sadly because I played for Begles in 1978 and Dad's great friend "Bambi" Moga, a charcutier by trade, had organised my trip. Bambi played second row for France in the late 1940's and was a huge presence. He played against Clem at Stade Colombes in Paris for Clem's 1st cap (1949). A natural bon viveur, trencherman par excellence, he became the soulmate of Peter Robbins. They played for Philippe Chatrier's Hertet Old Boys Teams that played a Press XV on the eve of Five Nation internationals and both regularly drank Paris dry after each match. Bambi was delirious with joy to see Clem and Peter and had organised a wine tasting for the two visiting gastronomes that Monday morning in two of the Medoc's most desirable vineyards: Chateau Palmer, a second growth Margaux, and Chateau Talbot, a fourth growth St Julian that belonged to his close friends Georges and Jean Talbot. I had the pleasure of meeting Jean and visiting the same Chateau with Bambi in 1978. It is one of the largest vineyards in the Medoc, with 102 hectares of vines under cultivation. The wine is assembled from four grape varietals, 70% cabinet sauvignon, 20% merlot, 5% petit verdon, and 5% cabinet franc. At our family Christmas lunch in 2016, held at my sister Caroline's home in Mumbles, we drank the last magnum of a 1965 Chateau Talbot brought back in the boot of Clem's MG BT. Bambi had generously gifted Dad and Peter a case each.

Of course, that Monday in the Medoc they did not exactly rush to get away, and they certainly did not lightly partake of the grape. "It was crazy," said Dad. "We were due on the boat at Calais for 8 o'clock that evening and we didn't leave Bordeaux until after lunch. I remember driving the MG BT as fast as I could without killing either of us. We were stopped and detained five times for speeding. Every time Robbins, a fluent French speaker, did his stuff with 'Le Flic', waxing lyrical and we got away with it. The cops sent us on our way. We very nearly came to grief though, whilst doing a hundred plus down a straight road and a horse and cart pulled slowly out in front of us. I had no time to react. I swear the horse reared and we drove plumb underneath it. After a few moments of stunned silence Robbins hissed at me to stop the car -- I might need to change my pants!" Clem's reckless driving was no accident. He had actually been properly tutored in the black arts of driving fast without killing himself. The terrible irony was that his tutor, friend, and customer, did actually die in a blazing inferno one terribly sad afternoon in Germany a mere few years later.

After Cambridge, Dad had returned home to Brynamman, but sorely missed the pace of life he had enjoyed whilst at university, especially the weekend jaunts to London. At that time he had fallen out of favour with the Welsh selectors. Not one to suffer fools gladly he vacated Wales for the 1951 Varsity match. Quite by chance he met a senior executive from Mintex, then the premier UK manufacturer of brake pads. The company was aggressively targeting growth, and used its support of various elite motor racing teams as its primary marketing strategy. Formula, touring, and sports car racing were the principal categories Mintex had decided to focus their commercial and technical support on. Clem was employed on the spot as a business representative. He took the opportunity to join the premier club in England at that time, Coventry. Dad's primary job at Mintex was to embed himself with the various leading drivers and their teams, and influence and sell them branded products. He worked closely with the legendary "Mintex Man", Lionel Clegg, a technical, hands-on expert mechanic. Clegg was also a fine photographer and had a unique perspective on the motor racing world of the 1950s.

Clem almost immediately became a brother in arms to the pin-up motor racing star of the day, Peter Collins. He cut a swathe through society at that time and is probably best remembered for his symbiotic relationship with Mike Hawthorne, the first British World Champion, each called the other "mon ami mate". Collins was from Kidderminster, and as a teenager he thrived in the rough and tumble of 500cc racing on abandoned airfields alongside the likes of Stirling Moss and Bernie Ecclestone. At a party in 1950 hosted by the pre-war racing sensation Kay Petre, the Toronto born 4' 10" lady racer, Collins met the Aston Martin sports team boss, John Wyer and managed to get himself a test drive at Silverstone. His career rocketed and he became a stalwart performer for them in endurance racing and rallies throughout the 1950s.

Clem was allocated the Aston Martin account at Mintex (1952), and his close friendship with Peter Collins was forged through a lust for life and the occasional legendary drinking session at The Duck in Birmingham. They would often spill out of The Duck and race each other down the Hagley Road. The finishing line was always the Bull Ring, where the two boy racers would indulge in hand-brake turns at great speeds at 1 o'clock in the morning. An entourage would leave the pub first, ready to be in pole position to watch the entertainment at the Bull Ring.

Dad told me that he drove the 1952 Monte Carlo

Rally for Aston Martin, as the back-up driver. Unfortunately, Peter Collins crashed out in the snow of the Auvergne Mountains, and that was the end of that. Clem remained great pals with Peter even when he returned to Wales for the 1953 rugby season. They would meet on occasion back in Birmingham, or at the track events that Dad attended during the summer months. It was Peter that taught Dad how best to drive a powerful sports car, lessons which undoubtedly kept him alive throughout his life. Clem's propensity for speed when behind the wheel of a car was legendary. I can recall the popular refrain used by all of his passengers, "For fuck's sake Clem…slow down!!!"

Peter Collins had a stellar career in racing. In 1956 Enzo Ferrari came knocking having seen Collins (with Stirling Moss) win the "Targa Florio" in a Mercedes-Benz 300SLR. The Targo Florio is an open road endurance race held in the mountains of Sicily, near Palermo, and is the oldest sports car event (founded 1906) of its kind. Collins became an immediate success with Ferrari and won both the Belgian and French Grand Prix. The two mid-season victories ensured that the World Championship boiled down to a mano-a-mano fight between the mercurial, film-star good looks and talent of Peter Collins, and his teammate, Juan Manuel Fangio, the legendary Argentinian and three-time World Champion.

At the final race in the Italian grand prix at Monza, Fangio's car suffered a steering failure, leaving Collins with a clear run to the title. What ensued was one of sporting history's most noble moments, sadly forgotten in the current era of pro sport with its self-regarding philosophy of 'win-at-any-cost.' Collins, spotting his teammate in trouble, immediately pulled over and gave the Argentinian his car. The thankful Fangio finished in second which sealed his fourth World Championship. After the race, Collins nonchalantly commented, "It's too early for me to become world champion…I'm far too young."

The great tragedy of Peter Collins' life is that he was a reluctant hero and champion, despite enjoying the high life to the full. He met American actress Louise King at Monaco: "a divorcee", his boss Enzo noted snottily, who should have been only a "passing acquaintanceship", for a young man enjoying life. But Collins chased King to Florida and by 1957 they were married and living on a yacht in Monte Carlo.

In 1958, Collins suffered early set-backs in Belgium, and argued with the Ferrari Scuderia in France, where his team-mate Luigi Musso was tragically killed in the Reims race. Of the twenty-one starters in Reims, five would die in racing cars within three years. The British Grand Prix saw the return of the old Peter Collins, who was inspired by Enzo Ferrari's attempts to drop him from the team, and drove an imperious race, pushing the car and himself to the limits in beating his teammate, Mike Hawthorne and Stirling Moss.

The next stop was the Nürburgring one week later for the German Grand Prix. Initially Moss led but his Vanwall's magneto broke, leaving Hawthorn and Collins out in front from a charging Tony Brooks in the second Vanwall, who duly caught and passed them.

Determined not to be caught napping twice at the 'Ring', the two Ferraris fought back, but at Pflanzgarten Collins ran wide, hit the earth bank, and was catapulted from his car as it somersaulted through the air. He was thrown head-first into a tree, snapped his neck, and did not survive the journey to hospital. Meanwhile, his car burst into flames nearby.

Peter Collins represented a set of moral values completely aligned with those endorsed by Dad. Whenever Clem spoke about Peter it was always with a tone of admiration and reverence, mixed with a glint in the eye as he remembered the mischief they got into at Birmingham. It was obviously a deep friendship, forged at racing circuits throughout England and Europe that Dad valued in many currencies. I often think Peter encapsulated the kind of guy Dad aspired to become.

Throughout his life Clem was always suspicious of what he termed "the Establishment", by which he meant those in positions of wealth, power, and authority, who had achieved such things not through meritocratic means, but by inheritance or a sense of entitlement. Dad was frequently approached for a minor honour by friends in high places who wanted to write letters of representation commending his services. He was always firmly consistent in warning that he would reject and refuse any such honour. As a Carmarthenshire lad, he was naturally both pro-nationalist and nonconformist by instinct, and it was the Liberal politics of a Lloyd George hue that he finally decided to fully support. His anti-establishment attitudes were fuelled by the personal struggle he had to win his Varsity cap for Cambridge, and by 1949 he had become sick and tired of a clique of older, lesser gifted colonial types who had managed to dominate Cambridge rugby just after the war. Dad understood that situation in 1947, with the large numbers of returning servicemen, but later he fell out with captain Kimberley, a four-time blue. He started to agree with Lloyd-Davies, the full-back from Ammanford, who lambasted the Kimberley regime as pure cronyism. Dad soldiered on and took real pleasure in physically dismantling Kimberley whilst playing for the LX Club (Cambridge University second team).

I have in my possession the St John's RFC annual dinner menu card from Friday, 12th March, 1948. St John's won the inter-college 'Cuppers' competition, beating Christ's, Trinity, Trinity Hall and, in the final Queens 4-0. The card is signed by all the players "for Clem", who by all accounts turned up for the dinner dressed in his striped pyjamas! It certainly documents a different age and includes some written comments from his fellow students:

"Gilbert and Sullivan would prefer, in for a penny, in for a pound Clem! Personally I prefer the pyjamas even if they were vaguely obscene!! Cymru Am Byth…Best of Luck," *Jack Fairhurst*

"Having tried to tackle you and failed miserably I can only say what a footballer!!!". *D.B. Weaver*

"A Blue next year Clem nothing is more certain!!! Every time it rains, it rains from heaven! She's pretty good Clem, but you're better! So long as I can have the bedroom, and you don't pinch that every Tuesday I'm happy. The best of roommates," *Geoff*

"Thanks for turning out! Smoke, smoke, smoke that cigarette Clem!" *J. Michael Simister*

"If you manage the girls (girl?) as well as you manage the ball, Gold help them." *Bob McGhie*

"Glad to see you didn't rot my socks…" *John Sharman*

"Never had so many near shaves since I flew in the RAF. Your driving is hell." *Harry*

"Keep fit - get BLUE!" *Alan Gregory*

By the time of the St John's annual dinner one year later, the exhortation for a Blue was evident from his peer group. This was only two weeks before Clem was due to win his first cap in Paris. Dad's selection had not been confirmed but the Welsh press had been advocating his inclusion for some time.

"Well played Clem. Your help in Cuppers has been invaluable – A Welsh cap and a Blue next year (Pass those exams. I tutor for 1 guinea per hour). *Nobby*

"A Blue and a cap next year, Clem. It ought to have been this year." *Dick Custance*

"From 'probable' in 1948 to certainty in '49'." *Mike Prosser*

"I sometimes wonder whether you do it because of or in spite of those knocks on the head." *Noel Bygate*

"You had better work hard or the whole rugger club will set on you (well, long to anyway)." *John*

"A chest fit to cushion the head of Venus! Twice nightly. Good on yer Clem! Here's to OUR next year." *Geoff Vaughan*

The 68th Varsity match (1949) between Oxford and Cambridge was held in front of a 50,000 crowd at Twickenham. In those days, the occasion was perceived to be the equal of any international match, with many of the players snapped up by national selectors. The Varsity was considered the preeminent finishing school for emerging rugby talent, and served as a draft for the larger English clubs. Scotland consistently used the 'grandmother clause' to cap any young talent from the Commonwealth. Sadly, Cambridge lost that day, 0-3. Dad said they hadn't played to their full potential, and had given the match away by not taking their chances. The captain, Arthur Dorward, the fine Scottish scrum half had assembled a close-knit group that term; a marked improvement from previous regimes where only the posh boys were allowed the limelight.

Included in the team was JV Smith, who won 4 caps for England (1950) on the wing, Peter Dalton Young who captained England in 1955, Geoff Vaughan, my godfather who later emigrated to New Zealand to enjoy a fine career as a GP, and Glyn Davies, the hugely talented outside half from Pontypridd who went on to win eleven caps for Wales (1947-51). All became friends for life, and were the reason that Clem looked back so fondly on his time spent at Cambridge. Their Oxford opponents featured numerous future England internationals including John Kendall-Carpenter CBE. He was the key player that day and would go on to win twenty-three caps for England, three Blues, and represent the Barbarians. Kendall-Carpenter later became President of the English RFU (1980-81), and was the Chairman of the very first Rugby World Cup (RWC) organising committee (1987). He played prop for Oxford that day and made the play of the match!

David Frost, the former *Guardian* rugby correspondent, a delightful man I always enjoyed meeting in the Press Box and who spent his honeymoon travelling with his bride on the Trans-Siberian railroad from Moscow to Vladivostok, recalled the famous tackle in the 1949 Varsity match when John Kendall-Carpenter preserved Oxford's 3-0 winning lead by smashing J.V. Smith, the Cambridge centre in the dying moments of the match:

Smith slipped his man, side-stepped two tacklers and seemed certain to score at least an equalising try. Cambridge hats and scarves were already in the air and Oxford's supporters were dumb with horror, but at the very last possible moment Kendall-Carpenter dived and took man and ball into touch, less than a yard from the try-line…

Dad was quite pally with Kendall-Carpenter, especially during the establishment of the first two Rugby World Cups. I had the pleasure of meeting this urbane, charming man on several occasions. John was responsible for selecting and procuring the RWC trophy. Sir Nicholas Shehadie, the Aussie representative on the RWC Committee, who played against Clem in a test match (1958), recalled,

> John Kendall-Carpenter rang to say we needed a trophy. No-one had given it any thought! John went down to Garrards, the Crown jewellers established in 1735, today based at 24 Albermarle in Mayfair and found the cup. He rang me to say he could buy it for £6,000. I had no hesitation in telling him to do it.

Kendall-Carpenter later added:

> I felt that a Victorian, not a Georgian trophy would be appropriate, made of silver - a masculine metal - rather than gold. The craftsmanship of the period and the beauty of the piece would have to project the past into the present. At Garrards, I was told by Richard Jarvis, a director that they had re-acquired that very day a piece of silverware, which was a copy of a Victorian cup which was made in 1906 in their workshop. When they brought the cup from the vaults, I immediately knew I had found what I was looking for. It was heavy, it was compact, and it was handsome...

Dad was always proud of his Cambridge heritage, especially his membership of the Hawks club, an institution only full blues may apply to join. Foolishly, perhaps, with hindsight, I made little effort to go to Cambridge, but Mark my youngest brother did his second degree there in Land Economy, winning two Blues in 1988 and 1989.

Dad retained many friendships from his links to Cambridge, and one larger-than-life character with whom he became great pals over the years is Ian Robertson, the doyenne of radio commentary for the BBC, covering both rugby and horse racing. Ian played for Cambridge University, the Barbarians, and London Scottish, and won 8 caps for Scotland (1968-70), but suffered a serious knee injury at only twenty-five years old. He became a prolific writer, publishing over thirty books including biographies of Bill Beaumont, Andy Irvine, and a "token" Welshman who Clem considered a close friend - Richard Burton. Ian, or "Robbo" as he is known to his friends, is also the premier rugby broadcaster of his generation, and has passed into that pantheon reserved for great BBC commentators, most notably for his memorable coverage of the climax of the 2003 RWC. Who can forget when Johnny Wilkinson kicked the winning drop goal?

Away from rugby Robbo's first love is horse racing, and over the years he became a catalyst, persuading a host of rugby players and administrators to join his annual racing syndicate. Whilst at Cambridge, Robbo had become close friends with Ian Balding, the accomplished trainer who inherited Kingsclere from Peter Hastings-Bass, his father-in-law in 1964. Balding had won a Blue for Cambridge in 1961, and went on to train horses for the American benefactor, Paul Mellon, The Queen Mother, and for The Queen (1964-99). He trained one horse who stood out from the rest of his stable: "Mill Reef was by far and away the best horse I ever had. He won the Derby and Prix de l'Arc de Triomphe in 1971. He is still thought of as one of the very best horses ever to have raced in this country. I've never had, nor would expect to have one as good as him again."

Dad always said that Robbo used to have him in fits of giggles when he explained how he discovered racing: "I was a student at Newmarket, sorry, excuse the Freudian slip I mean Cambridge. I met the trainer Ryan Jarvis, a rugby fanatic, and he gave me four horses running on four different courses that day and a two bob yankee won me

£78." That was in all intents the true origin of the syndicate.

Robbo spotted an opportunity to elicit interest from the rugby community in horse racing and together with Ian Balding, put together a series of consortia, investing a reasonable amount of money in a communally owned syndicate. The syndicate was operated by Robbo and advised by Ian Balding. The syndicate of 12 was comprised mainly of well-known players, Dad, Michael Steele-Bodger, Noel Murphy, Jeff Butterfield, Gordon Connell, Peter Yarrington, Peter Warfield, Robin Challis and Chris Martin Jenkins, the BBC's cricket correspondent.

The horses selected were supposed to be "sporting handicappers" which is race-speak code for a heap of crap normally. And although there were some extremely dodgy horses purchased in the early years: *British Lion, Triple Crown*...etc by the time Dad and I got involved Ian Balding had struck handicap gold by unearthing a horse, later to be named *Twickenham*.

You can imagine the dismay and objections of the Celtic fringe when they were informed that the nag was to be called *Twickenham*. There were Welsh mutterings to Robertson of "How can you expect to win with a name like that?" but the English influence was too strong and there were counter-objections of "Well, we can't possibly call it The National Stadium." Dad sardonically floated the snide suggestion of the rather more facetious name of Twickers but got shouted down.

Dad was thrilled to fly in a small plane from Blackbushe with Ian Balding, and the jockey John Mathias, to see *Twickenham* win the Prix Bayeux in Ostend. It was a heady experience to stand in the parade ring listening to Ian giving John Mathias his concise instructions on how to run the race. "Keep out of the rough track on the rails," he was told. "Just bowl him along down the middle of the course." Dad was a little put out when Mathias informed them a German jockey was saying his horse was one of the best two-year-olds in Germany, which made him a firm favourite at 6-4 on, while *Twickenham* was 2-1. However Ian remained confident and Dad put 600 francs on *Twickenham's* beautiful nose.

Never was such confidence rewarded as *Twickenham* made wurst-meat of the opposition to win by six lengths. Five minutes later Dad was having his photo taken with Ian and Twickenham in the winners' enclosure. He always said it was, "every bit as sweet a moment for a Celt as beating England at Twickenham."

The thing about handicaps is that the stable is always playing chicken with the Official Handicapper, and attempts all kinds of nefarious tactics to lower the weights. *Twickenham* got away with it for about a year, but it nearly always placed, and the syndicate would get an excited Robbo on the phone instructing Clem not to put all his money on at one bookie, but spread it about a bit. So Dad would then wait until Ian Balding was ready to expose *Twickenham* to the handicapper again. In fact *Twickenham* was such a good horse that Ian took it to run in Italy and Belgium where it won Group 3 races. Our last horse in that tradition was *Miller's Tale*, and whilst containing some fine genetics from the great Derby winner, it was not in the same class to win as regularly as *Twickenham*.

Robbo had not had an easy path to the winners' enclosure. Once he nearly bankrupted a previous illustrious rugby syndicate composed of names like Gareth Edwards, Barry John, Cliff Morgan, Mike Gibson, Andy Irvine, Gordon Brown, David Duckham, John Spencer and Michael Steele-Bodger, who was the only one kind enough to forgive and have the persistence to have another go.

On that occasion, the horse called *British Lion* started its first race as odds-on favourite, the second race as favourite, and well-fancied in its third and fourth races. However, it came nowhere, and for its fifth race a disgusted Robbo did not bother to inform the syndicate that he was running and *British Lion* promptly won by six lengths at odds of 14-1. Scotsman Gordon Brown's reaction was unprintable.

It was not surprising therefore, that when Barry John and Gareth Edwards were asked if they would like to join the new venture they replied in rapid guttural Welsh, which Robbo took to mean "No".

Dad used to love going to small tracks like Nottingham or Bath, and strutting around the Owners Paddock before the race, whilst I would pretend to know what the hell was going on around me, but for Dad, he was to the manor born. The sport of kings held great appeal for Clem, who appeared at home one evening with a fully equipped trotting horse and trap that he had decided to buy on a whim at Neath market. As for the kings themselves, Dad always held a consistently republican view, although he came up short of calling for the tumbril to the guillotine. My Mum was not amused as the trap now occupied the main garage, whilst the horse was put on Southgate farm which Clem leased in those days. I remember it well, since I always had the job of getting the hay into the barn during the hay harvest. Dad eventually embarked on lending out his pony and trap to every friend having a family marriage on the Gower in the early 1970's.

Clem may have liked the sport of kings but he was far from impressed by the prissy reaction of Prince Charles at a garden party he was forced to attend by my step-mum Joyce at Buckingham Palace. On being introduced, the Prince gestured to the tie he was wearing and said, "Same. Same. Are you a Hawk?" noting that both men were wearing identical Hawks Club ties. Dad quipped, "I couldn't help but notice you're having a spot of bother with the wife…" It was intended as a conspiratorial wink. The reaction was swift and brutal. Charles turned his back and shot off muttering, leaving his equerry and entourage flat-footed. For the sake of noblesse oblige I will not repeat the word Dad used to describe our future monarch.

It's 31st August 1997, and Diana, Princess of Wales has just died from her injuries suffered in a terrible car crash in the tunnels of Pont d'Alma in Paris. I was living and working in France at that time, and had become President of Paris University Club (PUC), (rugby section), we played in the second tier professional league. That Sunday we had a home game against Auch, the team then was ran by its effervescent President Jacques Fouroux, the ex-French rugby captain and coach. After hearing the appalling news of Diana's death, I decided to get to the clubhouse in Charlety Stadium early and was greeted to my horror by a sea of French news channels with live cameras, and dozens of print and radio journalists.

The French media were desperate to interview anyone from Wales in Paris that morning, hoping for any kind of connection to the Princess of Wales. Someone had mentioned PUC has a Welsh President, and that the Princess was the royal patron of the Welsh Rugby Union, so that link, no matter how tenuous, placed me under the firm scrutiny of the French press. We hastily organised a press conference at the entrance to the 30,000 seater Stadium, and I voiced my sympathy for the shocking turn of events that led to the death of the peoples' princess. Questions were flung at me, and I batted them away as best I could: "No, I did not know the Princess personally, but I had a friend who did." Bingo, the press had their tenuous connection confirmed as I outlined how an ex-player and teammate, Richard Webster (Swansea 1stXV 1987-88) who played wing-forward thirteen times for Wales, and was a British Lion, had engaged in a bit of 'cheeky chappy' banter with Diana at various pre-match presentations prior to anthems.

Diana was quite high profile in her role with Welsh rugby, in stark contrast to her husband the Prince. She would visit Swansea RFC to promote rugby in the community initiatives for school kids. The question often asked by us Welsh is why didn't the Prince show a greater interest in our rugby, the sport that's at the heart of the Welsh? Prince Charles last came to watch Wales at Cardiff Arms Park on 8th March 1969, the year of his investiture in Caernarvon Castle. Feelings about Prince Charles at the time were muted and not particularly enthusiastic. The general feeling was that he was distant and slightly monochrome. He had attended, albeit for one term only, my alma mater, the University College of Wales in Aberystwyth, studying Welsh History and Language. But he has never managed to establish any kind of special rapport with the people of Wales. Indeed the investiture itself was actively opposed by many in Wales; Mudiad Amddiffyn Cymru (MAC - the Movement to Defend Wales) and the Free Welsh Army, a paramilitary nationalist organisation formed by William Cayo-Evans (who incidentally went to the same prep school as me, Abermad near Aberystwyth) were among the opponents.

Bombs went off over the period of the investiture, two members of MAC blowing themselves up at Abergele social security offices, and an unexploded device was found at Llandudno pier, where Prince Charles was due to come ashore from the Royal Yacht Britannia. Today these events read like something out of the Theatre of the Absurd, but people died, the IRA was ferociously aggressive in Northern Ireland, and the prime minister, Harold Wilson, feared more widespread bombings, and a resurgence of aggressive Welsh nationalism.

The Welsh rugby team had, however, got its retaliation in first…Charles was targeted by the Wales front row prior to kick-off against Ireland. That front row consisted of three grizzled, diamond-hard, down-to-earth blocks of unsmiling granite, John Lloyd of Bridgend, Jeff Youngs of Harrogate and the veteran Denzil Williams, a steel-worker from Ebbw Vale. At the line-up before the anthems, Prince Charles was presented to the Irish, then

the Welsh players. The Prince came to John Lloyd, held
out his hand and...SQUEELLCH!!!

Lloyd had plastered his right hand with about three
inches of Vaseline and Wintergreen. The Prince looked
appalled and took the proffered hand from Jeff Young...
SQUEELLCH!!! The Prince demanded a handkerchief
from his equerry and wiped his hands. He turned to Denzil
Williams and... SQUEELLCH!!! Another handkerchief
was quickly procured. Prince Charles seems to have taken
the hint, and has never returned, neither to Cardiff Arms
Park, nor to the hearts of the Welsh.

4

THE GLORY YEARS OF
NO LONGER BEING
A BLUE BLOODED BASTARD

"Being part of a football team is no different than being
part of any other organisation - an army, a political party.
The objective is to win, to beat the other guy. You think
that is hard or cruel - I don't think it is. I do think it is a
reality of life that men are competitive, and the more
competitive the business, the more competitive the men.
They know the rules, and know the objective when they
get in the game. And the objective is to win - fairly,
squarely, decently, by the rules, but to win."
Vince Lombardi

From a promising schoolboy rugby player, by 1950 Clem
was one of the leading back row forwards of his
generation. His playing career now pursued a rather
chequered course after his days spent at Cambridge
University and the winning of his first cap in March 1949.
He would always describe himself as, "the most frequently
dropped Welsh wing-forward of all time." There were at
least two major periods when he was dropped following
intense public scrutiny and scorn, and in 1957, even trial

by television. Those were the early days of live televised internationals in the UK, and Clem was captured on camera swinging a haymaker at the England winger, Peter Thompson. There was the resulting brouhaha from the English rugby press that pressured the Welsh selectors to meekly omit him from the rest of the season. They recalled him to the captaincy for the match against Australia and he went on to lead Wales in nine consecutive tests.

After winning his first cap in Paris, the *Playfair Welsh Rugby Annual* (1949-50) commented: "R.C.C. Thomas, an undergraduate at Cambridge University, played occasionally for Swansea whilst on vacation and must be regarded as a little fortunate to get a cap on the strength of one or two performances." He had in fact been selected for the 'probable's' for the final trial match in 1949, and could equally consider himself unlucky not to be selected earlier in that campaign.

Clem's longest period spent out of the Welsh team was following his first cap. He was not selected in 1950 or 1951, and missed out in the two first matches in 1952, but he was eventually able to force his way back into the Triple Crown and Grand Slam team captained by John Gwilliam. Dad had played with him at Cambridge in 1947, 1948, and in his first game for Wales when Gwilliam played in the second row and not his favoured position of No.8. Whenever Wales played England at Twickenham, Gwilliam always made sure the dressing room door was open and he'd lead the players in a soaring rendition of 'Calon Lan' to make sure the English team knew who had the greater heart. After spending a year at Cambridge, he was commissioned as an officer in the Royal Tank Regiment and saw action in Europe during the war. The historian Max Hastings reported an incident at Rathau where John Gwilliam was carrying a small German soldier by the scruff of his neck. When asked why he didn't just shoot the man, Gwilliam purportedly replied, "On no, sir. Much too small."

Dad's return to the Welsh team had been advocated powerfully in the local press: "A strong contender for a Welsh cap as a wing forward, Clem Thomas has been the outstanding forward with the Whites in recent games... the eyes of the Welsh selectors are again turned in his direction."

He had to wait a good year later before the call came, and always gave the impression that he had been hard done-by in the selection process by the omnipotent Welsh selectors. Throughout both his playing career and his years covering rugby as a journalist, Clem had a fundamental distrust of the Welsh Rugby Union, a sentiment that was deep-seated, resentful, and very personal. Dad said the feud began at the after-match function in Paris in 1949, when an elderly, blazered, WRU alickadoo leaned across the dinner table in the sumptuous Gare du Nord Terminus Hotel and firmly clasped his grasping fingers around a bottle of Cognac that was intended as a generous gift from the FFR to the Welsh players. Rationing was still in force, and Clem was furious at the arrogance of the WRU committee man who told him, "You're too young to be drinking this stuff" as he brazenly bullied Clem into submitting the Cognac to him. For most of the forty-five years or so since that incident, an uneasy truce existed, interspersed with fractious incidents like his deselection from the team in 1957, or his whistle-blowing and accusations of corruption and incompetence that he levelled at the WRU in the late 1980s and 1990s.

In 1951, he felt he played outstanding rugby for Swansea, especially after his masterclass against the 1951 Springboks, who got out of jail with a late flurry of scoring to survive 11-3. Dad also blamed certain journalists for some ambivalent and hyper-critical reporting of his play. Most of his ire was aimed at J.B.G. Thomas, a dedicated, albeit dull chronicler of Welsh rugby for around 50 years. In JBG's day the power balance between journalist and sportsman was weighed heavily in favour of the former.

The son of a Pontypridd butcher, who joined *The Western Mail* in 1946 as chief rugby writer and left it 36 years later as assistant editor, influenced the game as much as he reflected it.

In JBG, The Big Five – the legendary Welsh team selection panel – had a secret sixth member. The effect his writing was able to generate is best illustrated by the fact his editor once told him to "make a few mistakes" when predicting the Welsh team so that the readers of *The Western Mail* would not think it was he who picked the national side.

Dad said JBG was at least honest enough to begrudgingly concede his mistaken criticism:

> There are moments in a critic's career when he feels, on reflection, that he has been too severe in his criticism of a young player making his entry into representative football... one of these is Richard Clement Charles Thomas, proving the point that no matter how stern may be the criticism, an outstanding player can always rise above it. The occasion was the France v Wales match of 1949 at the Stade Colombes. Wales lost, but only narrowly, and the Welsh back row of Thomas, Stephens and Stone experienced a rough time, being continually called upon to cover against brilliant Frenchmen.
>
> It is a difficult job for any opposing back row operating against the French, for three players who had never played together before, and with two of them new to representative football, It was a nerve-wracking job, and perhaps on reflection was too harsh in my comments, but happily Thomas was to prove me wrong, for he was a player with a colourful future ahead of him, although he had to wait three seasons before being recalled to the colours to share in a brilliant

⸱ Crown triumph at Dublin in 1952.

ıny is the time we have chatted together about 1949 match, and now that Thomas spends his ɔaturdays reporting for *The Observer* we spend many happy hours discussing the game and its players... He bears no malice, but admits that at the time he was made all the more determined to do well by the criticism."

Now Dad was very fond of JBG, as he was affectionately called by all in Welsh rugby, but he never forgot, and he never trusted anything JBG ever wrote or pontificated on regarding a player's qualities. He didn't rate his judgement or his journalism.

Of Clem JBG did however continue in his confessional, mea culpa:

Clem was a 'hard' wing-forward, as good in attack as in defence, although his sternest critics said he was not a good passer! He was capable of putting the 'evil eye' upon opposing outside halves, and of all his great performances I saw him give none was better than his play for Swansea against the 1951 Springboks, and again against the Barbarians every Easter Monday. As Cliff Morgan readily admits, "He was one of the hardest players in the position to play against!" and then adds with a wicked twinkle in his eye that makes Thomas laugh heartily, "I never held on to the ball when Clem was near!"

JBG was considered, "Rugby's Man of a Million Words", no other chronicler of the oval ball was so prolific. He wrote 28 books between 1954 and 1980 – including the jauntily titled *Bryn Thomas' Book of Rugger*. He continued his assessment of Dad:

Thomas was ideally made for the position, being big, strong, fast and intelligent and always a keen student of the game. He was brimful of confidence, and the better the opposition, the better he played, which is the true hallmark of a great player. Yet he was conscious of his own limitations, and knew when he had not played well or had not done enough for his side.

Clem then had two seasons with Coventry...maturing fully as an openside wing-forward and re-entered the Welsh XV against Ireland in 1952, to play in what (at that time) must be the best Welsh post war pack, for in it were several players of whom the tag, "great" can be applied: JRG Stephens, E.R. John, and W.O. Williams plus Gwilliam as captain. This match established Thomas as an international and he was to make 24 more appearances for Wales and two Tests for the British Isles..."

E.W. "Jim" Swanton, the *Daily Telegraph's* chief cricket and rugby writer, described JBG as "a historian who writes about rugby football with discriminating enthusiasm." But it's often remembered that JBG wasn't all that discriminating with his enthusiasm. This was, after all, the journalist who admitted he abandoned the journos' code of conduct to thump the press box and yell, "Go on Ken!" as Jones the Olympic sprinter dashed for the line in Dublin (1952).

Clem's playing career for Wales in the 5 Nations:
Country and Result (Wales score first)

1949	France L 3-5			
1952	France W 9-3	Ireland W 14-3		

1953	France W 6-3	Ireland W 5-3	Scotland W 12-0	
1954	France W 19-13	Ireland W 12-9	Scotland W 15-3	England L 6-9
1955		Ireland W 21-3	Scotland L 8-14	
1956		Ireland L 3-11	Scotland W 9-3	England W 8-3
1957				England L 0-3
1958	France L 6-16	Ireland W 9-6	Scotland W 8-3	England D 3-3
1959	France L 3-11	Ireland W 8-6	Scotland L 3-6	England W 5-0

Clem's overall 5 Nations Record is: **P 24, W 15, D 1, and L 8**

In addition to these 5 Nations games he played against two southern hemisphere touring teams for Wales winning both.

> 1953- New Zealand W 13-8
> 1958- Australia W 9-3

Clem's final record: **P26, W17, D1, And L8: THIS IS A WIN RATIO OF 65%**

Also,
1955- South Africa, 3rd Test for British Lions W 9-6
South Africa, 4th Test for British Lions L 8-22

Clem said, "My three greatest moments in the game were, firstly the Triple Crown triumph of 1952, secondly winning the Third Lions Test at Pretoria and finally the great Welsh victory over New Zealand." There were two other players who shared all three occasions, Cliff Morgan and W.O. "Billy" Williams, who along with Ken Jones, Bleddyn Williams, Bryn Meredith John Gwilliam, and R.H. Williams, constitute the pantheon of players who Clem himself rated as possessing all the hallmarks of greatness in that era of the 1950s.

R.H. Williams was simply the best Welsh tight forward Clem thought he played with, although he also spoke in the highest terms of Courtney Meredith, the Neath prop. "RH", as he was known, is one of the giants of British rugby from the 1950s, and it was on successive tours with the British Lions, to South Africa in 1955 and New Zealand in 1959, that the Llanelli lock earned worldwide respect for his powerful play. His performances in the Test Series in New Zealand brought praise from arguably the game's greatest lock, Colin Meads, who described him as the strongest opponent he had ever played against. *The New Zealand Rugby Almanac* of 1960 voted him one of their five players of the year. Few, if any visiting forwards, are afforded such elevated status, and the Almanac stated, "He was the outstanding forward of the Lions side. Had he been a New Zealander he could well have gained selection as an All Black. He had as much energy at the end of the tour after 17 appearances as he did at the start."

RH was from Cwmllynfell, only three miles across the mountain from Brynamman, and Clem enjoyed a long and deep friendship with him. Sadly the two men fell out over South Africa (RH served for 15 years on the WRU Committee) when Clem savagely criticised the WRU over its ambiguous policy towards apartheid in the early 1990s. But it was as a player that RH will be best remembered - a powerhouse of a man who won 14 of the 23 games he played for Wales. His record with the British Lions was remarkable, playing in 10 test matches, winning on 5 occasions. The respect with which he was held can best be summed up by the tribute the All Blacks paid him in 1959. The Kiwis invited him into their private post-match function and presented him with an All Black jersey. No greater mark of respect could a forward ask, no greater compliment or tribute be paid. JBG wrote of him:

> R.H. is a hard man, perfectly built for his job in the engine house of the scrum; lithe enough to jump freely in the line-out and move rapidly in the loose; strong enough to maul with determination, and resilient enough to hold his own with the toughest of Commonwealth players. His approach to the game was immaculate, for at all times he played the ball and not the man, and preferred crisp, clean play to that of the rough and undisciplined. Yet he was not loath to protect his colleagues when they were on the receiving end of unnecessary punishment.

Of all the great players Clem played with, his closest friend both during the time that they played together, and after they had moved onto new careers, was the incomparable Cliff Morgan. Over a period of seven years (1952-1958), they played on eighteen occasions together for Wales, including the famous 1953 win over the All Blacks, and the 1952 Triple Crown match with Ireland. I was lucky enough to know Cliff, not through Dad's friendship with him, but because in my last year at Aberystwyth University in 1979 I shared a house with his son, Nick, a good ball player with whom I became great friends. Nick is an orthopaedic consultant in Canada these days.

My fondest memory of Cliff is when he invited us both to the BBC Sports Department Christmas party, held at Broadcasting House on Portland Place. I was in the process of applying for articles with the large accounting firms at that time. I would often hitch a ride with my uncle, Ian Jones, who travelled regularly to London in his chauffeured limousine, attend my interview, and charge the firm a full return fare to Aberystwyth! I recall that I arranged to meet Nick around midday outside the BBC, and we duly trundled up to go and see his Dad. Cliff was Head of Outside Broadcasts at that time but his real allegiance lay with the stable of quixotic sports reporters. They were all superstars to me and I was enthralled to meet David Coleman, John Motson, Jimmy Hill, Peter O'Sullivan, Peter Alliss, Harry Carpenter, Eddie Waring, Bob Wilson and Barry Davies - all legends. Cliff was very generous and gave Nick a big wad of cash to buy ourselves an early lunch, and suitably lubricated we crashed into the department's party at around 2.30. A good few hours later, feeling more than a little mellow I was jogging up from the underground somewhere west of the City. I realised that I was already a half hour late for my interview with Coopers and Lybrand. On arrival at their plush offices, I swallowed three or four extra strong mints, and drank as much coffee as I could persuade the pretty secretary to make. I waited a half hour... then an hour... when the door finally burst open, and a partner in a very wide pinstripe suit, fit for a Borsalino type character shouted at me in a cut-glass Oxford accent how absolutely delighted he was that I was still there. He assured me the job was mine, and that I seemed to be a splendid fellow having been to school at Blundells and that I should give my expenses claim to his PA. He was twice as pissed as I was, in fact he could barely stand up. So using the think of a number technique...then doubling it, I wrote my expense claim on a chit and gave it to the secretary, who came back some minutes later brandishing large numbers of high denomination bank notes. It was a startling demonstration of the power of the old school tie.

Cliff went on to play 29 times for Wales, 18 of the matches with Clem in the Welsh backrow, his final game being the frustrating 3-3 draw at Twickenham in 1958.

Clem rates this game as one of the most disappointing of his entire career, as the draw meant that he missed the accolades of being a Welsh Triple Crown winning captain. He referred to the occasion as, "my greatest personal tragedy". With the scores tied going into the final minutes, Wales were awarded a penalty 40 yards out. Terry Davies delivered what seemed to be a perfect strike of the ball, it looked to all present as if bound to go over, the game won. Unfortunately the 'cussed Twickenham wind' caught the ball, it hit the upright, and the glory was lost, the moment gone forever and the ultimate honour denied to a great Welsh team.

Clem had first played with Cliff in the Triple Crown winning match against Ireland in 1952, a game in which Cliff announced his special talents to the world with a world class display that he would consistently deliver over the next six years, culminating in his domination over the Springboks in South Africa in 1955. After that Triple Crown win, Pat Marshall of *The Sunday Express* wrote, "It wasn't just the Welsh pack...Behind them they had Cliff 'Pimpernel' Morgan. He showed the Irish that Jack Kyle has been deposed as prince of fly-halves." Cliff's Dad was at the match that day and became so excited that he spat his false teeth 15 rows in front and never saw them again.

Cliff often confided in Clem that the fly half's job is complex; a jigsaw where cunning, skill, awareness, daring, courage, and more than a little arrogance are all part of the make-up. Cliff Morgan, by common consent, had all these attributes in spades. It was once said of him that he had "an agility that made Harry Houdini look arthritic".

Of his first international, against Ireland in Cardiff, Cliff recalled, "I felt a hand gently touch my shoulder. It was the man I was having to mark, the maestro Jackie Kyle. He put an arm around me and whispered as fondly and genuinely as an uncle would: 'I hope you have a wonderful, wonderful first cap today, Cliffie'." Frank Keating wrote of this episode, "Thus, like all true romances, was the baton passed on." Kyle, who later became a missionary in Zambia, always described Cliff as "the best fly half there can ever have been, thrusting, darting, always unexpected".

Cliff admitted to me later in life that he never enjoyed playing against Dad. He said that Clem was blessed with both pace and stamina, and had the ability to track him as he began to run with the ball, and that any collision or tackle which inevitably followed would be aggressive and painful. Dad told me that he loved to play against Cliff, because it was the ultimate challenge for an open side wing-forward. To pit yourself against the electric, dancing feet of Cliff, knowing that he had the gas to burn you if you got the angle wrong, or allowed him to slip inside. Dad claimed he always knew when Cliff was going to attempt the outside break, because in the step before he accelerated he would dip his shoulder as if to give himself impetus into the break. That gave Clem just enough time to block the channel, and deliver another smashing tackle.

Peter Stead, the Swansea historian and broadcaster, wrote of this great rivalry in his insightful essay about Cliff:

> Who spent his whole rugby career working endlessly for an extra yard of space. Someone who often tried to deny him that space was the Swansea flanker Clem Thomas who accompanied Cliff on that 1955 Lions tour and who was subsequently to remind readers that in those days before the rules were changed flankers had a license to kill outside halves for it was legally possible to arrive at the outside-half before the ball by taking a flyer as the ball came out of the scrum.

For Clem, it was Cliff's vitality and effrontery which allowed him to flourish even in an age of flying flankers. Cliff always credited his inspirational teacher, ER "Ned"

Gribble of Tonyrefail Grammar School, with setting him on the right path: "He changed my life. He converted me from being a 'Soccer-mad Joe', as he referred to me, to a game he loved, coached and understood. He saw to it that his charges developed a deep and abiding passion for the game which, he claimed, 'sweats the vice out of you'. He was a gale of humanity and cared for standards of performance, skill, behaviour, discipline and fair play" – all qualities for which Cliff himself became noted, both on and off the playing field.

With Gribble's encouragement, Cliff moved from school to village rugby, turning out on a windy hillside for Coedely Coke Ovens XV at Llantrisant. "Before the game we had to drive a herd of cows from the pitch; there was little we could do about the cow pats. That is how we learned to swerve and sidestep. Those who failed to develop these skills smelled horribly for weeks."

Cliff must have been tackled in every match, but photographers preferred their man in space and that is why their collective work allows him to thrill us even today. In shot after shot we see him in the space he has earned by pure skill, his opponents well and truly frozen, as much by surprise as by the camera, whilst Cliff, gasping with anxiety, is still quite obviously on the move.

After the famous win in the first Test against South Africa, Vivian Jenkins wrote: "Cliff Morgan it was who started it with an unforgettable try from a scrum 20 yards out. With the entire Springbok back row and his opposite number converging on him he veered outwards and flashed past all of them, plus an apparently stock-still full-back, to score a magnificent try between the posts".

Despite his success Cliff always resisted the temptations of Rugby League. One chairman arrived at his parents' terraced house in a white Rolls-Royce and placed £5,000 in fivers on the kitchen table, along with a cheque for £2,500. His mother, a powerful figure, said money was not important and she wanted her son to stay at home. She cooked the chairman breakfast, then sent him on his way, saying, "It's been lovely to have you down here, but on Sundays we go to chapel."

Cliff once memorably said, "Rugby is a nonsense, but a very serious nonsense." The sport certainly defined the lives of a group of Welshmen in the 1950s who went on to achieve success both on and off the field. Later, in Hollywood, whilst dining with his great friend Richard Burton, they astonished staff who had placed them at the best table at the Beverly Hills Hilton by proceeding to order egg and chips.

My final memory of Cliff is at my father's Memorial Service held in St Bride's Church, Fleet Street, where he delivered an off the cuff eulogy to Clem that had everyone present both laughing and crying at the same time. Alas, no written record exists, but those who were there will retain that emotion forever.

Clem's philosophy of the game of rugby football was that it allowed fit young men the perfect release. That combined in a team, a group of guys could pull together, and through physical commitment, individual skill, and collective competitiveness, achieve great things. His reputation was that of a footballing, skillful wing-forward, and Clem, whilst appreciating the darker arts of forward play and the drive needed to play back-row, always preferred to accentuate the creative parts of the game, believing from a very early age that a passing game was preferable to a kicking game. This philosophy was famously put to one side when in 1959, he captained Wales against England on a flooded, boggy, straw strewn pitch at Cardiff Arms Park. Such was the quagmire that Clem gave strict instructions to his players, especially the forwards, to allow England to have the ball, and then hound them down in the loose. Clem said that they beat seven bells out of the English forwards as they scrambled backwards in the mud, with the crowd baying for blood, he said it was at times like performing in the Coliseum such was the physical intensity with which the Welsh pack hunted down their brown shirted opponents. The match is remembered in rugby folklore for the fervour of the Welsh crowd which intensified its passion in eager anticipation of a Wales win. Thousands of supporters began to spontaneously sing *Maen Hen Wlad fy Nhadau,* the Welsh National anthem. This galvanized the team into ever greater efforts as they set about the English. It is believed by most historians of the game that this was the first occasion that a crowd broke into song during the course of a rugby match anywhere in the British Isles. The match introduced the public to a new cap, the young Swansea winger Dewi Bebb scored the only try of the game, as Wales won 5-0. It was the start of an illustrious career that saw Bebb score 11 tries in his 34 appearances for Wales.

Dad believed that you needed to play rugby with extreme physical intensity and commitment whilst staying firmly within the rules. Many of his contemporaries and people who saw him play say he is still one of the hardest men who ever played for Wales. Dad viewed it all in black and white - if another player wanted to start something, then Clem was always ready to finish it – he was pretty uncompromising in that respect.

One of the truly hard men who played with Clem was the Pontypool second row, Ray Prosser. "Pross" was a single-minded monster, a rock in the second row who played 22 times for Wales between 1956 and 1961, a lock converted to prop for international duty. Later, he transformed Pontypool's fortunes as a revolutionary coach during the 1970s and 1980s. He was tough and crude, skilled and analytical. Pross's way of showing he cared about you was to subject you to a tirade of verbal abuse, usually based on how you looked physically or what you did for a job. He would love to take the piss out of the more white-collar types, "We've got more bloody medical men, lawyers, students and teachers than University Challenge. We're keeling over with eggheads!" was how he once memorably described Pontypool RFC.

Pross was an enforcer and a technician. And yet despite being one of the hardest men ever to don a Club, Welsh or Lions shirt, Ray was very down to earth, as befits a JCB driver, and in his own inimitable way had little or no time for the "glamour boys" of rugby. In his mind, Clem Thomas, with his Public School, English and Cambridge background was one of those glamour boys. That was until Wales v England in Cardiff (1957), first game of the Championship, with England bringing a very strong side that included in the forwards, Ron Jacobs, the top-class prop from Northampton who had gained a reputation as 'the iron man of English rugby', the captain and hooker, Eric Evans, and Currie and Marques (Harlequins) in the second row. At six feet five inches David Marques was the tallest man in rugby at that time. Behind they boasted Dickie Jeeps, who Cliff Morgan rated as one of the greatest scrum-halves to ever grace the game of rugby. Jeeps, a Cambridgeshire fruit farmer of stocky build, with a ruddy complexion and thin fair hair over a domed head, was jokingly said to resemble one of his own apples. He had a talent for mischief and his practical jokes – using a water pistol, a catapult, putting raw eggs in pockets, or just shoving people into the hotel swimming pool – became notorious on rugby tours. His pièce de résistance, came in Paris when, tiring of an interminable after-match speech by the President of the French Federation – and an even more prolix translation by the interpreter – he crawled under the table and let off a firework under the tedious official's feet.

Outside Jeeps was Ricky Bartlett, a gifted fly half who made 276 appearances for Harlequins and was awarded seven caps for England where he never played for a losing team. The peerless centre three-quarter, Jeff Butterfield, who Dad thought a master of all the arts of centre play, was ably accompanied by Peter 'Nijinsky' Jackson. The match was on a razor edge, incredibly physical, and it boiled over amongst the forwards on several occasions. Prosser said at one point there was a suicidal maul, but in went Clem yelling his old Blundells chant of "blood on the boot", giving his all and taking quite a bit in return. Pross was at first amazed, then went in with him, uttering the classic remark, "the Blue Bastard's one of us after all, let's get with him." From then onwards they became best of pals, and it was Pross who said at the conclusion of the failed 1959 Lions tour to New Zealand, that if Clem had gone as captain, the Lions would probably have won. They missed his leadership, physical intensity, and combativeness. RH Williams and Tony O'Reilly were of the same opinion and both said much the same thing.

Clem loved playing with skillful players and he lauded two of the great centres he played with, Bleddyn Williams, who Dad called the Prince of centres, and Jeff Butterfield, who had an outstanding tour to South Africa for the Lions. In terms of playing tactics, Clem believed in a fast, open, passing game, and he encouraged his half-backs to put the ball wide to stretch defences, creating opportunities for strong support runners to back-up the three-quarters. He toured France with both Cambridge University and Swansea, and played against some of the great French players of the late 1940s, most notably, Jean 'Manech' Dauger, the great Bayonne three-quarter centre, and French captain Jean Prat, the outstanding blindside flanker who was born in Lourdes, which prompted some to suggest that he was a miracle player, giving rise to his nickname, 'L'extraordinaire'. Such was the high esteem in which Jean Pratt was held in world rugby, that when the final whistle blew in the last game of the Five Nations (1955), the Welsh players were delighted with their 16-11 victory over France in Paris. Not only did it mean a share of the title, they had also denied the French their first Grand Slam. But, instead of celebrating among themselves, they walked over to the French captain, lifted him shoulder-high, and carried him off the Stade Colombes pitch to huge acclaim.

Dad also played against French rugby legend Robert Soro. The formidable second row was nicknamed the "Lion of Swansea" after a towering performance against the Welsh in Swansea, where on a snow-covered St Helen's pitch, he was credited with inspiring his side to their first ever win over their hosts in Wales alongside his second row partner, the incomparable Alban 'Bambi' Moga. Dad admired the French flair and outrageous tactical risks they took, being a close friend of Jean 'Manech' Dauger, the first of the great mercurial three-quarter geniuses and the archetype that set the standard for the Boniface Brothers, Jo Masu, Jean Trillo, and Dennis Charvet who were to follow - all of them 'Le Souris' for the ability to squeeze through the smallest hole in any defensive line. Dad learned the tactical benefit of a cross-kick from studying Dauger and his playing experiences in France with Cambridge University. But even armed with this positive ambition to play expansive rugby, when he tried to implement such tactics with Swansea in 1954, the year he was voted to the captaincy, the club suffered its worst start to a season in living memory.

The Whites lost the first 10 matches of the season and there was much consternation amongst the public. Clem gave an interview to the local press following the eighth successive defeat:

> The early fixtures have been the hardest I've known: Newport (twice), Bristol, Harlequins, Cardiff... and all away. Llanelli, Neath and Ranji Walker's XV... We want to revert to the classical style that gained the All Whites a high reputation in the old days... the style that developed such men as W.J. Bancroft, Billy Trew and Dickie Owen and Dick Jones, the "Dancing Dicks". We are building along the lines of Cardiff, the best example of open, attacking, confident football.

Since the war the spirit engendered by the Cardiff club and their approach to the game has been the finest in the British Isles. It has paid them handsome dividends in attracting the right kind of player and the largest crowds for club matches in the history of the game. It might be argued that Cardiff have players with outstanding ability for playing open, attacking football. What has been done at Cardiff Arms Park can be done equally as well, and perhaps better at St Helen's. But it cannot be done overnight. It will take time. As the town is being rebuilt into one of the most attractive in Great Britain, so the All Whites are being rebuilt into a team worthy of the town. When this is achieved the young men of West Wales will no longer go east for the type of football they wish to play. It will be a case of "Go west, young man. Go to St Helen's."

Sadly, the revolution never quite caught hold in that era, and Dad never captained Swansea again after that season was finished.

Clem however stuck to his principles and attempted to play open rugby whilst the press and the pundits on the terraces continued theorising about the situation. Most rugby people did not wish to disagree with the new 'Clem Thomas philosophy', but there was a groundswell of opinion which called for a modified approach. Ron Griffiths, *The Evening Post* reporter, argued that modern tactics be employed. By that he meant closing up the game and only launching attacks from inside the opposing half. There were, too, those who argued that Clem Thomas was the victim of his own playing policy, in that opposing teams, being aware of the Swansea tactics, set out to negate their open play and strike them on the counter-attack.

The final record was fairly average, Played 38, Won 14, Drew 3, Lost 21. But the underlying philosophy that

Clem applied in justification of playing a fast, loose, handling game which would ultimately thrill and appeal to spectators and rugby fans, was the right one. Today, the two professional franchises in the West of Wales dominate Welsh rugby and the Welsh team selection. From 2005 to 2017, The Ospreys and Scarlets have contributed 75% of all Welsh caps, and that's with only 25% of the rugby playing population, which is quite remarkable when you stop to consider it. The Blues have consistently failed over the past 20 years to make any impression on the game, and the tag that Cardiff RFC enjoyed in the mid-1950s of being the best rugby club in the world, has, sadly long since gone.

Clem would have been immensely proud that the 2017 British Lions featured no less than six Swansea schoolboy's in their ranks: Dan Biggar, Alun Wyn Jones, Leigh Halfpenny, Justin Tipuric, Liam Williams and Ross Moriarty; its quite staggering when you stop to think about it. Swansea continues to produce great, world class rugby players in the tradition of Gowerton schoolboys, Haydn Tanner and Willie Davies.

Clem's season as captain started with great hope and an ambassadorial rugby tour to Romania, the first tour ever to go behind the iron-curtain during the cold war. The Swansea club had been invited by the Romanian Rugby Federation to play the matches there because of its "fame and tradition". The Swansea party flew from London to Prague, and then split up into three planes to Bucharest. Unfortunately, the weather was so bad that lightning strikes forced two of the aircraft to make emergency landings, as Clem wrote:

> I doubt if any rugby team has had a tour of such hardship. We struck an electrical storm over the

Carpathian Mountains and were forced down at a small town on the Yugoslav border called Arad, where we were promptly arrested, another unfortunate habit of Swansea touring teams. We were marched off at gun point and locked in an airport building under armed guard for over 3 hours. Finally word must have come through from Bucharest that we were not an invasion force sent from the evil capitalist West, and we were afforded the hospitality of the town, which was not very much! But they opened up a hotel for us and we spent the night with cockroaches the size of large mice. That was not the end of our trials, for a few days later we found ourselves playing before a 90,000 crowd in a temperature of 110 degrees.

There is an iconic photo of Clem grasping an enormous bouquet of flowers leading out the Swansea team into the Romanian Olympic Stadium that day. Not surprisingly the 'Whites' melted in the second quarter of the match, during which the Romanians scored 15 points. In the second half, the Swansea side made a comeback in the cooler conditions, but Lokomotiv were the victors in the first ever game between a Romanian side and a British team, 23-12. In the second match, Swansea beat Constructors club by 16-5.

Clem had enjoyed a break from playing for Swansea when he went to join Coventry for the 1952-53 season. But by September he was back in Wales and had rejoined Swansea, as he focused on the All Black challenges to come, not only with the Whites but also with Wales. The press headline complimented his performance in the first Welsh trial - "CLEM LEADS THE WAY" - and commented:

> Discriminating spectators at the rugby trial played at St Helen's considered that R.C.C. Thomas is now the greatest wing-forward in the four countries. His play in the trial was one of the greatest individual performances by a forward seen for many a year and it was common talk that Thomas made more openings in attack than any other player. New Zealand will find him a real problem.

Propitious words from the Welsh rugby press indeed!

On Saturday, December 12 1953, Swansea mounted a desperate challenge that gave them a highly creditable 6-6 draw with the All Blacks. JBG Thomas reporting in *The Western Mail* wrote of the game:

> Rising to the occasion magnificently and performing almost as well as did their great predecessors in 1935, who beat the All Blacks, Swansea gained a draw with honour against New Zealand…
>
> The result will hold a high place in the pages of rugby history…Swansea's heroic effort, with RCC Thomas the bravest forward of them all, exposed the limitations of the New Zealanders… the darkness of their present attacking football matches the colour of their jerseys…
>
> The All Blacks had the advantage in the tight, but in the loose it was a different tale, for Swansea contained them…and the big, burly and hard-working All Black forwards found men their equal in Thomas, Blyth and Billy Williams.
>
> The forward play was often fierce, and a few blows were struck. The players themselves must know whether or not it was in the interests of the game…

Ron Griffiths also added, "Swansea owed a great deal to their forwards, whose terrier-like work in the loose clearly rattled the New Zealanders as it did the Springboks two years ago."

In the match programme that day the Honourable Judge Rowe Harding wrote of his view of amateurism which dominated the ethics of rugby football at that time, and which Dad certainly adhered to:

> The days when a man was looked down upon because he was paid for playing a game are gone. We in the rugby game stick to amateurism not because we look down on a professional sportsman, - indeed, a professional cricketer may be an amateur rugby player or a knight - but because we consider this tough game of rugby is meant for the young and care-free; it is short-lived, too joyous, too bound up with the giving and taking of hard knocks in good spirit, with playing to win but not caring overmuch if you lose, to be the subject of a pay packet; and this is the point of view, not only of the business man or professional man, but of the miner, the steel-worker, the impecunious Varsity student, and even of the "out-of-work" now fortunately rare, who loves the game.

I have another curious memento of that game played in 1953. It's the Swansea Cricket and Football Club's official Dinner menu, held at The Osborne Hotel in Langland Bay. The dinner card is signed by the players of both teams, and I can clearly make out the autographs of AEG Elsom, Peter Jones, Dixon, R Jarden, Bob Stuart (the tour captain), Haig, and RA White, amongst 24 other signatures. The rather grand menu consisted of - iced grapefruit or cream of tomato soup, grilled fillet of lemon sole and shrimp sauce, roast Welsh turkey, bread sauce, savoury stuffing, with roast potatoes, creamed potatoes, brussels sprouts and swedes. The main course was followed by strawberry melba, assorted cheeses & biscuits, celery, and coffee. The wines: Bouquet d'Or. The extraordinary thing is I also have the menu from the Wales v Ireland match played at Swansea the previous March, and it's identical in every regard!

The Western Mail reported the following Monday, "NEW ZEALANDERS WANT FLAG BACK" and commented:

> The New Zealand tourists are upset at the disappearance of their official flag from the flagpole at the Swansea Pavilion during the game last Saturday. It is the only official flag they have brought with them, and it has flown at all the grounds they have played on during the tour. It could not be found after the match against Swansea despite a thorough search and inquiry. The Swansea club have issued an appeal to any enthusiasts who might have "captured the flag" as a souvenir to return it. As the tourists cannot obtain a replacement immediately, they would like to have the flag back for the Welsh match at Cardiff on Saturday.

Alas, I can find no record as to whether the New Zealand flag flew over Cardiff Arms Park the week after.

The match for Wales against the All Blacks at Cardiff represented one of Dad's greatest sporting triumphs, particularly as he made the instinctive footballing play that created the scoring opportunity for the Olympic sprinter Ken Jones to convert by catching the ball on the bounce and cutting inside the last beaten defender to score under the posts. That moment encapsulates the full armoury that Clem brought onto the field of play. His pace on the ball, handling skills to scoop it off the ground, strength to hold off the physical challenge, rugby guile, balance and poise in the heat of battle, all combined with the clarity of purpose to switch the direction of play so dramatically and unexpectedly. And in 2017, Wales, who are due to play the world champions in Cardiff in November, have not won since. It's a ridiculous statistic that all Welshmen of subsequent generations should be deeply ashamed of.

The build up to the game was an unmitigated disaster for Dad. Pat Marshall in *The Daily Express* explained:

> Millions watched spellbound on TV at the glorious spectacle of Wales beating the All Blacks. The 56,000 crowd went crazy at Cardiff Arms Park as Clem Thomas banged a magnificent cross-kick eight minutes from time to pave the way for a wonderful win. What millions who saw the game did not know was the before-the-match drama with hero Thomas the central figure.
>
> He had been involved in a fatal car accident on Friday, but still wanted to play. Everyone wanted him to play… except the selectors, who felt Clem might still be suffering from shock. One man talked and persuaded the reluctant Welsh selectors round - Bill Ramsay, treasurer of the Rugby Football Union. Now it will be a wonderful, wonderful Christmas in the valleys and hills of Wales, but Welshmen everywhere should send the biggest Christmas card they can find to Bill Ramsay.
>
> When musing over the incident after the game, "Why did I cross-kick just at that moment? Well, I had to do something. There I was, alone on the touchline, looking for someone to pass to, and there were two All Blacks bearing down on me. So I just booted and hoped I'd done the right thing.

The Times reported:

> The crowd, one cannot help thinking, would have been content with a draw, but not so the Welsh team. They out-rushed their opponents even if they got the ball. It was the smothering of Elsom which offered R.C.C. Thomas his great chance. Gathering the ball on the left touchline, he had a quick look about him and saw that across the field spread a wide open space occupied by Ken Jones. Thomas placed his long kick across the field well and it bounced nicely for Jones whose speed and swerve easily beat his only opponent. Rowlands then made no mistake with the kick and, for the last five minutes, New Zealand were too shocked by the two blows which had suddenly befallen them to strike back in force.

The final word on this match belongs to the truly great cricket and sports correspondent, E.W. Swanton, who covered the match for *The Daily Telegraph*, and who summed up proceedings thus: "It was the intuitive skill of the Welsh rugby footballer that won the day, and I think it is not ungenerous to the All Blacks to remark that it is a good thing brain was not bettered, broadly speaking, by brawn."

In the era that Clem played, the team he had the most respect for were the South African Springboks whom he encountered in Wales in 1951, and then in South Africa in 1955. At that time, in the mid-1950s, it was South Africa who were perceived to be the best team and rugby nation in the world. The British Lions tour of 1955 was greeted with such acclaim when the tour party returned to the British Isles to excited applause. It was considered a heroic and ground-breaking event, the 2-2 drawn series rubber represented far more than any honourable draw in the eyes of the rugby fraternity.

The next chapter is the story of that particular tour told in Clem's own words. It was a life changing experience and my father always credited the tour as a significant formative event. This was partly the reason that Dad was so forthright in always defending the benefits of both British Lions tours and short Barbarian tours as being a key part of the structure within the institution of rugby union football. The Springboks represented the very pinnacle at that time and although he only played 3 times against them, as he did the All Blacks, it was the South Africans who always commanded his total respect, that's not to say he didn't appreciate the competing qualities of New Zealand rugby. Today as we approach the next World Cup in Japan, with the All Blacks reigning world champions since 2011, a period of brilliance that can be traced back to the Wayne Shelford era post the 1987 World Cup, won by New Zealand, it is often forgotten that it took the All Blacks up until 1996 to win a test series in South Africa. Up until the start of the professional era, from the first test played in Dunedin in 1921, the Springboks had won 21 tests to the All Blacks' 18. But since 1995, the situation has been reversed with the All Blacks winning 36 tests to 14.

The All Blacks hegemony of the professional era is due to numerous factors, most notably the massive social and economic changes wrought on two very different "frontier" ex-colonies. The years of sporting isolation eventually caught up with South Africa, as the country meandered to full democratic political independence, the ending of the hated apartheid regime, and the gradual brain drain of the educated middle classes which continues to this day. This has been further exacerbated by the high playing salaries on offer in Europe, particularly in the French and English leagues. In 2017, with ex-Springbok coach Jake White coaching Montpelier in the French Top14, there were 17 South Africans on contract there.

Dad had some good rugby friends from South Africa,

particularly Dr Dannie Craven, who played scrum-half for the Springboks before the war, winning his first cap against Wales at St Helen's in 1931. Later, Craven coached the Springboks, achieving a 74 per cent win record (1949-56), and going on to serve as President of SARFU (1956-93). He had the intelligence and grace to appreciate that the years of isolation were draining South Africa of its rugby reputation and its vitality, and whilst making a last play with the white Nationalists with the botched New Zealand Cavaliers tour in 1986, by 1988, in the face of massive Nationalist opposition and criticism, Craven met leaders of the African National Congress in Harare in a bold move to return to global competition. An unprecedented deal was done to create a single South African rugby association to field integrated teams. Danie Craven was attacked by many white South Africans as a traitor for meeting the ANC, and the prime minister, PW Botha, denounced the move. But it worked, and in 1992, South Africa returned to international competition. Clem's last visit to South Africa was for the 1995 world cup, and I remember him telling me that he had visited Danie Craven's office in Stellenbosch, and that to his surprise one of the photos on his desk, which has been kept as a time capsule since his death in 1993, was a photo of Dad and Danie Craven.

Clem had a more prosaic view of New Zealand rugby. He loved their passion for the game and the all-embracing rugby culture that permeates parts of New Zealand society, but deep down he was always suspicious that there was too much emphasis placed on winning at all costs, that whilst he admired their physical intensity and frontier-like hardness to absorb physical pain, such singular attitudes could and did lead the All Blacks down dark corridors to achieve a win. Dad had noticed in 1953 that New Zealanders are bad losers, that at the end of the Swansea and Wales matches, there had been dirty play and cheap shots thrown.

From the 1970s onwards, the All Blacks became the "unsmiling giants", and every tour to Wales seemed to end with acrimony, whether out of brutality in 1973 (Murdoch), or downright cheating to con the referee (Andy Haden). The famed New Zealand rugby correspondent Terry Maclean who was affectionately nicknamed "poison pen" by friend and foe alike in the press box, wrote of the 1972-73 All Blacks tour that, "The team took on the character of a body of graceless and humourless men."

With psychopaths like Murdoch selected, touring teams to New Zealand ridiculed, humiliated, and virtually spat at by the rugby public, Clem came to regard any tour to New Zealand as a penance for any fine living he may have enjoyed in-between. By the 1980s he began to baulk at having to cover yet another wet, windy, graceless trip around an island where the clocks seemed to have frozen at midnight in 1947.

By the late 1980s he had taken up the cause of the Fijian, Samoans, and Tongans, who were being denuded of all their young talent which began to appear in the New Zealand jersey. The Maori have traditionally enjoyed a separate status and respect for their rugby traditions which started in 1888 in Dublin against Ireland, but up until the 1980s an All Blacks team would consist of white New Zealanders plus the most talented Maori players of their generation. Indeed, some of New Zealand's best players are Maori, whether Sid Going, Zinzan Brooke, Wayne Shelford, Christian Cullen, Eric Rush, George Nepia, and Dad's great buddy, the original "black panther" Waka Nathan. What irked other countries and their administrators by the late 1980s was a clear effort to pull in talent from the Pacific islands, and award caps to prevent the Pacific islanders from playing for the land of their birth, or their parents. The great Jonah Lomu was Tongan although born in Greenlane Hospital in Auckland, he was typical of a shifting migrancy which led him back to Tonga for his early childhood where he lived with his aunt and uncle. A cycle of gang violence led the family back to New Zealand via Wesley College. And his freakish athletic talents were identified and developed by Eric Rush in the 7's arena.

The situation is also evidenced by the Samoan influences over the past 25 years, beginning with today's President of the New Zealand RFU, the great winger of the 1970's and 80's, Brian Williams. And a further 70 or so world class players that includes the likes of Joe Stanley, John Schuster, Julian Savea, Ma'a Nonu, Mils Muliaina, Kevin Mealamu, Aaron Mauger, Chris Masoe, Pat Lam, Josh Kronfeld, Michael Jones, Christian Cullen, Jerry Collins, Frank Bunce and the Bachop brothers. It's an incredible list that goes some way to explaining why the All Blacks have dominated the world game. With a "draft" of such outstanding athletic talent on their doorstep it is hardly surprising. We can only be jealous, but should admonish New Zealand for not putting back into the island communities what they stripped out.

To this day, New Zealand has not played one full test match in Apia, Samoa or in Nuku'alofa, Tonga. Fiji has not escaped the player drain either, the latest freak athlete is Waisake Naholo, but in recent years, Joe Rokocoko, Siteveni Sivivatu, and Jerome Kaino continue the relentless New Zealand adoption of Pacific island talent. Clem often commented that if the three islands of Fiji, Tonga, and Samoa had been off-shore of Swansea, then Wales would be winning Grand Slams and World Cups in a manner now accustomed by New Zealanders. But it wasn't jealousy that provoked him to criticise the New Zealand RFU, it was simply their wanton indifference to putting something back into the Pacific Islands' development pathways, or even just to say a simple thank you, by playing the odd match in Apia, to secure some much-needed funding for the Samoan RFU. The New Zealand Herald wrote in 2013, "The All Blacks' refusal to play a test match in the islands has long been viewed as a source of contention, given the number of players with Polynesian, and Melanesian ancestry who have made such telling contributions to the game in New Zealand. A host of reasons ranging from a lack of infrastructure in the islands, cost, fear of injury on substandard pitches and too many other fixture commitments have all been used by the NZRU to justify their position."

Unfortunately, World Rugby led by Bill Beaumont continues to turn a blind eye to the islands' predicament, which is worsened by French Top 14 clubs seeking alliances with so-called rugby schools in Fiji and Samoa with the intent of signing any young talent. Clem called for a halt over 20 years ago, but the system is still under abuse in the professional era. The indentured "farm" system of virtually enslaving young talented athletes is an issue rugby is yet to deal with. The migrant populations that access New Zealand from the Pacific for work, education and healthcare, have become second and third generation New Zealanders. Their children may embrace a family's Samoan culture, but they are born New Zealand citizens, and good luck to them. But New Zealand needs to take fellow tier one rugby nations with it, and its own people too. For whilst the composition of All Black teams changed over the last decades of the 20th century, with a greater and greater preponderance of islander influence, the commitment towards rugby football from the white section of New Zealand society has waned dramatically, especially when the All Blacks kept choking on a 4-year cycle by failing to win another World Cup until 2011 and 2015. I notice among my New Zealand friends that many have moved away from the game, although most are happy to lend some support to the All Blacks if a game is up on the TV. But their kids are playing soccer or cricket, they're swimming or doing athletics, or skate-boarding. There seems to be a general distrust of the New Zealand brand, and it stems from the type of experience Clem had when playing against them in the 1950s.

At the end of the Swansea v New Zealand (1953) game, Clem and the outstanding full-back, Bob Scott, enjoyed a stand-up exchange with a flurry of fists in front of the main stand and VIP box, a brawl that Scott started with a cheap shot thrown at the back of Clem's head. The fight continued as the players left the field at full-time, brawling along the corridor at the narrow entrance to the changing rooms as you turn sharp left, just outside the All Black changing room. Fortunately, sense prevailed and Clem continued walking into the Swansea showers! This was partly the reason Clem wrote in *The Observer:*

> If the total object of a game of rugby is to win, then the least that can be said of New Zealand is that they succeeded. They will be happy but the manner of victory is also part of the folklore and in this they would be regarded without affection…

One of Dad's favourite rugby quotations which he used on many occasions was the viewpoint Tony O'Reilly held of Welsh rugby, who, with his typically whimsical wit commented, "Whether we like it or not, and most of us don't, rugby football is simply not a game without the Welsh." Dad often said that his favourite opponents were the Irish, and his favourite ground, outside Cardiff was Lansdowne Road, for he always tended to play well there against the Irish teams he faced over the years. In 1952, Dai Gent of *The Sunday Times* commented on the Triple Crown game that "Wales put in glorious counter-attacks…Roy John and RCC Thomas both handled and ran beautifully…"

Whilst *The Sunday Express* was of the opinion:

> Clem Thomas, recalled to the side after four years had the good sense to dog John's footsteps, content to pick up the crumbs from the master's

table…and what a crumble - a pass in the first half after a great burst from a line-out which Clem handed onto Rees Stephens to touch down and another ten minutes after half-time when John smashed through the Irish pack and left their three-quarters behind, This time Clem went on himself for the try…

Dad often reminisced about playing at St Helen's - a ground he preferred to Cardiff because the surface was always firm under foot which suited his pacey, metronomic, running style. He thought one of his finest personal performances was against the Irish, led from fly-half by the iconic Jackie Kyle, who Dad remembered "dismantling" one afternoon. Wilf Wooller, the famous Glamorgan cricketer, writing in *The News Chronicle* declared: "THOMAS BLOTS OUT KYLE - Wales well deserved their victory which could have been more convincing in terms of points had the bounce of the ball gone their way… Clem Thomas so subdued Jack Kyle that, apart from his superbly accurate kicking he might not have been on the field."

Every player has a bogey team, and for Clem it was Scotland. In particular, two bad losses in his career stand out, both at Murrayfield in 1955 and 1959. Wales had beaten England and went to Scotland as firm favourites to repeat their 1952 Triple Crown triumph, but, "Scotland, the underdogs of the international championship series, caused the upset of the season when they halted Wales' Triple Crown progress… Hurried passing and some indecisive running allowed the Scottish back row to get in some effective spoiling and Wales was a thoroughly rattled and disjointed side."

Wen Davis further commented that: "Wales, beaten by a poor side, have only themselves to blame…there was little life, and they were never together as an eight or used their weight to crush the lively Scottish forwards. Billy

Williams worked tremendously hard, ably supported by Bryn Meredith and Clem Thomas… in all a day for Wales to forget - the game was thrown away."

In 1959 Clem was captain, and again had won a famous victory over England in the Cardiff Arms Park quagmire. They went to Murrayfield with great hope, but lost 6-5, with Ken Scotland kicking the key penalty goal. Clem said that the Welsh half-backs had some success with a short kicking game in the first half, but then Cliff Ashton overdid the kicking in the second half - contrary to his instructions! Wales had planned to get the ball into their new star winger's hands more (Dewi Bebb), and the all-Swansea back row of Clem, John Faull, and John Leleu performed powerfully. His abiding memory of the match was the Saturday night in Edinburgh, when a group of around a thousand Welsh supporters gathered outside the Welsh team's hotel and started singing the Lonnie Donegan hit song, "Hang down your head Tom Dooley, Hang down your head and cry….", although they replaced the words "Tom Dooley" with "Clem Thomas"! To his dying day he thought that this result cost him the captaincy of the 1959 British Lions tour, but the politics were against him, notably the ban on taking any player over the age of 30 years old.

One of the great characters Dad played against was Sir Ewen Alastair John Fergusson GCMG GCVO, second row for Scotland in 1954, who played in the last international match ever to be played at St Helen's, in front of a 50,000-capacity crowd. Sir Ewan, a sixteen stone, 6' 6" second row from Oriel College, Oxford University, later joined the Foreign Office. Famously, Sir Ewen is the only candidate to have passed the notoriously difficult Civil Service exams with full marks. I can personally vouch that he had an attractive personality and self-confident manner which enabled him to be an outstanding diplomat. Of the match itself, JBG Thomas commented in *The Herald of Wales*:

> Wales established herself as one of the season's leading rugby countries by defeating a poor Scottish side at St Helen's, Swansea, with considerable ease…Scotland were no better than an average club side, and it is no exaggeration to state that several of the leading Welsh clubs could have beaten this team. The pack worked hard, and none did more than RKG MacEwen, A Fergusson and JW Kemp, but they could not do enough to dominate the Welsh forwards.

Sir Ewen is probably best remembered for his role as the British Ambassador to France (1987 – 1992), and it was whilst staying at the Paris embassy at the Rue du Faubourg St Honore' that Margaret Thatcher heard the news that she had failed to win enough Tory votes to avoid a second ballot for the leadership. Watched by the ambassador and others from a window, she emerged dramatically into the embassy courtyard to announce in front of the TV cameras her determination to fight on. It was to Sir Ewen that she turned for solace and advice during a series of limousine trips to and from a state banquet at the Palace of Versailles. Sir Ewen diplomatically as ever said, "I regarded the gossips that I had with her in the car…as an absolutely fascinating bonus to my professional experience…" He had an outstanding career in the Foreign Office, and was Private Secretary between 1975 and 1978 to three successive Foreign Secretaries: James Callaghan, Anthony Crosland, and David Owen. Sir Ewen served in Addis Ababa, Brussels, and New York, and was Ambassador to South Africa (1982-84). In the land of the Springboks, as in France, his prowess as a Scottish rugby player proved a "great help" for diplomatic relations. He shared with Clem a healthy appetite for living, and was regarded as "the epicurean British ambassador to France who led a renaissance in diplomatic entertaining". Sir Ewen made it his business to be personal friends with every top chef in Paris.

I had the distinct personal pleasure of meeting Sir Ewen in 1991. As the Deputy-Director of Welsh Development International for Europe - responsible for attracting inward investment to Wales - I had to organise a promotional dinner hosted by the Embassy. I got summonsed by the ambassador, who wanted a detailed briefing on the occasion, and who wanted to be brought up-to-speed on the reasons for the success we had at that time in attracting record levels of foreign investment into Wales. During the 1990s we won major job-creating investments from top French industrial groups like TOTAL, Elf, and Valeo. After my allotted 30-minute briefing with Sir Ewen, he asked me if I had ever played rugby, being of a somewhat similar stature to himself. When I told him I played for Swansea, he enthused about taking part in the very last international match played at St Helen's, and I mentioned that my father, Clem, had played in the same match. Excitedly, he jumped to his feet and led me through various corridors, finally pushing open a large Louis XV11 door leading into a sumptuously decorated fin-de-siecle Napoleonic bathroom and WC. It was a vibrant purple, and, attached to the walls, were a series of walnut cabinets containing the story of Sir Ewen's brief but well-documented international rugby career. There were framed Scottish and 5 Nations jerseys, all the Match Day Programmes carefully opened in the middle to reveal the team names, and an assortment of newspaper clippings, match reports, and photographs. It was jaw dropping in its unexpectedness, and I had to remind myself that I was in the loo of the British Embassy, right next door to the Élysée Palace itself. Sir Ewen knew damn well the effect it had on people and just chuckled away like a cat who'd eaten all the cream. The best of friends, we retired back to his private study, talked rugby for over an hour, and drank the entire contents of a crystal decanter of fine malt whiskey. He was a lovely man who sadly passed in the Spring of 2017 in the beautiful village of Vaison-la-Romaine, Vaucluse.

Clem loved touring, and bought into the adage that a rugby tour is like sex. When it's good it's great, and when it's bad - hey! It's still pretty good. During his career he toured with Cambridge University, The Woodpeckers, the Barbarians (his favourite moments), the British Lions, and Swansea, plus he "guested" as a player with the Harlequins on a tour to Romania in 1958. The major trips he made with Swansea were to Tarbes in France, Romania, and Italy. The Italian tour almost ended in disaster, as Dad and John Maclean - who had been Clem's fag in Francis House at Blundells - set another Swansea rugby club fashion by being locked up by police in Padua for shooting out all the lights in a rifle range at a travelling fair. Fortunately, on that occasion, they were represented by no less a figure than Judge Rowe Harding, who happened to be the team's tour manager, and who with all the regal bearing of the British legal system, managed to bail them out at four o'clock in the morning. Clem and Johnny 'Mac' managed to get back into the Judge's good books by being the only members of the touring party to attend an official reception held by the Mayor of Rome. Unfortunately, the rest of the team had missed the train. Dad and Johnny Mac were, of course, left over in Rome from the night before.

The Woodpeckers were formed in October 1948 with a membership drawn mainly from Oxford and Cambridge Universities. The formation of the team was in response to a letter sent to *The Playfair Rugby Football Annual* by Major CH Johnston, the Honourable Treasurer of the Swedish Rugby Union. *The London Evening News* helpfully published the appeal: "It would be a godsend if a British club would tour our country." The hastily formed Woodpeckers duly picked up the baton and arranged a ten-day visit with five matches at the start of September 1949. Dad went on the tour and had the wonderful experience of dining with the King of Sweden, Gustav V. The Woodpeckers were set up by Sir Colin Figures, who attended Pembroke College, and later became Chief of the Secret Intelligence Service (MI6). Figures' self-effacing personality masked both an incisive intellect and firmness of purpose. He won the affection and trust of his subordinates, who valued his sense of humour and found him approachable and free of pomposity. He also inspired confidence in both Whitehall and Downing Street. In April 1982, Figures found himself immersed in the Falklands conflict, mounting an operation in Paris against the Argentine Naval Procurement Office, which had been asked to trawl the international arms markets for Exocet reloads. SIS also played a significant role in neutralizing a three-man team of enemy saboteurs sent from Buenos Aires to Spain to attack British naval targets in Gibraltar as well as a BP oil tanker, British Tamar.

The Cambridge University tour to France in 1949 was an opportunity for Clem to highlight not only his rugby footballing talents, but also his flair for entrepreneurship and black market dealing. Games were played in Dijon, Clermont-Ferrand, Brive, and Paris, which is where Dad was when news of his selection for Wales for his first cap was received. Geoff Vaughan, Dad's closest friend at Cambridge, and my godfather, answered a relentlessly ringing telephone on the Tuesday before the match in their hotel room in Paris. My grandfather DJ excitedly shouted down the line that Clem had been selected. Unfortunately, Geoff was unable to wake Clem who was sleeping off the previous night's excesses. Dad stayed on in Paris to meet up with the Welsh team and committee on the Friday at the Hotel Terminus. Before the Cambridge tour began, Clem and Geoff had volunteered to take the kitbag with the playing jerseys. They managed to smuggle into France 50 pounds of fresh Fortnum & Mason coffee beans, which Geoff said they sold for a small fortune, as France was still in post-war rationing and coffee was impossible to find, even in 1949.

I'm not sure when Clem played his very last game of first-class rugby in 1959. I know he played on Good Friday in the Barbarians versus Penarth match, a tour that he always loved to participate in, and when not selected, could deliver a performance for the ages for Swansea against the Baa-Baas each Easter Monday. Dad played nine times for the Barbarians between 1952-59, but he made his reputation in the games he played for Swansea against the touring team, most notably in 1956.

In 2000 I was returning from the Sydney Olympics with my close friend, Robert Davies, the leading investor and benefactor of the Ospreys since inception. We had stopped off in Hong Kong to break the trip and to indulge in some bespoke shopping. I recall we were in the foyer of the Mandarin Hotel, and stood in front of us was a tall, elegantly dressed senior executive, surrounded by eight other corporate types. I recognised him immediately as AJF O'Reilly, the legendary Irish and British Lion international, a good friend of my father since the 1955 Lions tour. Tony O'Reilly was Chairman of Independent Newspaper Group, Waterford Wedgewood, and previously President of the Pittsburgh-based Heinz Corporation. He recognised me immediately, and said in his clear Irish brogue: "This guy's father is a very old friend of mine, and is the only player I know who took his profession onto the field of play... he was a butcher both on and off the field..."

Tony regaled us with tales of the legendary 1955 Lions tour for the next 15 minutes as his group awaited their transport to a Waterford Wedgewood event. Finally, as he turned to leave, he added with a twinkle in his eye:

> And your Dad was the only player who I felt
> actually tried to kill me one day, because he

certainly frightened me to death. I was playing for the Baa-Baas against Swansea, and I received the ball in space on the left, on the grandstand side, so I aimed for the corner flag, but coming across like a train was Clem who got to me five yards out, and got hold of the collar of my jersey. Instead of pulling up as we crossed the touchline, I realised that he hadn't decelerated but was, if anything still accelerating, towards a small waist high red brick wall. And he ran me straight into it which luckily my survival instincts somehow made me hurdle, only to clatter into the enclosure...That's why Clem was a butcher both on and off the field.

5

A HOLY CRUSADE: CLEM'S
1955 LIONS TOUR TO SOUTH AFRICA

"There is no passion to be found playing small - in settling
for a life that is less than the one you are capable of
living." *Nelson Mandela*

Clem's selection for the British Lions tour was a life-
changing event; the experience was enriching both
professionally and holistically. Dad recognised that it
helped shape him for the rest of his life – it was the
making of the man. Whilst he relished the extreme
challenges and physical demands necessitated by such a
tough tour, he always felt frustration at having missed out
on the first two Tests due to appendicitis. He had his
appendix removed on June 25th and returned to play in
the match versus Central Universities on August 10th,
where according to Viv Jenkins of *The Sunday Times*, "he
played a thoroughly good game". He also played against
Boland before captaining the Lions to a win over Western
Province Universities, where he again enhanced his Test
claim. But he missed out on selection for the Second Test
when Tom Reid was chosen ahead of him. Many
commentators thought that Reid frankly lacked the pace to
play Test match rugby in the back-row against such

athletes as fielded by the mighty Springboks. This factor, combined with the below-par playing of the tour captain, Thomson, led to a physical mismatch against the violent assault launched by the Springbok forwards that day - who ground the Lions up!

Dad confided in me often that the reason the Lions failed to win the series was because of selection errors and bias, and that many of the Lions players thought his omission in the second Test was an appallingly bad call, consistent with the conservative nature of the tour manager and unofficial head of selectors, Jack Siggins. Despite his personal misgivings, Dad always regarded Jack Siggins as a top-class manager and a first-class bloke, and would never criticise him in public. Reid was moved into the second row for the third test, where he replaced Thomson - who was injured - and played a blinder! Clem was recalled and added his pace and aggression to the back-row, and they famously won the third test in Pretoria.

Here I have edited Clem's own version of this now forgotten, but historically successful tour, an extended essay which he published in his *HISTORY OF THE BRITISH AND IRISH LIONS (1996)*. Consider the magnitude of their task: the Springboks were unbeaten in a rugby test series by any country in the world, either at home or abroad for 59 years. It was a massively daunting challenge, and required the dedication and focused belief of a medieval crusade to the Holy Land to secure a winning series.

The 2017 Lions experienced much the same challenges and almost symmetrically left New Zealand with only the second drawn series in the history of the British Lions. They would have experienced the same frustrations that Clem would have felt upon leaving South Africa in 1955: so near and yet so far. I personally believe that the Lions of 2017 lacked two or three world-class players to make the difference, like a Cliff Morgan in '55, a Barry John in '71, or even a Gareth Edwards in '74 - that

155

little bit of magic eluded us. But it must be said that as a collective, and especially in defense, the 2017 Lions were immense, heroic, and a credit to the British Isles.

***

I now come to my own Lions tour, which I intend to cover in some depth, in an attempt to give you a more intimate insight into the mechanics and character of such a tour, and my own thoughts on some of the pleasures and problems encountered.

First came the extreme delight I felt at being selected for such an adventure, and then crept in the personal doubts about taking on a country who were the undisputed world champions, and whether I was good enough to measure up to the challenge and make the Test team. I was given huge support by my club and my parents. The Swansea Rugby Club, in their generous Welsh fashion, gave Billy Williams and me a suitcase and £50, a handsome sum of money in those days, which, in fact, contravened the International Rugby Board's laws on amateurism. The Welsh, like dominions, were always pragmatic in such matters.

I left with the rest of the Welsh Lions by coach for Eastbourne, where we were to meet our fellow adventurers, to be kitted out for our four months' trip of a lifetime and to be instructed on what would be expected of us. I had not a care in the world apart from the prospect of the huge challenge which faced us, for the Springboks had not been beaten in a Test series by any country, either home or away, for 59 years.

When we congregated at Eastbourne, we were unaware of any problems, and our first rude awakening came when we were addressed by a man from the Foreign Office. He told us that we were to be careful how we behaved with non-white people in the recently formed

Republic of South Africa, which had embarked on the disgraceful path of apartheid which was to bring them so much grief for over 40 years. We were instructed that on no account should we invite these people into our hotels and warned that any sexual contact with people of a different colour would put us in grave danger of imprisonment. We were surprised, even astonished, but at the time, made light of it. On the whole we were a bunch of politically agnostic young men, who had not thought too deeply about politics either at home or abroad and, being more or less apolitical, we were determined to go ahead and enjoy ourselves.

At that time, immigration from the West Indies into the UK was increasing, the Mau Mau were being offered an amnesty in Kenya and 60,000 blacks were evicted from their homeland west of Johannesburg. We were probably more interested in other things, such as Joe Davies making the first 147 break on television, and Marlon Brando winning an Oscar for *On the Waterfront*. Churchill resigned that year and Albert Einstein, James Dean, Thomas Mann and Henri Matisse all died. The Warsaw Pact was created and Tito and Krushchev made up. Ruth Ellis was sentenced to be the last woman hanged in Britain, and independent commercial television was launched, with toothpaste as the first advertisement.

Later into our week at Eastbourne, we were told by our big bluff manager, Belfast man Jack Siggins, what was expected of us in terms of behaviour, and we thought that the ground rules he set out were pretty generous. Basically, he said that we were to be well dressed at all times, particularly at functions, that we were adults and that we should keep our own hours, but that the two nights before a game he expected us to be in the hotel and in bed before midnight. He also told us, more enigmatically, that we should always make sure the water was clean before we dived in. All good advice which, on the whole, we heeded.

It was amusing to recall how we were on our best

behaviour with Jack and each other for the first week. Nobody misbehaved, we went to bed reasonably early, no one had much to drink and our fitness level improved considerably. We were kitted out with two pairs of boots each from a well-known manufacturer, but a couple of us had handmade boots by one of the finest makers of football boots, Law of Wimbledon. They were as light as a feather and, seeing their quality, a number of players immediately made phone calls and arranged details for measuring and having the boots sent out to them. We had all given the outfitters our measurements but, when we tried on our blazers, it was apparent that somebody had paid insufficient attention to detail, so, amid ribald comments about shapes and sizes, the next couple of days saw fitting sessions with tailors, who were kept working flat out.

The training sessions began, and it was evident that there were as many as half a dozen players who simply were not up to the standards required for such a hard tour, an assessment which was borne out by subsequent events. I have also asked members of many other pre- and post-war tours whether they experienced the same problem. Invariably the answer was unequivocal 'Yes'. Therefore, there has always been a problem with selection on Lions tours, which is not surprising considering the horse trading that goes on between selectors drawn from four different countries. Wild horses would not drag the names of these inadequates from me, but I remember hearing that mighty lions forward, Rhys Williams, saying 'Some of these guys could not get into Llanelli seconds'. It meant, of course, that these players had to be used sparingly, thus causing huge problems for team selection during the tour. From the start, that delightful man and great centre Jeff Butterfield assumed the responsibility of fitness coach and he took over the training sessions.

In terms of tactics and strategy, there was soon established a natural pecking order of those who really knew their rugby and those who did not, and a sort of senior unofficial committee evolved, to which, wisely, the management and captain listened. People like the hard-bitten Scot Angus Cameron, the elegant and brilliant Jeff Butterfield, those 100 per cent forwards Rhys Williams, Jim Greenwood, Bryn Meredith and the irrepressible Welsh wizard Cliff Morgan were among the better rugby minds of the tour and set the agendas to follow.

Another feature of a Lions tour was that you were able to assess a player's ability and, by the end of the tour, you knew every player's strengths, weakness and capabilities, both on and off the field, to the nth degree.

It was soon apparent, in that first week spent training at Eastbourne College, that there were some remarkably talented players and people of considerable substance on the tour. There was also an immediate sense of fun, emanating mostly from the Irish and that remarkable man Cliff Morgan, who became a household name. We were highly amused when, at a team meeting, the ubiquitous Trevor Lloyd, the third scrum half, suddenly said in his high-pitched Welsh accent, 'Hey, Jack!' (which was very brave, for we were still thinking in terms of Mr Siggins). 'What if a player has a girl and somebody tries to muscle in? Now, that could cause a great deal of trouble on a tour. I think that we should have a rule that nobody interferes with another player's girl.' Jack Siggins, for once, seemed lost for words, but the laughter relieved him from making a response. Thus 'Lloyd's Law' was born, which was invoked, more in jest than seriously, throughout the tour and has entered into the vocabulary of most Lions tours ever since.

I remember, too, that great character Reg Higgins creating another catchphrase of the tour. As we were walking along the tarmac to our plane at Heathrow, a gorgeous air hostess wiggled her way past us and, as we all stopped to admire her as young men will, he suddenly said in his broad Lancashire accent, 'Eh, Dad! Buy me that!'

Again, it was to be used many times in a country so rich in wildlife and lovely girls!

We left our shores virtually unheralded and unnoticed, and the next morning the papers only had the briefest accounts of our departure for what turned out to be an experience of a lifetime. We were the first Lions team to travel by air, thus shortening a tour to South Africa by about a month. We flew in a Lockheed Constellation and the flight took 36 hours, stopping at Zurich, Rome, Cairo, Khartoum, Nairobi, Entebbe and, finally, Johannesburg.

It was the first time that most of us had been to Africa and one will never forget the thrill of that flight, the humidity of Cairo and looking forward to getting out at Khartoum for a breath of air, only to feel the blast of oven-hot air as the 140-degree heat rolled into the aircraft off the tarmac and one was immediately drenched in sweat. On the flight onwards to Nairobi, we finally cast off our deference to the management and, in the ladies' powder room at the tail of the aircraft, half a dozen of us started a small party, and proceeded to drink the plane dry. In no time we were joined by others, and eventually there were about 20 of us crammed into an area designed for a quarter of that number. Finally the captain of the aircraft appeared and breathed a huge sigh of relief, because for the last hour he had been trimming the aircraft as it gradually became increasingly tail-heavy.

There were 30 players, none of whom were aged over 30, because Jack Siggins made that the criterion of his selection policy. Consequently, some famous players such as Jack Kyle, Bleddyn Williams, Ken Jones, Noel Henderson, Rees Stephens and Don White were left at home. Our captain, Robin Thompson, was, frankly, not sufficiently experienced. The vice-captain was Angus Cameron, a strong character with a fine football brain who, fully fit, would have been a tremendous asset, but he came on tour with a wrecked knee and he really should not have played. Angus was finally rumbled by the Springboks in the second Test, when they played on him with disastrous results. The captain of the tour should have been the immaculate Jeff Butterfield.

The stars of the tour were Cliff Morgan, Jeff Butterfield and the precocious baby of the team, Tony O'Reilly, who had his 19th birthday in the Kruger National Park and who was the most mature teenager I have ever seen, both in intellect and in playing ability. The friendship of the Dubliner with the equally amusing Northerner Cecil Pedlow was one of the features of the tour, particularly as they conducted a friendly running battle with the Ulster hard-liner, Jack Siggins. O'Reilly said of Pedlow, when he was late for his 50th birthday lunch at the O'Reilly mansion in Kildare many years later, 'Did you know that Pedlow is a rear-gunner on a bread van in Belfast?' he also related the story of Pedlow asking a guy at a cocktail party, 'What do you do?' the reply to which was that he was a writer, currently writing a book about Belfast. 'Then you'd better hurry up,' said Pedlow.

Another find on the tour was the uncapped Dickie Jeeps, who was really Cliff Morgan's choice, for he knew that you could not have two conductors in the band. He got four Tests for the Lions before he played for England. Danie Craven, however, always maintained that had the Lions played Johnny Williams, a reserve scrum-half, in the Tests, then the Lions would have won the series.

It was the forwards, for my money, who were the unsung heroes of this tour: that remarkable front row who sounded like a firm of solicitors, Meredith, Meredith and Williams (the last only 6ft 3ins tall but a giant), backed up by Tom Reid and splendid back-row men like Jim Greenwood, Russell Robins and Reg Higgins, the last until he got injured. I also loved the play of Johnny Williams and the admirable Douglas Baker, and, in the background, the young Arthur Smith was learning the trade which was to make him into a fine player and goal kicker.

The South Africans were kindness personified to us. No people are prouder of their country, which is not surprising considering its great beauty and enormous variety of climates and contrasting regions, from the tropical North East Transvaal and east coast to the Indian Ocean, to the Savannah of the Karoo and the temperate Cape. They were always in my view, aware of the flaws in their politics and were, as a nation, uneasy with their politicians and their appalling policy of apartheid. They wanted us to ignore the bad element and love them for themselves, their country and their great hospitality, which has been the hallmark of the Afrikaner since his trekking days. It was not surprising, therefore, that so many rugby people were beguiled by them and became so ambivalent over their racial policies.

It was to have a profound effect on many of us, and the first time that I really began to think about apartheid and worry about our role in it was when a number of United Party women, who had organised themselves into an anti-apartheid organisation called 'The Black Sash Women', picketed our hotel in Port Elizabeth. I also observed at the games how the black people were segregated behind the goalposts, and I saw how they were treated in so many other aspects of normal life.

I learned recently from Tony O'Reilly, who is a good friend of that marvellous South African leader Nelson Mandela, that Mandela was one of those who stood in support of the Lions under the huge advertisement for Quinn's bread at Ellis Park, as a gesture of defiance towards the nationalist regime. When we won that unforgettable first Test, and at other times, our black supporters lit newspaper bonfires whenever we scored. We would always run over and applaud them at the end of a game, in recognition of their support.

After our exhausting flight from the UK, we arrived at Jan Smuts airport in Johannesburg and were astonished at the number of people who had come to the airport

simply to see us. In turn, we surprised and delighted them
when we sang Sarie Marais in Afrikanns, which we had
bothered to learn under our choirmaster, Cliff Morgan. We
were then taken by coach to Vereeniging on the Saturday
night, for ten days acclimatisation before the first game. I
was so tired after the flight that I fell on my bed fully
clothed and was woken the following morning by Angus
Cameron, to be told that I was expected on the first tee at
nine o'clock against some of the locals. Once again, we
had an insight into how rugby-mad the country was, as
thousands came out from Johannesburg to see us, and they
lined the fairways of the golf course as if it were the British
Open.

That week, the details of touring were worked out,
the duty boy rosters were organised and the policy of
changing room-mates every week or fortnight was put in
place. On the following Wednesday, we were taken to
Pretoria to see Northern Transvaal beat Western Province.
It was our first glimpse of provincial rugby in South Africa
and we were shocked and appalled at the power and the
pace of it all, together with the liveliness of the ball, which
bounced like a mad thing on those hard grounds. We
could not believe how far the ball travelled in the thinner
air of the high veldt. I can remember Tony O'Reilly, who
was to score a record number of 16 tries on the tour,
sitting behind me in the stand and whispering in my ear,
'When does the next plane leave for home and shouldn't
we be on it?' We were pretty quiet that evening, and the
next day in training it was apparent that everybody was
working twice as hard.

We were fortunate that we were a fast side, with
quick-thinking backs in Cliff Morgan at fly-half, the
peerless Jeff Butterfield at centre with the powerful Phil
Davies, and fast and intelligent wingers in Cecil Pedlow,
Tony O'Reilly and Gareth Griffiths, with quick back-row
forwards and a mobile front row.

The hospitality was overwhelming. One farmer,

whose wife was the daughter of my tutor at St John's College, Cambridge, actually kept a leopard, which had been decimating his cattle, alive for a couple of weeks so that I could shoot it! Jack Siggins, the manager, heard about it and decided to ban my involvement, but the farmer shot it anyway and gave me the cured skin. It was not so politically incorrect in those days but, alas, the skin was stolen from my hotel room in Nairobi on the way home. On another occasion, a farmer pitched up at our hotel, the old Carlton in the centre of Johannesburg, and again, to the chagrin of the management, presented me with a lion cub. Siggins insisted on my donating it to a local zoo, which I did with some relief. South Africa was unsophisticated in those days and there were still some dirt roads between Johannesburg and Pretoria.

For the first time, the Lions were accompanied throughout the tour by two journalists, Vivian Jenkins of *The Sunday Times* and J.B.G. Thomas of *The Cardiff Western Mail.* They were both popular with the team and were virtually accepted as members of the party, as was the equally likeable Roy McKelvie of *The Daily Mail,* who arrived in time for the first Test. As the press contingent grew to astonishing levels on later tours, they were never able to enjoy the same intimacy that these early journalists achieved, particularly when the tabloids began examining aspects of the tour other than those connected with rugby.

We were to play 25 matches in 15 weeks with 19 wins, one draw and five defeats and, in the process, we drew the series at two-all. Strangely, we gave the lie to the theory that it is difficult to perform at altitude, for we won both our Tests at altitude (Johannesburg and Pretoria are over 5,000 feet) and we lost the two at sea level. We got off to the worst possible start as we lost the first game against Western Transvaal, a team of no consequence at the time and one that we should have been able to put away quite comfortably. They won 9-6 after the Lions had led by two tries to nil, but a drop goal by Peters, and the

Lions' first encounter with the prodigious kicking by van der Schyff, who dropped a huge goal and then kicked a penalty, both from the half-way line, severely dented the Lions confidence.

I had been selected for that first game, but I was feeling poorly, and spent the day in bed with what seemed an upset stomach. Picked again for the Saturday game against Griqualand West, I was determined to play but, again, felt desperately ill on the morning of the game. The manager saw me and, realising that I was in a bad way, asked Norman Weinberg, the president of Griqualand and a prominent surgeon, to have a look at me. He promptly diagnosed appendicitis and shipped me off to Kimberley hospital where, after attending the match dinner, he arrived to perform the operation – but not before I had questioned his sobriety. He laughed and said that I had ruined his evening, because he was unable to drown the sorrow of his side's defeat by 24-14. He did a great job on me, for I missed only the first ten matches of the tour and returned to play against Rhodesia five weeks later.

It was a pretty bleak moment when the manager and a few players came to see me the next day, before they left for Johannesburg to play the Northern Universities and then on to Orange Free State and Windhoek in South West Africa, before I was to join up with them again in Cape Town. That night, however, two men arrived in my private ward with a crate of beer and announced that they would leave only when it was finished. They were Sailor Malan, the World War II ace fighter pilot who shot down the record number of 32 enemy aircraft, and a local businessman called Sam Armstrong, who was a dead ringer for Victor McLagan, the film star. They came in every night for five nights and, on the fifth, Sailor told me that the next day I was going to convalesce on his farm. In the meantime, the town of Kimberley avalanched my ward with crates of booze, cartons of cigarettes and dozens of boxes of chocolates, enough to open a large shop. Such was the hospitality of those South Africans, both English-and Afrikaans-speaking.

I had a week's convalescence with Malan, who had led the Torch Commandos for Oppenheimer in opposition to the nationalist policies and, as a reward, had been given the lease on his showpiece property, a de Beers farm of some 600,000 acres which was as much a game farm as anything else. Almost every day we went out shooting the high-flying partridges coming into the dams, or shooting other game such as springbok, and I was as fit as a fiddle when I rejoined the team in Cape Town some twelve days later.

Meanwhile, the Lions had begun to show their quality with strong wins over Northern Universities, Orange Free State, whom they shattered by 31 points to three, when they became angry after a Free Stater had knocked out two of Rhys Williams's front teeth, and South West Africa, now known as Namibia. Wins over Western Province and South Western Districts followed, before the Lions were brought down to earth with their biggest provincial defeat of the tour. They lost by 20 points to nil against Eastern Province, but the result was pre-ordained, because by now the Lions had accumulated a dreadful list of injured and sick players. We played Tony O'Reilly at full-back and Bryn Meredith was unfit, so we had to play Robin Roe with two cracked ribs at hooker. We lost 35 out of the 41 scrums, as Amos du Ploy bored in on Roe, thus winning a Test cap which he had not really earned in light of the circumstances. He was not to survive after playing in the first Test at Ellis Park.

The Lions bounced back and won the next eight games in a row, including the first Test. That Test was never to be forgotten by all who saw it, and it attracted the biggest gate in the history of the game. An official record 95,000 spectators paid to see the match, many from the most rickety scaffolding stands thrown up for the occasion which, nowadays, would give any building inspector or ground safety officer a nervous breakdown. They also estimated that another 10,000 got in with forged tickets, or one way or another. The black market got up to £100 a ticket, a fortune in those days, but the sheep farmers coming in from the Karoo would pay anything to see that match. The Lions sold their surplus tickets to the hotel barber at £50 a time and everybody made a killing.

The selling of those tickets was, for some, their only income during a four-month tour, apart from one pound and ten shillings a week pocket-money, so they had no compunction in breaking the amateur laws. In future Lions tours there would be a team fund organised by the players, which was shared out at the end of the tour, and it usually amounted to enough to buy presents for their families and wives or girlfriends.

Those hard Afrikaner cases, from Transvaal and throughout the high veldt, had come to see the Lions thrown to the Christians, but were astounded when 45 points, the most ever in a Test in South Africa at the time, were scored and the Lions got one more than their beloved Springboks. To add insult to injury, the Lions had lost Reg Higgins with a knee injury soon after half-time, and played most of the second half with only 14 men.

The Lions won 23-22, and it was, without question, one of the greatest Test matches ever played anywhere in the world, in any era. There is a famous photo of van der Schyff letting his head drop in dejection, when he failed with the last kick of the game to convert a last-ditch try. Like most of the team and their supporters, O'Reilly could not look at the kick, and when somebody asked him in the dressing room what he was thinking of at the time of van der Schyff's kick, he said, 'I was merely in direct communication with the Vatican.'

Ernie Michie, immaculately turned out in his kilt, had led the Lions on to the field with his bagpipes wailing what some thought was a lament for the Lions, and Robert Thompson, clutching our tour mascot, a large toy Lion named Elmer, had run the team out to the huge roar of a crowd waiting to see the first British side play their invincible Springboks for 17 years.

It was a nail-biting thriller of a game, and it was no wonder that a total of 678,000 flocked to see all 24 matches during the tour. The hallmark of these Lions was their direct, simple play, their speed of pass, their speed of running, and their philosophy of ignoring whether it was good or bad ball; they merely used whatever was available. Above all, they were adventurous and ran everything they could.

The Lions scored a dazzling opening try, when Butterfield, or 'Buttercup' as Cliff Morgan called him, collected a poor pass and classically broke on the outside and drew the full-back, to put Pedlow over in the corner. Van der Schyff then kicked two penalties with two superb kicks, which people forgot in the recriminations which were to follow. The diminutive scrum-half Tommy Gentles, the smallest ever Springbok and the smallest player I ever saw in Test rugby at 5ft 3ins, broke and Stephen Fry, the Springboks captain, put Theunis Briers, a Paarl farmer, away on one of his powerful runs for a try. It was converted by van der Schyff, and South Africa led 11-3. An eight-point lead was never safe from these Lions and Butterfield now contrived another try, scoring at the post with a clever change of direction, and Cameron converted to make it 11-8 at half-time.

Immediately after the restart, the Lions lost Reg Higgins for the rest of the tour with torn ligaments, but this misfortune only seemed to inspire them, and the pack played like men possessed. In a ten minute period, the Lions scored 15 points, to roar into a commanding 23-11 lead. First, from a strike against the head by Bryn Meredith, Cliff Morgan weaved some of his magic and I can still see him sticking his neck out and rocketing past the great Basie van Wyk with a devastating outside break, to score an inspirational try. Two more tries swiftly followed when, from two kicks ahead, the bounce deceived van der Schyff, and the indefatigable Greenwood and the alert O'Reilly went over. Angus Cameron converted all three and the Johannesburg crowd were stunned. In the last quarter, the seven Lions forwards inevitably began to tire and the Springboks began to get back into the game.

The Lions continued to hold until the last few climatic minutes when, with only a couple of minutes to go, that mighty forward Chris Koch picked up and stormed his way over from 20 yards out and van der Schyff banged over the conversion. Then, late into injury time, with the massive crowd screaming deliriously, Stephen Fry picked up a loose ball and flipped it to Briers, who beat both Pedlow and Cameron with an inside swerve to score about half-way out. Agonisingly, the Lions stood there waiting for a conversion, which was difficult only because of the pressure. The scoreboard read 23-22 and the last number then disappeared, as the scorer prepared to put up 24. That photograph will remain a monument to van der Schyff's despair, as the ball swung to the left of the posts. It was van der Schyff's last game for South Africa and he turned to making a living by crocodile hunting in Rhodesia.

Danie Craven put the defeat of his beloved Springboks down to the fact that they were not motivated. 'You must be keyed up for the big occasion, and the belief among old Springboks that a team which sings before a Test is destined to weep afterwards is not a silly superstition.' He was to ban singing by the team on the way to future Tests.

It was the match of that generation and all who saw it will never forget it. The Lions were jubilant, for they knew they had achieved the minor miracle of putting South Africa on the back foot in a Test series in their own country. One man in the crowd dropped dead from excitement. The South Africans took it very well and it was to revive back play in the Republic, as the Lions quickly found to their cost.

Three more games were won against Central, Boland and Western Province Universities, the last providing one of the best games of the whole tour, which was not surprising as 11 of the students subsequently won Springboks colours. I happened to be captain that day, and I remember that they matched us try for try at four each, and that I was sweating. Only a try by Tom Reid in the dying moments saw us through by 20-17. I recall they had a lovely pair of half-backs in Richard Lockyer and Brian Pfaff and they had Butch Lochner, later to become a Springbok selector, in the back row. At that time Butch was a farmer, but on subsequent visits to that country I found that, in turn, he became a lecturer at Stellenbosch and then a colonel in the army.

The great Johannes Claassen, who played against us that year, had a similarly chequered career, first in the university, then the army, and at one time he even became a bishop. I often wondered about this, and I concluded that it was a system by which the Afrikaner brotherhood rewarded their famous sons.

For the next Test, South Africa dropped five of the team. Wilf Rosenberg, a really sharp centre, came in to partner Des Sinclair in the centre and van Vollenhoven was switched to the wing. Swart and van der Schyff were the backs dropped, with Roy Dryburgh drafted in at full-back. The three forwards dropped were Amos du Ploy, C. Kroon and the legendary Basie van Wyk, who played his last game for the Springboks. In their place came the immensely strong Northern Transvaal prop Jaap Bekker, Bertus van der Merwe, and the fast flanker Dawie Ackermann, who played so well for Southern Universities against us. The Lions made only two changes; Gareth Griffiths, flown in as a replacement after Arthur Smith had broken his thumb in the first game, was preferred to Pedlow, and Russell Robins was moved to flanker, to accommodate Tom Reid at number eight.

Apparently Stephen Fry, the Springbok captain, was too nervous to address his team before the kick-off and asked Danie Craven to do it for him. The Lions on the other hand were cheerful, but the back-row and the unfit Angus Cameron were to be our Achilles' heel, and we lost by the resounding margin of 25-9, a big score in those days. Van Vollenhoven had found his spiritual home on the wing, as Gerald Davies did a couple of decades later, and the Springboks wing, later to play rugby league for St Helens, scored three magnificent tries.

The seven tries scored by the Springboks at Newlands constituted a record number for a Test in South Africa. There was no hint in the first 20 minutes of the avalanche to come and, at that stage, the Lions led with a penalty goal by Cameron. Jeeps and Morgan were unhappy at half-back and the Lions pack was far from its best. Nevertheless, it was not until three minutes before half-time that the Springboks scored, when Sinclair kicked across field for van Vollenhoven to steal the ball from under O'Reilly's nose and score. At half-time it was 3-3.

The Springboks had now spotted how slow Cameron was at getting into the corners with his crook knee and they played on him, in what was to be his last game of the tour. Inexorably the tries came as the Lions, for the only time on tour, really cracked. Van Vollenhoven got two more quick tries for his hat-trick, and Rosenberg, Dryburgh, Briers and Ackermann all added tries, although Dryburgh converted only two of them. The only response by the Lions was a couple of tries by Butterfield and Bryn Meredith, two of the most outstanding players of the tour.

It was the Lions' turn to lick their wounds, as the South Africans had picked up the gauntlet of running rugby and had beaten us at it. We journeyed north, sadder and wiser men, for what should have been an easy game against Eastern Transvaal at Springs but, with a side mostly composed of the midweek 'dirt-trackers', as they are called in Lions parlance, we nearly came to grief again and only scraped a draw at 17-17. We only had 14 men in the second half, for Doug Baker pulled a muscle and, as he was needed for the Test as a makeshift full-back, he could not be risked. To make matters worse, Doug lost his contact lenses the next day and we had to enlist the aid of the British High Commission to get a new pair flown out from Germany.

There was now the prospect of the harshest week of the tour, as we had to play Northern Transvaal one Saturday and the Springboks the next, which was almost the same as playing back-to-back Tests. I was fully fit again and I was delighted to be included in the team against the Blue Bulls, as Northern Transvaal are known. I was renewing my 1951 Swansea confrontation with Hansie Brewis, that great Springboks fly-half. He was now at the end of his fine career, as was Fonnie du Toit, his scrum-half in the fantastic Springboks side which toured Britain in 1951. In addition, Northern Transvaal had van Vollenhoven in the centre and Bekker, Retief and 'Salty' du Rand, their captain, in the pack.

The Lions were expected to lose, but we won another famous victory by only the narrow margin of 14-11. I shall never forget Butterfield's try that day when, with a couple of minutes to go, he juggled the ball from somewhere behind his back inside his own 25, and shimmied his way through a gap to race 80 yards to score, with the local hero, van Vollenhoven, chasing him every step of the way, but unable to make up an inch of his three- or four-yard lead.

So we had set the scene for another battle of the giants in the third Test. The Lions made four changes, with Doug Baker coming in for Cameron, and I came into the pack at flanker, for Tom Reid to revert to the second row in place of the injured Thompson, and for Russell Robins to return to number eight. Cliff Morgan was given the captaincy and Billy Williams, the indestructible prop, was given the leadership of the forwards and the vice-captaincy.

South Africa made only one change, bringing in the Free Stater Coenraad Strydom, known as 'Popeye', for the tiny Tommy Gentles. Later, Dan Retief withdrew with an injury and he was replaced by Butch Lochner at number eight.

This Test became known in South Africa for a remarkable training session as Danie Craven, obsessed by the idea that the British press were spying on him, took his players off the field and, when they had gone, took them back again for a session under bright moonlight. The press dubbed it 'the moonlight sonata'.

It did them no good, as the Lions now changed their tactics and decided to attack the Boks where they least expected: through the forwards, with heavy support kicking from the backs. We made a few mistakes, but we were well worth our 9-6 margin at Loftus Versveld, another of those magnificent grounds which abound in South Africa.

There were 63 lineouts, which illustrated how we decided to make it a kicking and not a running game and took the Springboks forwards on up front. It was a hot, enervating day and some of the forward exchanges were particularly fierce. The scrummaging of our front row of Meredith, Meredith and Williams was quite magnificent, and I well remember Jappie Bekker talking to Chris Koch and swapping places for a few scrums. I asked Chris Koch at the after-match function what happened, and he told me that Bekker was having trouble with Courtney Meredith and asked him to change. After a couple of scrums, Koch said he told Bekker to do his own dirty work.

During this match, Courtney Meredith picked up one of the worst mouth injuries I have ever seen. He came up to me at half-time and, with blood streaming from his mouth, showed me his tongue, which was almost severed half-way back to the root, and asked me, 'How bad is it?' I said, 'It's bloody terrible, but keep your mouth shut and stay on the field for the second half or we are done for.' He was in great pain but, to his undying credit, he did just that and, after the game, was rushed to hospital to have it stitched. He was in trouble with his injury for a couple of weeks and did not play again until the final Test.

As often happened on these Lions tours, players like Courtney Meredith and Rhys Williams were, in the Orange Free State match, victims of what is known as 'the cheap shot'. It became necessary to have a fixer to stop such unprovoked attacks. Tony O'Reilly became the principal spotter from the safety of the backs and I was made the avenging angel. Tony would come up to me and say, 'Number four' or whatever, and I was supposed to go in and mete out the punishment at the next opportunity, preferably at a nice loose maul. I don't know how I got such a difficult job! It was merely, as Tony often explained, that I could hit harder than the others, even though I was one of the smallest forwards at about 14 stone. It was all about having been taught to fight on the coal tips in Brynamman during the school holidays and having boxed a bit at school.

The first Test ever to be held in Pretoria was an unpretty, dour game and out of character with the normal style of the 1955 Lions, because our strategy was to win at all costs, to go one up in the series with one to play. In a grimly fought first half, the only score was a left-footed drop goal by Jeff Butterfield. Twelve minutes into the second half, Baker increased our lead with a penalty, before Dryburgh replied with a huge 50-yard drop goal from a penalty. Sustained Lions pressure finally brought reward, when I managed to pick up a loose ball and gave to Butterfield, who crashed over for a try. Although Dryburgh then kicked an orthodox penalty, the Lions finished strongly and were attacking fiercely at the end. Everybody, including Danie Craven, said that they deserved a win, a fact which shook South Africa and, indeed the world of rugby, to the core.

After the enormously successful fortnight in Pretoria, we then took off in high spirits to the Kruger National Park for a well-deserved break. On the way, we lunched at Crocodile River at the home of Ivan Solomon, a millionaire citrus grower, who typified the massive hospitality we received whenever we went in the new Republic by laying on a braai or barbecue of such quality that it was something to remember. We spent the next four days in this extraordinary game reserve which is the size of Wales, and most of us saw lions, leopards, elephants, buffalo, crocodiles, hippopotamuses and almost every type of game. It was magic, and I will never forget the first night, for we were celebrating O'Reilly's and Danny Davies's birthdays. Remarkably, it was only the former's 19th, for his maturity of mind and body was equal to anyone on tour. What a grand party it was! The next day we had to send our truck, which accompanied us full of cases of beer, back to Nelspruit for new supplies.

We had three matches to play before the final Test, and the first was against Natal in Durban which, in many ways, was the most English of all the provinces we played. Unthinkingly, we offended them by resting most of the Test team and trotting out the dirt-trackers, including none of our stars like Morgan, O'Reilly and Butterfield. The local press, *The Natal Mercury*, called us the 'Insult XV', but then we had to rest our top players who had just finished a tough campaign in Northern Transvaal.

I was made captain of what was considered to be a rag-bag side and, frankly, we played as though we were, although there was no criticism of the forwards, for it was the backs who squandered one opportunity after another. I remember we snatched our 11-8 win against a very lively and young Natal team only in the closing seconds of the game, when Tom Reid, bless his big heart, picked up and fed me, so that I put Tug Wilson over for the try.

We now played the Junior Springboks at

Bloemfontein, which was virtually as hard as any Test match and, again, the temperature reached 80 degrees. It was also evident that the Lions were beginning to get travel and tour weary, and we struggled to win a dour game by 15-12. Worse was to come, for next we lost 14-12 to Border in East London, who were a really tough outfit. They were a bit like the Llanelli or Swansea of South Africa: always guaranteed to give any touring team a hard time.

It is easy to make excuses, and some of them were true, for we were by now a tired side and beleaguered with injuries, and some of the selections for the final Test were disastrous. Tom Reid should have been retained after his great game in the third Test, but tour politics saw the captain, Robin Thompson, brought back, and O'Reilly, who played on the wing for most of the tour, was brought into the centre in place of Phil Davies. Cliff Morgan was not really fit to play after an ankle injury sustained against the Junior Springboks but, as it was unthinkable both in his own mind and those of the other members of the team that we should take the field without him, he decided to play.

The only changes made by the Springboks selectors, Chairman Frank Mellish, W.C. Zeller, Danie Craven, Maurice Zimmerman and Basil Kenyon, who refused to panic after Pretoria, were to bring back Tommy Gentles at scrum-half and the formidable Daan Retief into the pack.

The major factor in the final disappointing defeat was, of course, the Springboks spirit, which dictated that they were not going to lose a Test series at home and, on the day, they were magnificent. The Lions had the chance of being the first team since the turn of the century to win a Test series, but were simply not good enough, on that day, to do it.

The Lions threw everything they had at the Springboks in the first 20 minutes and scored first when, from a sweeping three-quarter attack, Gareth Griffiths kicked ahead; the always energetic Greenwood won the race with Tommy Gentles, and Pedlow converted. In the first half, the Lions looked good to win and created many scoring chances which were not taken. Ulyate then began to ply Pedlow with high balls where his eyesight was suspect and Briers, chasing up, stole a ball from under his nose to score a try. At half-time it was 5-3 to the Lions.

In the second half, Ulyate applied the same tactic and, again, Briers stole in for a try. A break by Gentles brought a try from Ulyate, converted by Dryburgh, and the Lions had no petrol left in their tank, as van Vollenhoven scored a try in the corner and Ulyate dropped a goal to make it 17-5. The Lions showed that they could still bite back when O'Reilly scored, breaking his shoulder in the process, but, with a minute to go, Retief scored under the posts and Dryburgh converted, to make the final score 22-8.

And so ended a dream, and a tour which was measured as much by its friendliness, great humour and comradeship as by the standard of play, among one of the finest bunches of players to represent the British Isles. They were popular wherever they went and Danie Craven, who, in his famous office in Stellenbosch University, granted me the last interview he gave to a pressman shortly before he died in 1992, said they were the team he always admired most for their attitudes both on and off the field.

The South African media were no less flattering. One newspaper said that they were grateful to these Lions for reminding them that the skull was still a receptacle for brains, rather than just a battering ram.

No wonder thousands of South Africans turned up to say Tot Siens (goodbye) to us, and as we walked out on to the tarmac we turned and sang *Sarie Marais, Sospen Fach* and *Now is the Hour* for them, before heading home, via one game in Nairobi.

After leaving the UK unheralded all those weeks ago, we were to arrive home to a fanfare of plaudits, as far finer players and better men for such an amazing and fulfilling experience. We had enjoyed a crash course in the University of Life.

Results of the 1955 lions in South Africa

P 25   W 19   D 1   L 5   F 457   A 283

Western Transvaal	L	6	9
Griqualand West	W	24	14
Northern Universities	W	32	6
Orange Free State	W	31	3
South West Africa	W	9	0
Western Province	W	11	3
South Western Districts	W	22	3
Eastern Province	L	0	20
North Eastern Districts	W	34	6
Transvaal	W	36	13
Rhodesia (Kitwe)	W	27	14
Rhodesia (Salisbury)	W	16	12
South Africa (Johannesburg)	W	23	22
Central Universities	W	21	14
Boland	W	11	0
Western Province Universities	W	20	17
South Africa (Cape Town)	L	9	25
Eastern Transvaal	D	17	17
Northern Transvaal	W	14	11
South Africa (Pretoria)	W	9	6
Natal	W	11	8
Junior Springboks	W	15	12
Border	L	12	14
South Africa (Port Elizabeth)	L	8	22
East Africa XV (Nairobi)	W	39	12

Robin Thompson's 1955 Lions team

Full-backs

A. Cameron	Glasgow HS FP	Scotland
A.G. Thomas	Llanelli	Wales

Three-quarters

J. Butterfield	Northampton	England
W.P.C. Davies	Harlequins	England
G.M. Griffiths*	Cardiff	Wales
H.T. Morris	Cardiff	Wales
A.J.F. O'Reilly	Old Belvedere	Ireland
A.C. Pedlow	Queen's Uni	Ireland
J.P. Quinn	New Brighton	England
A.R. Smith	Cambridge Uni	Scotland
F.D. Sykes	Northampton	England

Half-backs

D.G.S. Baker	Old Merchant T	England
R.E.G. Jeeps	Northampton	
T. Lloyd	Maesteg	Wales
C.I. Morgan	Cardiff	Wales
J.E. Williams	Old Millhillians	England

Forwards

T. Elliot	Gala	Scotland
J.T. Greenwood	Dunfermline	Scotland
R. Higgins	Liverpool	England
H.F. McLeod	Hawick	Scotland
B.V. Meredith	Newport	Wales
C.C. Meredith	Neath	Wales
E.T.S. Michie	Aberdeen Uni	Scotland
T.E. Reid	Garryowen	Ireland
R.J. Robins	Pontypridd	Wales
R. Roe	Lansdowne	Ireland
R.C.C. Thomas	Swansea	Wales
R.H. Thompson(c)	Instonians	Ireland

R.H. Williams	Llanelli	Wales
W.O.G. Williams	Swansea	Wales
D.S. Wilson	Metropolitan P	England

Manager: J.A.E. Siggins
Assistant Manager: D.E. Davies

*Replacement
This team believed in open rugby and revived the whole concept of back play in South Africa, whose teams had been becoming too engrossed with forward power. They never differentiated between good or bad ball and they played some of the most direct running rugby ever seen, unsurpassed until those great Lions teams of 1971 and 1974.

***

Dad's series ended in a 2-2 draw but the sporting impact on the rugby public in South Africa was far more profound. *The Eastern Province Herald* roared in its leader column, "The visit has brought a tremendous amount of excitement and happiness to the Union. They have taught us that the skull is still a receptacle for brains, and not merely a battering ram". *The Cape Times* adopted a statesman-like stance, "South Africa owes a manifold debt to the British Isles rugby team. They have provided us with superlative sporting entertainment; they have rescued our rugby from becoming a matter merely of boot and brawn, and they have exorcised the arrogance which our so-long undisputed supremacy in the game was breeding in us. They enabled us to forget for a while our bitter internal political divisions in common anxiety about our country's prestige, and their spirit both on and off the field has strengthened the bonds of goodwill between their country and ours. Though they provided inspiration, the credit is not theirs alone. South Africa's rugby representatives in this crucial year of our rugby history responded magnificently to the challenge. Perhaps this rugby renaissance will have a wider influence, reminding us that "the game is the thing" and that rewards for "playing the game" are more enduring if, for the moment, less tangible than those for merely winning,"

Whenever Dad talked about the tour, especially with fellow Lions like Cliff Morgan or Tony O'Reilly, he always dwelt on the almost unbelievable physicality and athleticism of the large Springbok forwards, and emphasised the reserves of physical courage needed to be called upon when confronted by them in the heat of battle. A Cardiff business executive, Tom Lyons, who worked for the large grocery business *OK Bazaars* in Johannesburg, attended the first Test match and wrote a wonderfully colourful letter to his wife back in Cardiff an hour after the match ended. He stated in admiration:

> The South Africans are most famous for playing the hardest and most vicious rugger in the world. Today they excelled themselves in playing so hard and vicious a game that their own supporters were stupefied. Every tackle was given with a stretcher in the back of the tacklers' minds. These Springboks are nearly all farmers, well off and university educated. It is my firm belief that before they get to the universities they are taught that to take the bulls to the abattoir is a sissy's way of slaughtering beef. I am sure that their approved method is to tackle the bull, and when it is down, twist his bloody head off... This was not really a Test. It was for the rugby supremacy of the world... hence such a berserk performance.

The other aspect of the tour that Dad enjoyed was the sheer adventure involved in taking a charabanc along country dirt roads throughout the Transvaal and Orange Free State, finally arriving in a dust cloud in some 'dorp' town in the middle of nowhere, and running out in front of 20,000 plus screaming Afrikaner rugby-mad supporters. Often, sitting in the stands were the grandparents of the local players who had been interned in British concentration camps during the Boer War fifty or so years earlier. And when the opposition team ran out onto the field it would consist of a bizarre uniformity of physique, with every player from No1 to No15 being 6ft tall, blonde cropped hair, 15 stone per man of pure muscle, with the scrum-half looking identical to the second row or prop. This was considered payback time, and Tom Lyon described the feel of such crowds, "The roar of an Afrikaner crowd cannot be repeated unless it be with a full orchestra. It's full throated and seems to tear the vocal chords asunder. Just like a lion roar, without words and quite a jungle sound. It not only chilled my blood, I felt a horror creep over me at its bestiality. When the Springboks are pressing they start up a chant, roaring… "NOU, NOU, NOU!!!" The ferocity and menace in their voices is a part of sport beyond my ken. It actually made me quite afraid for the boys in red. It was an inhuman sound."

As Dad so aptly and often remarked, the tour had been a crash course in the University of Life.

6

THE SPORTS REPORTERS: A CAROUSING BUNCH OF PUB-LOVING, LAID BACK TROUBADOURS

"If you obey all the rules you miss all the fun... Life is to be lived. If you have to support yourself, you had bloody well better find some way that is going to be interesting. And you don't do that by sitting around."
Katharine Hepburn

Clem was hired to join *The Observer* sports desk by Chris Brasher, the Melbourne Olympics Steeplechase gold medalist, and creator of the London marathon. Brasher, in turn, had been recruited by David Astor, one of the outstanding editors of the post-war period, transforming his family's newspaper from a staid organ of the Establishment into the leading forum of English liberalism. Astor was a colossus of the golden age of a long-vanished Fleet Street, before Pilates and San Pellegrino came in, when any semi-educated reporter was capable of writing crisp and concise English; when Dickens, Shakespeare, and Tolstoy could be discussed knowledgably by typesetters; when everyone smoked and drank themselves comatose and a newspaper had brilliance and bounce.

When Astor took over *The Observer,* its circulation was 360,000. He doubled it in a decade. The aristocratic Vita Sackville-West did the gardening column. Kenneth Tynan went to the theatre. Kim Philby was employed to cover the Middle East because, "he seems an extremely reliable chap and he created a good impression", Astor said. Though Anthony Burgess was sacked when he started reviewing his own novels favourably in *The Yorkshire Post,* Terence Kilmartin sensibly got him back. The foreign editor was appointed "on the basis of an essay he'd written on one of the Brontë sisters". The Washington correspondent filed his report on Bobby Kennedy's funeral before it had even taken place.

Dad's first copy was not a piece on rugby… it was on Joe Erskine, the Welsh heavyweight boxer from Butetown in Cardiff, and was headlined, "STILL AN ENIGMA". His first rugby match report followed a week later, a 3-0 win for Newport over Clem's alma mater Cambridge University. By January 1960, he was covering the Final Welsh Trial match and started his journalistic career by voicing clear, strong opinion - a trait he became known and respected for up until the end of his writing days. "A dismal day at Cardiff Arms Park, and trial football as dreary as the drizzle which persisted all morning…Here we were, back to that unimaginative pattern of play which is contemporary international football…"

Chris Brasher, a man not known for his patience with people, spent hours coaching and mentoring Clem on the fine art of crafting a match report that had structure and clarity. Brasher delivered to his acolyte an educational crash course in sports journalism and Dad rated the equivalent, or better than any degree course. I know that Dad was genuinely forever grateful for the help and assistance he was offered. Brasher would constantly berate him for two negative aspects of his journalistic qualities. Firstly he was consistent in always overwriting the requested length of any match report, and in the early days he would overdo the metaphor or simile. In his Cardiff v Barbarians (1960) match report he wrote, "The forwards got among the Baa-Baa flock like so many killer sheepdogs. JD Evans, D Harris, and H Norris were always there, and, most savage of all was the inimitable Hayward... whilst... M Roberts stepping inside the sparse cover defence, he darted under the posts like a disturbed fish..."

The status of being the Chief Rugby correspondent for *The Observer* was amongst Dad's proudest accomplishments, and it really defined him for that period from 1959, when he stopped playing, up until his death in 1996. He held a proper affection for both the paper and the people whose energies and creativity contributed to make it the finest broadsheet on Fleet Street until large investments from *The Sunday Times* and *The Telegraph* bullied the paper aside.

Chris Brasher had been hired as the sports editor in 1957, with no real experience as a journalist. This was straight out of the deputy-editor, Michael Davie's formbook; in that he was inspired and revolutionary to some, amateurish and incompetent to others. Alan Hubbard, another of Brasher's successes as a future sports editor, commented: "Ron Atkin, who became sports editor in 1972 got on badly with Chris, whom he thought was unmanageable. Brasher somehow convinced Trelford (editor of *The Observer* 1975 - 1993) that Atkin should go and that Atkin be offered a different job, so Ron Atkin told Trelford that his choice was tennis correspondent, with the result that Shirley Brasher (Chris's wife) was demoted to being a column writer."

You might imagine that dinner at the Brasher household was quite frosty that particular evening!

Brasher was another with a tendency to overwrite,

and whilst brilliant, he could also be very obstinate and bloody-minded to deal with. When Peter Corrigan was sports editor Brasher wrote a piece about Steve Ovett, the 800 metres gold medalist, suggesting that some of the problems that he had with his psyche and attitude was because his mother was only fifteen when she had her son. This was of course subbed out. Trelford wanted it out. Corrigan wanted it out - and the lawyer duly took it out. A tremendous row ensued. It was an indication of the obstinacy of Brasher that he dug his heels in, but Trelford as editor had the last say.

Donald Trelford and Chris Brasher were great friends, and Clem got on famously with both. Brasher had commissioned Trelford's first sporting article for *The Observer* in 1959, a report on a rugby match, while Trelford was still at Cambridge. Brasher, always the eccentric, also got Trelford to cover the first ever Oxford v Cambridge tiddlywinks match. As great a friend as he was, even Trelford had to concede that Brasher often had difficulty in his relationships with colleagues, "Cantankerous, obstreperous, cussed and abrasive were just some of the principal descriptions I recall from around the sports desk. He was not the most accommodating of colleagues.

The man who invented the London Marathon had an unquenchable appetite for stretching himself to the limit. There was something of the great Victorian about Brasher. A manic energy and bustling single-mindedness that brokered no opposition in pursuit of diverse interests and campaigns that included the environment, mountaineering, fly fishing, race horse breeding and the technology of running shoes."

Trelford once asked Brasher, in the course of yet another office row, "Are you so big-headed because you won an Olympic gold medal, or did you win the gold medal because you were so big-headed? Brasher looked at Trelford and growled, then he looked a little chastened. "A rare occurrence" Trelford noted. Brasher then chewed on his filthy pipe and said, "Good question. I don't know the answer."

Dad loved the institution that was *The Observer* back in those halcyon days. Astor managed to give the diverse talents – and there were many – their heads, while at the same time maintaining a distinct *Observer* identity, composed of a combination of high thinking with an almost amateur approach to the business of producing a newspaper. Dad was exactly the kind of journalist who met the criteria that Astor once famously expressed, "I had no interest in conventional journalism and don't to this day...the governing principle was that it should be written by amateurs", on the grounds that "journalism is too important to be left to journalists."

Katharine Whitehorn, author and columnist, in a moment of exasperation, once remarked of Astor, "the editor's indecision was final". But there was steel beneath Astor's diffidence. For example, he decided that, for reasons of internal politics, Cyril Connolly, whose reputation was then at its zenith, would have to forfeit control of the arts page. The two men met at White's, to which Connolly had just been elected. Astor put his point politely but firmly; Connolly stormed out apoplectic with rage.

Astor drank very little, but the boozing was prodigious; Patrick O'Donovan and Philip Toynbee led the pack, but even they were eventually out-drunk by Clifford Makins, of whom the original epithet, "A legend in his own lunchtime" was created by his colleague, Christopher Wordsworth.

As a supporter of the Liberal Party Clem felt very much at home working at *The Observer*. Astor once stated, "In the character of this paper, ethics matter more than politics. The particular ethics could be roughly defined as doing the opposite of what Hitler would have done." And he saw the paper as "an extended conversation with the readers, always intellectually lively but never snobbish, exclusive or insiderish. My aim has been to be militant in fighting for tolerance, freedom of expression, non-prejudice - all causes of moderation - here and abroad. What's wrong with moderates is that they lack militancy".

Peregrine Worsthorne, ex-editor of *The Sunday Telegraph* and doyen of the conservative, libertarian right wrote of Astor's *Observer*: "his paper was wrong on most of the major issues - absurdly unrealistic about prospects for democracy in black Africa, about the blessings of permissiveness, about Suez and so on. But it was wrong with such intelligence, such an abundance of seriousness and knowledge, that even those who disagreed preferred its friendly minted arguments on the wrong side to a routine repetition of truisms on their own."

As a young boy, I remember the impact a weekend visit from Clifford Makins would have on my parents. It was like watching them plug into an energy socket, for the house would reverberate with ribald laughter and gaiety for hours on end. 'Uncle' Clifford had a gift for making everyone feel better about themselves, and after his ascetic apprenticeship under Chris Brasher, Dad felt the brakes were finally off under the free-wheeling cavalier stewardship of Clifford's editorship. He joined as sports editor in 1962 to succeed Chris Brasher, and may have been the heaviest of all the *Observer's* heavy drinkers. Clifford had worked as a stage manager and his experience in journalism was as editor of the inspirational children's comic of the 1950s, *The Eagle*. Clifford also wrote *The Happy Warrior*, the life story of Sir Winston Churchill, as told through *The Eagle*. To so many British children growing up in the 1950s and 1960s, Friday meant only one thing – thousands of youngsters would race to their local newsagents, pennies in hand and sometimes parents in tow, to buy the latest edition of *The Eagle* comic. Each issue was choc-a-block with adventures and exciting new pastimes for boys – from Dan Dare, to Extra Special Agent Harris Tweed, from tips from the pros on rugby, boxing and jiu jitsu, to advice on the care of goldfish.

Hugh McIlvaney, the legendary sports writer, who also started at *The Observer* in 1962, recalled that although Clifford "looked like one of the homeless", he introduced him to champagne. On one occasion, when the VIP guest at an editorial lunch dropped out at the last minute, David Astor announced that, "We will do without the drink – it will be good for us."

"It might be good for you David, but seriously harmful to me," Makins retorted, and headed off to El Vino's in Fleet St, from where legend has it, he commissioned his sporting articles. I quite recently bumped into an old friend of Clem's, the legendary cricket broadcaster Henry Blofeld, at a Lashings charity cricket match in Potterne, and after bestowing, "my dear old thing", which I'll cherish to the end of my days, he nostalgically recalled the long afternoons spent in El Vino's with Clifford Makins holding court and conducting editorial business over countless glasses of claret along with his chosen tipple of the day.

Towards the end of his time at *The Observer,* Makins stupefied colleagues by marrying Nora Beloff; "It's the best news since the Fall of Rome," exclaimed David Astor when he heard the news, but then added, "But was that a good thing?"

Nora, who I also remember coming to stay with us in Swansea, married Clifford in 1977. She and Clifford would fascinate us kids with their colourful storytelling told with such elegance and depth. Nora was obviously the boss, and loved to wind up Dad discussing the finer points of Liberal party politics, and always insisted that the Liberals could make a comeback as a major radical force in British politics. One thing I do remember is her sharing Dad's scepticism over the trade union domination of the Labour party which she regarded with extreme suspicion. I think she forecast the emergence of the New Labour movement under Tony Blair twenty years ahead of time.

So Clem had joined, like Robert Chesshyre before him, the esteemed Washington correspondent of *The Observer* "an organisation that floated on alcohol. There was Kim Philby, who Astor admitted he had never seen sober; Patrick O'Donovan, whose face glowed like a setting sun and Clifford Makins, the original legend in his own lunchtime". Another who joined *The Observer* in 1960 was Geoffrey Nicholson, who was brought up in Mumbles, Swansea, and attended Bishop Gore grammar school where he struck up lifelong friendships with Paul Ferris, the biographer of Dylan Thomas and Richard Burton, and John Morgan, one of Wales' leading TV journalists.

Nicholson's first lecturer was Kingsley Amis who awarded Nicholson the Principal's prize for the best essay of the year and confessed he had not expected to find such talent in his new post at Swansea University. Despite embarking on a career in advertising, in the late 1950s Paul Ferris helped Nicholson establish a connection with *The Observer* sports desk. Geoff once told Dad that in all his time with Crawford's advertising agency he wasn't really happy apart from the time he noticed a colleague had written an ad for Daks which read "The Trousers that Stand Out in Front". He neglected to draw attention to the possible misconstruction and it appeared in a newspaper. He also confided that his only achievement in five years of advertising was coining a slogan for fruit gums: "Hey Fella, Fruitella!!!" at which point he decided to seek alternative employment. It is a measure of how far sports coverage has evolved in the broad sheets that when he first began work for *The Observer* he answered to someone with the title of 'Sports and Religious Affairs Editor.' It is not a coupling of functions that could be envisaged these days.

Nicholson became deputy Sports Editor to Chris Brasher in 1960, but moved onto *The Sunday Times* as their Sports Features Editor where he was shocked to find a physical fitness regime imposed on all sports journalists.

As an unreconstructed chain-smoker himself, and doubtless recalling the more bilious ambience of *The Observer* sports room, he was eventually enticed back to *The Observer* in 1976, rejoining as Sports Editor. Religious affairs had been dropped from his title by then but there was a devout cult following for the quixotic stable of sports writers; a talented but generally untamed bunch including Hugh McIlvanney, Arthur Hopcraft, Chris Brasher, Peter Dobereiner, Peter Corrigan, Richard Baerlein, and of course my Dad, Clem. An impressive gang of writers and dazzling characters who needed a strong force at their centre to help marshal their considerable talents; his two years in the job were vitally important because at that time *The Sunday Times* was flexing its muscles, which in the battle for sports page readers amounted to *The Times* sponsoring a nationwide keep-fit frenzy.

This was in complete contrast to the image of *The Observer* sports department as a pub-loving, carousing, bunch of laid-back troubadours. The difference in quality of the work they turned out hardly needed emphasising such was the superior level of reportage, Nicholson once famously remarked: "What *The Sunday Times* could do with is a deep breath of foul air". Nicholson and his troubadours are credited with transforming the character of sports journalism from the 1970s onward by eschewing tabloid clichés and public relations hype and introducing a quality of writing that matched, and was sometimes superior to, that on the arts and foreign pages.

Dad adored Geoff Nicholson and they became the best of friends; his wife Mavis became a much-loved double-act as well as becoming the queen of day-time television in the 1980s.

Mavis Nicholson, who was born and brought up in Briton Ferry on the east side of the Neath estuary, is also a celebrated author, her published works include *Martha Jane and Me: A Girlhood in Wales* (Seren 2008) and *What Did You*

Do in the War, Mummy?: Women in World War II (Chatto & Windus 1995)

Peter Corrigan wrote in his obituary of her husband, that Mavis and Geoff "became a much-loved double act. Kingsley Amis did not always approve of their views and claimed to have invented the word, "lefties" during one little set-to with them. While it was true that the Nicholson's didn't have dinner parties as such - they invited people for an argument and threw some food in - they were by no means belligerent but had in abundance the Welsh love of debate."

Mavis made her reputation as one of the leading interviewers on British television from 1971 onwards. Her guests included all the great 'A' list stars of the day and right up to the millennium. David Bowie, Elizabeth Taylor, Peter Cook and Dudley Moore, Bette Davis, Liberace, Rudolph Nureyev, Charlton Heston and Lauren Bacall were just some of the illustrious names she sparred with. The Welsh journalist Caroline Hitt wrote, "the alchemy of her interviews was part journalism, part psychotherapy plus the relentless curiosity which is perhaps peculiar to a certain kind of Welsh working class upbringing. Anyone who, like Mavis, grew up in a household where strong women constantly chatted, gossiped and debated will recognise it."

Maya Angelou, the great American writer and poet, described as "the black woman's poet laureate" said of Mavis, "I like her a lot because she doesn't laugh at people: she laughs at herself. I like that she's tough, tough as an old walnut - a black walnut. And she's tender as a grape. That's how I want to be. She can't bear pretension, she would laugh it out of existence if she could."

As Mavis said to me recently as we discussed Dad, "I smile the moment I think of Clem who loved laughing and who loved making us all laugh."

For many years, Geoff Nicholson was the number two rugby writer in support of Clem, but the quality of his writing was always superb, and the two combined in 1980 to publish their account and analysis of Wales' glory years in their co-authored book, *WELSH RUGBY The Crowning Years (1968 - 1980)*. Geoff handled the match reports and statistics, whilst Clem penned Part One of the book, focusing on the reasons behind this successful period. Nostalgically, he wrote of Cardiff Arms Park:

> The congregation produces the ultimate sound of their personal expression of nationhood, a combination of the lively fortissimo of grand operas and of the doleful hymns of Welsh Tabernacles, Ebenezers, Siloams and Gibeas. The more lachrymose hymns draw out the best descants and harmonies from what is the largest and most skillful choir of its kind in the world, so funereal at times that they have buried the expectations of many a fine foreign team before the kick-off. I remember it well, for although it is almost twenty-two years since I last appeared as a Welsh gladiator waiting to be unleashed at English, Irish, French, Scottish, Australian or New Zealand Christians, I can still recall the feeling of the hair rising at the nape of the neck, bristling like a wolf waiting to lunge at his prey, for the first fifteen minutes of an international, no Saxon, French, or Celtic boot or bone seemed capable of penetrating a mystic armour.

Clem concluded in the book that:

> The Welsh teams from 1969 to 1980 reached heights of success and produced rugby of a quality that has probably never before been bettered in the British Isles. One can only say that it has been a marvellous privilege to watch them play. In the final analysis, it was all achieved by collective

purpose and organisation, induced by the advent of enlightened administration; by men dedicated to the cause of coaching and organisation; by the revolutionary concept of the squad system; by the coincidental arrival of players with single-minded loyalty to the cause and huge talents for rugby football; and, finally, by the eagerness and zeal that Welshmen at large possess for a game which they admire before any other.

Geoff wrote a great number of books, the best being his classic observation of the compelling Tour de France, *The Great Bike Race (1977),* and his co-authorship of Cliff Morgan's autobiography, *Cliff Morgan: the autobiography - beyond the fields of play (1997).* I remember Dad going up to Llanrhaeadr-ym-Mochmant in Powys where Geoff and Mavis lived, and returning very jealous not just at the beauty of the village they lived in, but at the fact that they had both made their debuts for the silver screen in the Hugh Grant movie comedy, *The Englishman Who Went Up a Hill but Came down a Mountain.* Incidentally, my publisher reports that this was the first movie he ever worked on as rushes runner, running the daily raw footage from the set in Wales to be processed at the lab that used to lie in the bowels of the old Arsenal stadium at Highbury, and then motoring back to Llanrhaeadr stopping off en-route to collect Hugh Grant's mail and his clean underwear.

Dad really thought the world of Geoff. Donald Trelford once said, "Journalists being a cynical lot, few of its abler practitioners escape their critics and detractors, even enemies. Geoffrey Nicholson is one of the very few I have come across, after four decades in the trade, about whom I have never heard a bad word".

Geoff was also an old friend of Kingsley Amis who had become his lecturer in English at Swansea University (1949 – 1961). I can remember Kingsley visiting Mumbles in the 1990's, when he would decamp from London during the summer months and stay with Stuart Thomas and latterly Michael and Virginia Rush (both of whom became Lord High Sheriff). I had helped a business associate, Vince Moreno, along with others like Rob Davies, Rosemary Morgan, and Terry Francis - the original Swansea "Godfather" - to set up what became the best bodega north of San Sebastian, a tapas pub on the Mumbles road called *Vincent's*. For the duration of Kingsley's visits, Vince would have to order 10-year-old Macallan single malt whisky by the case load. I can vividly recall Dad and I spending many a lost afternoon in the company of Kingsley Amis and his gang of minders. Kingsley's seduction days were long over, but he was by his own admission a serial adulterer, a major contributing factor to the breakdown of his first marriage. There is a famous photograph of a sleeping Amis on a Yugoslav beach with a slogan written by his wife Hilary in lipstick on his back, "1 FAT ENGLISHMAN – I FUCK ANYTHING".

During one memorable long, boozy afternoon at Vincent's, Kingsley confided in Dad and I that he had cast Dad in his 1958 novel, *I Like it Here* as the hero, 'Garnet Bowen' - talented socialist and Welshman. I remember Dad putting him straight on his Liberal affiliations. The novel reads as a satire on a British family living abroad and the strongest element of the book is Bowen's sense of himself, for he is a Swansea Jack who took a First in English at Swansea University before working on the local rag, during which time he played wing-forward for the All-Whites, his last game being a victory over Llanelli at St Helen's in which he had managed to punch an opponent in the final line-out. I remember Dad laughing about that.

Kingsley was very fond of Swansea natives Stuart Thomas and his wife Eve, who for some years had a flat in Onslow Square in South Kensington. It was there, that sometime in the 1960s, they gave a party for Daniel Jones, Swansea composer and lifelong friend of Dylan Thomas.

The occasion was the first, possibly also the last, performance of Dan's opera, The Knife, at Sadler's Wells. Amis was in hysterics that Dan had eschewed Welsh themes, clearly as part of his image-remoulding drive, and concocted a sort of taffy spaghetti western complete with lynching. Amis recounts in his memoirs that he was desperate not to say anything unkind to Dan when the moment came: "Well, Dan, I thought I could hear the tones of your master coming through what you wrote there." Dan waited mutely in his porcine way, expecting 'Handel'. "Old Evans Parry Parry-Evans of Llantwit Major after his stroke" was Kingsley's considered opinion.

Summer after summer, Amis visited Stuart and Eve a great deal at their bungalow in Mumbles, considering it the perfect retreat from London: "I have spent a tranquil, planless three or four weeks, working for an hour and a bit every morning (just right) while Stuart went to the office and did some of what solicitors do, being swept off to the unchanging Yacht Club (a little Garrick beyond Wales) by the great bay, or joining an occasional minibus trip inland – no outdoor stuff. In the more distant past, Stuart and Eve saw me through some nasty bits by the same means as, before and ever since, they have used in making the good bits better: the application of much kindness, good sense, whiskey and hilarity. Thanks chiefly to them, Swansea has again become what it was further back still in my life: the piece of earth I know best, better than any part of London, and feel most at home in."

Amis was a boozer of boundless enthusiasm. Drinking came to define him and he turned it into an art form. As a critic of all things alcoholic, Amis held many unconventional views. He was not a fan of French white wine, Tequila, sake, or bland lager - all were dismissed with utter contempt - while gin and tonic was a "mawkish drink best left to women, youngsters and whisky distillers". He championed cask ales over keg, but kept cans of Carlsberg Special Brew in the fridge: the super strength lager was recommended as a morning pick-me-up, but he warned that "after a certain amount of it you do tend to fall over".

His personal tipple was always the Macallan 10 year-old, which he apparently discovered on a trip to Speyside in 1978, and loved for its signature Sherry flavour. This possibly accounted for the warm glow with which he confided in me one afternoon, "that a good pub is like a good friend, in that it can stay with you for life and never let you down...and Vincent's is a good pub Christopher!"

The fact was that Amis enjoyed a drink, and spent a good deal of time in pubs. Amis was quite brilliant in capturing the world of West Wales drinking in *The Old Devils*, which won the Booker prize in 1986 and was later made into an exceptional TV series by the screenwriter Andrew Davies. The novel is satire of the very highest quality. One of the main story strands, for instance, follows professional Welshman Alun (born Alan) Weaver and his return to "this land of river and hill" from a successful career he has carved out in London by banging on about his affinity to "Brydan" (a thinly disguised stand-in for Dylan Thomas). Cue countless barbed riffs on Pays-De-Gallic posturing. "If you ask me all the proper Welshman are leaving Wales," someone remarks. "I say, are they really? Well that's splendid news, by George," comes the reply. Most blunt (and wonderful) is the invitation: "Show me a Welsh nationalist and I'll show you a c***."

Clive James, writer, poet, and critic once said: "All on his own, he had the weekly drinks bill of a whole table at the Garrick Club even before he was elected. After he was in, he would get so tight there he could barely make it to the taxi." But his writing never suffered as for many years he imposed a rigorous daily schedule upon himself in which writing and drinking were strictly segregated. Mornings were devoted to writing with a minimum daily output of 500+ words. The drinking would only begin around lunchtime when this output had been achieved. Nevertheless, according to Clive James, Amis reached a point when his drinking ceased to be social, and became a way of dulling his remorse and regret at his behaviour to Hilly, his first wife. His friend Christopher Hitchens said, "The booze got to him in the end, and robbed him of his wit as well as his health".

As a boy I can vividly remember visiting *The Observer* offices and print works in 1967. I was in London for a treat - a visit to the pantomime to see *Peter Pan* at The Mermaid theatre - and Fleet St was just up the road. In those days *The Observer* used hot metal printing, the method used to set the pages and create plates from which each edition of the paper was printed. It involved casting the words in the stories and headlines out of molten lead using Linotype and Ludlow machines. I remember a lot of noise, which was more like a factory than the office of a national newspaper. The noise was made by the linotype machines which were like giant typewriters fed with ingots of lead, and the compositors would bang down the type on the stone with mallets. It was intimidating, almost like something out of Dickens, and it seemed dirty and smelly. Clifford Makins walked Dad and I around the plant, and he insisted that I had my name cast in molten metal - *Christopher Thomas* - and I kept the heavy souvenir for many years.

Deadlines were everything. The sports department off stone print deadline was 5.20pm on a Saturday. If this deadline was not met, the paper would fail to be on the train which connected with the ferry to Ireland which left at 6.30pm. Four additional editions were printed. This 5.20pm deadline was the reason why the football league matches had to kick-off at 3pm. The rugby reporters like Clem had a bit more time, as most matches kicked off at 2.30, finishing around the 3.55pm mark. Clem would be given around 20 minutes to finish penning his 600 to 750-word report, and then had another 30 minutes to find or locate a telephone, dictate his report word by word, comma by comma, to a copy taker who would set out the match report, with the sub-editor forever hovering, responsible for the fit and grammar. Clem was instructed to deliver the article in full, on time, and be pretty much spot-on the word count. Otherwise the sub would cut the transmitted article, and the following day Dad would blow a gasket, and start a rant when he realised that the sub had cut out some flowery, lyrical intro he had lovingly crafted.

The one writer who Dad considered to be the best in Fleet St during his time there, was unquestionably Hugh McIlvanney, who wrote about boxing, football and horse racing with equal excellence, resulting in him winning the Sports Journalist of the Year award seven times, and becoming the only sportswriter ever to have been voted the Journalist of the Year. Hugh recently said, "Over 30 years at *The Observer*, I always felt fortunate to be among so many people who were exceptional at what they did. As for the sports department, there were too many colleagues of humbling talent to be listed, and if I mention Richard Baerlein it's on the grounds of eccentricity. He thought nothing of trying to ad-lib a feature while eating a pheasant in his bed."

David Randall, in his book *The Great Reporters*, described McIlvanney thus:

> Although his features were sometimes filed to a deadline that bore no relation to the one we in the

office were working on, he could, if it came to it, ad lib down the phone a 2,000-word report of a major event that was, when you received it, as inventive, lucid and considered as if it had been written with a goose-quill pen over three weeks. To this talent, he added a capacity for reading and research that bordered on the compulsive. His quest for precision and talent for getting to the essence of anything was best shown in his report on the death of the young, painfully shy boxer Johnny Owen following a bout in Las Vegas:

"Boxing gave Johnny Owen his one positive means of self-expression. Outside the ring he was an inaudible and almost invisible personality. Inside, he became astonishingly positive and self-assured. He seemed to be more at home there than anywhere else. It is his tragedy that he found himself articulate in such a dangerous language."

Dad reckoned that McIlvanney considered sport an art form, as worthy as any of the arts, although he once told Donald Trelford, "If I had to choose between having read King Lear or having seen the Brazilian football team of 1970, Pele would have to yield to Shakespeare."

Dad enjoyed his boxing, and indeed covered various fights and fighters for *The Observer* in the 1960s. He often told the story about the time he met Mohammed Ali in an elevator in the Hilton Hotel in Park Lane, when he shoved his way into the lift to find himself standing toe to chin with the champ. Ali winked at him and said, "You so big you take up all the room!" Dad said he was embarrassed, and was relieved when Ali got out before him. But he loved to tell the story of the Rumble in the Jungle featuring McIlvanney, who rebutted the original theory put forward by Norman Mailer and George Plimpton that Mohammed Ali had planned his infamous rope-a-dope tactics ahead of the fight with George Foreman in Kinshasa, Zaire

(October 30, 1974).

"There is no question," McIlvanney insists, that only during the fight itself did Ali make his decision to abandon his famed dancing style and go to the ropes "The idea that it was some premeditated plan is nonsense, he says. "It was more of a triumph that such a brilliant improvisation had come to him in a crisis."

Hugh states this opinion with the absolute authority of a dedicated sports journalist who realised after the fight that Ali would not be able to sleep. So Hugh drove (accompanied by Ken Jones of *The Sunday Mirror*) to Ali's villa in N'Sele, 40 miles from Kinshasa. They were invited indoors and for more than two hours given a detailed explanation of Ali's winning tactics in one of the most iconic heavyweight fights ever fought.

"Truth is I could have killed myself dancin' against him," Ali revealed - "He's too big for me to keep moving round him. I was a bit winded after doin' it in the first round, so I said to myself, "let me go to the ropes while I'm fresh, while I can handle him there without getting' hurt…"

Clem watched, read, debated, and learned an enormous amount from Hugh McIlvanney over the entire period of his rugby writing career, and whenever we travelled anywhere on a Sunday, invariably the first article I would be asked to read out as he drove, would be the McIlvanney piece. There was also an informal, highly competitive horse gambling culture that featured Clem, Hugh, Ian Robertson, and others who were constantly sharing tips, more often at the bookies' expense, especially when they got close to certain trainers like Ian Balding who would generously share some accurate piece of stable gossip, like the fact that a particular handicapper would be trying that day!

Dad loved the social status that being the Chief Rugby Correspondent afforded him, especially in a place like Swansea, and in Wales. He took the responsibility extremely seriously, and Alan Watkins, the political essayist and part-time rugby columnist, illustrates this in his semi-autobiography, *A Short Walk Down Fleet Street:*

> Clem took as much pride in his connection with the Observer as chief rugby correspondent for over 30 years as he did in his achievements on the field - perhaps more. He never claimed to be a fine writer in the manner of his predecessor Bert Toft. Indeed, I once remarked that it was sometimes difficult to say whether Clem was writing like a butcher or a wing-forward. But in his generation his knowledge and understanding of the game were unrivalled. He both spoke and wrote his mind, a complete honest witness, his own man. Perhaps the outstanding example of his independence was provided during the disappointing British Isles Lions tour of New Zealand in 1977, when he told the readers of *The Observer* in convincing detail about how the management were not doing their job properly.

Alun was a good friend of Dad's, whose presence on certain occasions when he was able to swop the Press Gallery in the House of Commons for a rugby press box, would galvanise the usual rugby writers to launch into political jokes and epithets. I remember he borrowed Dad's house in St Vivian in the Medoc, whilst writing his acclaimed *A Conservative Coup: The Fall of Margaret Thatcher*, and we all went down to cover the semi-finals of the French rugby championship at the end of May 1991. My old team Bordeaux-Begles played their semi-final in Toulouse, beating Beziers 13-12 in a brutal encounter under a burning sun, in front of a crowd who would not have been out of place at a bull-fight. Bernard Laporte played scrum-half for Begles, the current President and ex-head coach of the French Rugby Union (FFR). The front row consisted of the ferocious trio: Simon, Moscato, and Gimbert, more commonly known as "les rapetous" (the rape and burners!).

I recall escorting Alun down into the bowels of the stadium in Toulouse, and being a fluent French speaker, I conducted a few interviews for Alan to scribble down, in the hope of getting a decent quote to add to Clem's match report. For years after, Alun wrote of this moment as one of the most bizarre that he, as a British rugby writer, had ever witnessed. He was gobsmacked that the entire front row union, "les rapetous", were wearing jock straps with cricket boxes inserted to protect their crown jewels. He simply could not fathom the sporting culture that required players to take such extreme risk management measures, and it confirmed for him his suspicion that the French simply lack the ethical and moral standards to play a game like rugby football. Alun was absolutely right about the moral compass going somewhat astray that fine day and later. Gimbert and Moscato were both involved in some pretty dreadful head butting exchanges with the English front rowers, Probyn and Brian Moore, in the 5 Nations match at the Parc de Princes 10 months later. Moscato was sent off for persistent head-butting, Lascube for stamping, and how Jeff Tordo and Gimbert survived was a mystery to everyone in attendance.

Alan Watkins wrote again and again that he owed his greatest debt - in terms of being accepted and embraced into the brethren of rugby writers - to Clem. When Alun began to write his "colour" column in *The Independent* he was surrounded by kindred Welshmen like his sports editor, Geoff Nicholson from Swansea, Tim Glover, and Steve Bale from Neath. Alun was an Ammanford boy, and was friendly with the quixotic Hugh Lloyd-Davies who played with Clem in his first year at Cambridge. He wrote that, "Clem understood the purpose of the column: that it was intended to be, as he puts it, "eccentric", the work of someone who loved the game even though he might not know everything there was to know about it and might not have been much of a player himself (although, as I do not want to be unduly modest. The last limitation applies to many full-time rugby writers as well)."

He continued, "I can only say that Thomas behaved to me as another Welshman, the late Sir Trevor Evans of *The Daily Express*, did when I attended my first TUC in 1960: buying me drinks, finding me seats, introducing me to colleagues and performers, and - most flattering of all - asking my opinion. Clem has even been known to ask me who scored the crucial try. I am most grateful to him."

Extending a welcome and helping hand to young aspiring rugby writers is a theme that runs through Clem's career. Many of the accomplished Fleet St rugby correspondents passed through *The Observer* and worked with Dad as researchers, sub-editors or, as in the case with Eddie Butler, groomed to take over from Dad. Although Dad, was not happy with that arrangement when first put in place, just before his Paris heart attack.

Huw Richards, writing of Clem in his *Dragons and All Blacks* account of the 1953 Wales v New Zealand match said, "He was occasionally impatient of the routine disciplines of journalism. One particular personal memory is of hearing him in conversation with a harassed sub-editor on *The Observer* sports desk one Saturday in the late 1980s. "But Clem, you've written 650 words and we only wanted 450," said the sub. "I know," said Clem, "but it was such a great game." Though not wholly appreciated by a sub-editor with a deadline and 200 words too many, that enthusiasm was always a trademark along with a generosity and warmth I greatly appreciated as a novice writer, flattered that someone of Clem's standing should take the trouble to get to know and encourage me."

Huw also wrote, "It is a matter of great regret that someone whose experiences and knowledge of the game was quite so broad-ranging - Clem seems never to have maintained anything so journalistically mundane as a contacts book, he just knew everybody in the game and where to find them when he needed to - never wrote his memoirs…"

I recall that one project Dad thoroughly enjoyed contributing to was an off-the-wall, behind the scenes documentary by film maker Kevin Allen. The project was made for BBC as an irreverent look at the 1991 Rugby World Cup. Kevin was destined to go onto Hollywood, and directed that seminal classic *Twin Town*; the iconic dark crime comedy that helped launch Rhys Ifans' career. Clem was supposed to have acquired formal accreditation for Kevin and his crew, but he completely forgot about this promise he had made one late evening at the Groucho club. Nevertheless, Clem took great delight in serving as Kevin's bridgehead, barreling his way forcefully into various changing rooms at Cardiff Arms Park, Lansdowne Road, Murrayfield, and even Twickers, closely followed by Kevin holding a microphone, with a cameraman in tow. This quickly became the Clem Thomas TV Show on the move, and so without any kind of press accreditation, Kevin got more access than the rest of the world's largest broadcasters put together.

The hallmark of Clem's journalism was strong opinion, written with the authority drawn from the credible reputation he had earned firstly as one of the world's leading players, and later from his exposure and witness at the forefront of the sport, notably in the press box, radio, and TV studios. *Observer* readers and BBC Wales listeners and viewers became familiar with his tendency to voice trenchant opinion, written in solid, broadsheet English, or spoken in his drawled, Cambridge accent. The rugby-loving public took what Clem said at face value, respecting his wisdom and sagacity in most matters. I cannot recall any critics of my father's commentary on the game. Invariably he would mirror the public frustrations of the day, and he maintained this reputable credibility of opinion until the day he died - sadly only an hour after completing a radio interview at the BBC Swansea studio on Alexandra Road.

Dad liked to recount the time he was having dinner with my sister Caroline and her husband Roger at the Groucho Club in Soho; it was early in the 1990s and he was approached by Jon Holmes, a sports agent who ran SFX in the UK. He handled David Beckham and, the only rugby player to have an agent at that time, Will Carling. Holmes introduced himself to Clem, and then asked him bluntly, "Why is it you never write anything interesting about Will?" To which Dad replied equally bluntly, "Because there's nothing interesting to write about…"

Over the 36 years he wrote for *The Observer*, *The Guardian*, *The Independent on Sunday* and the *South Wales Evening Post*, he also contributed hundreds of articles to rugby magazines around the world, as well as international Match Day programmes. Dad also worked in radio and television, starting on February 27th 1960 when he introduced a programme on the Home service called *Sports Medley*. He went on to become a regular contributor to the BBC's *Sports Parade* programme, where for over twenty years he would dissect and analyse the latest Welsh performance in tandem with Bleddyn Williams. Some of Dad's most insightful analysis was eloquently voiced in debate with Bleddyn on a Saturday evening. It was always balanced, informative, diagnostic, in-depth intellectual rugby commentary of a quality that is sometimes lacking in today's pundits.

Clem and Bleddyn rarely made any personal criticisms of players, but would not sit on the fence over a particular failure of technique or application. The production values of these halcyon programmes were high, both in content, and in presentation. Unfortunately, rugby television in Wales today is increasingly dumbed down to the lowest common denominator. Flagship programmes like Scrum V, favouring the Taffy, is a daffodil approach to serious rugby comment, do a great disservice to Welsh rugby aficionados. This is a great shame because some commentators are highly knowledgeable, and could contribute a more intelligent, responsible tone to the sport from which they earn their living. Dad would have sent the same message years ago.

There are a great deal of Clem's writings to study and they are often as vibrant and cutting today as they were when first published. There are far too many to include in this book, but I intend on publishing a companion limited edition in the not too distant future, that will include a lot more of Dad's articles, photographs, and memorabilia. I've selected some drawn from a 30-year period that provide an insight and flavour of how he reported certain key events and debates, like the apartheid question, and the positions he took over the development of the game, professionalism, the Lions, foul play, some excerpts from the great games, and some of the great fun he had. What is indeed remarkable is that in most instances - "plus ca change" as they say in Pontypool - his critique remains as relevant and fresh today, as it was then.

Dad was always Wales' number one fan, although the Omerta code of the press box precluded anyone from ever demonstrating any partisan support or displays of emotional joy. The only time Dad showed any real emotion in a press box was the occasion Mark, his youngest son, scored the match winning try in the Varsity at Twickenham. The TV camera caught Clem leaping up like a salmon from his seat in the press box as Mark squeezed in at the corner flag. He was already being dragged back into his seat by his peers, when the cameras cut to him. But what was funnier was the bollocking he got from his wife, Joyce for having a cigarette dangling from his mouth!

When analysing the Welsh dominance over England in January 1976, he wrote:

It may seem that in Wales these days it is simply not enough to beat England - you have to crush them. After Wales had won by their biggest margin at Twickenham, the pronouncement by John Dawes that Wales had played badly, and that he hoped they had put their one bad game of the season behind them, visibly irritated many and smacked of arrogance. But in truth the Welsh coach, a man more disposed to honest opinion than the niceties of life, was only reflecting the immediate thoughts of the Welsh team and their supporters...

The sustained success of Welsh rugby over the last six years is due to three factors. Changes in the laws have suited the Welsh style - there has been a tremendous crop of great players with four of the current side, namely JPR Williams, Gerald Davies, Gareth Edwards and Mervyn Davies - ranking as the best Wales has ever produced in their respective positions. The performance of JPR at Twickenham will remain a privileged memory of all those fortunate to have witnessed it. But above all it is the coaching which has allowed these great players to develop and express themselves.

The appointment of Ray Williams as the first national coaching organiser in the United Kingdom was the best decision ever reached by the Welsh Rugby Union (WRU); he more than anyone developed the framework for prosperity. He began with the basic philosophy of positive, effective rugby and developed the four principles of play, namely Go Forward – Support – Continuity - Pressure. Possession being an objective, not a principle.

Eighteen months later, wrapping up his thoughts on the disastrous 1977 Lions tour to New Zealand, Clem was forced to confront the shortcomings of the tour management, especially the performance of John Dawes, the coach:

> Not even as I sit luxuriating and pampered on the balcony of the fabulous Fijian Hotel on the island of Yanuca, contemplating the exotic beauty of coconut-laden waving palm trees and the magnificence of the great Pacific breaking on the coral reef, fringing a clear blue lagoon, can I relive the disappointments and sadness constituted in the 1977 Lions tour of New Zealand.
>
> History will record it as the unhappy tour, dogged and ill-fated by the combustible ingredients of bad weather, poor crowd behaviour, deficiencies in key positions and, above all, by a management that was uncongenial and unsatisfactory.
>
> From the start they were hag-ridden by the graceless and galling goddess of success, and instead of facing her with the disarming weapon of geniality they became hypersensitive to criticism and established a climate of such hostility that they and the team became the target of greater pressures than the importance of winning.
>
> They opened the way for scurrilous attacks by the insanitary fringe Press in New Zealand who printed contemptible front-page headlines like, "Louts and Animals" and "Lions are lousy lovers".
>
> No-one is going to pretend that these Lions any more or less than other touring teams were angels. They certainly did some damage and when the NZRU presented the bill for breakages at the end of the tour both the innocent and guilty paid £20

each. The few involved tried to justify their foolishness by saying that the damage was done only where their hosts had put them in bad accommodation.

The NZRU who grossed over two million dollars in gate receipts and showed an enormous profit, were intransigent in many of their dealings, particularly in regard to the itinerary and many of the hotels provided for the team. Surely these amateur players, who receive no other rewards, are worthy of the very best... Another recommendation is that in view of the innumerable scenes involving John Dawes throughout the tour the authorities should think twice about appointing him to a similar position in the future...

The disappointment of the 1977 tour became something of a default mode for Lions rugby after the tremendous successes of 1971 and 1974. They were destined to not win another test series until Australia in 1989, under Sir Ian McGeechan, a fallow period that then extended to include the 1983 and 1993 losing tours to New Zealand. By then the halcyon days of Carwyn James' winning tour of New Zealand was a distant memory. That was arguably the greatest Lions tour of all, albeit against a waning All Black rugby presence. This was quite possibly due to the lack of preparedness of the Kiwi forwards to engage the scrummage with any sort of technique, and the superb level of three-quarter play marshalled by the best fly half Clem ever saw, Barry John. The Lions won the 1971 series 2-1, with the last test drawn thanks to some ridiculously political refereeing ensuring there was no further humiliation heaped on the All Blacks. Clem thundered:

The Lions made history when they recovered

gallantly from an eight-point deficit to draw a mighty game and became the first British Isles side to win a test series in New Zealand. It was a moment to be savoured for, as All Black captain Colin Meads said, it is one that will probably never be equalled by any British team in the future.

In 30 years of watching and playing rugby, I have never felt an atmosphere charged with such emotion as that at the final whistle of this grim and rugged test match, and the scenes in the Lions' changing rooms afterwards were enough to draw tears of joy from even the most massive and hardened of rugby men.

It was not the greatest of games, but by heaven, it was one of the most exciting and excruciating games I have ever seen... Unhappily the game had a dark beginning, for the approach of the New Zealand forwards was reprehensible. Some of them had decided to use the mailed fist and the start was brutish and medieval. Whiting smashed down Brown with his fists and Muller's conduct was beastly... The Lions were in trouble, like a boxer out down in the first round. There followed more ugliness and open warfare broke out among the forwards. Willie John McBride led the retaliation, and this was perhaps the turning point of the match...

This was the backbone of the Barbarian team that came up against the All Blacks in the most famous rugby match of the Twentieth century, played at Cardiff Arms Park on Saturday, January 28 1973. The Baa-Baas won by 23-11, and Clem eulogised:

Of all the previous legions of Barbarians, none have struck a greater blow for the cause of rugby than those who brought the massed choir of

Cardiff Arms Park to a pitch of ecstasy yesterday. It was one of the greatest games seen at the national ground. I never saw a greater first half as the Barbarians, with dazzling speed of limb and wit, tore gaping wounds in the New Zealand defence to lead 17-7 at half-time. The euphoria began with perhaps the finest team try seen at Cardiff. Bennett began it by breathtakingly beating three men with fire-cracker sidesteps from deep inside his "25", and then swinging into the open where John Williams took it up and, with a speed which deceived the eye, Dawes, David and Quinnell hungrily carried the ball to the halfway, finally putting Gareth Edwards away for a try in the corner. This struck the note, and the Barbarians played rugby which recaptured the rapture of the 1971 Lions tour of New Zealand.

Clem enjoyed a love-hate relationship with New Zealand rugby. He was always respectful of their incessant high standards, and ability to produce superb rugby players with sublime footballing and ball-winning skills. But at times, he would launch into them when he felt it was merited, albeit on the physical nature of their play, in an era where they invented fast ball through rucking, driving over the tackled player, he was always prepared to give them the benefit of the doubt. In 1967, he marvelled at one of the finest All Black teams ever to tour the UK:

> The deficiencies of British rugby have been exposed brutally during the last three weeks by the sixth All Blacks, yet strangely the atmosphere has been one of resigned acceptance of the inevitable and the type of admiration that the small boy has for a big and stronger brother. There has been little recrimination or anger that a small country of some two and a half million should batter and

subdue us into subjugation. Unhappily submission seems to have become a feature of British sport... They are powerful physically but individually no cleverer than ourselves but their mental processes are so uncompromisingly dedicated to the habit of possession, giving absolute support and making no mistakes that they are proving themselves invincible. Winning and winning ways are not necessarily synonymous and their previous two tours of the British Isles the All Blacks have been adept at the former but less impressive in the latter. On this tour however they have behaved splendidly, been less dour and beyond reproach in terms of sportsmanship. This to me is a greater success than their splendid record. It is a relief to find them departing from being too physical, for I am certain that they were in danger of ruining the game by over-stating power rugby. They have loosened up their play, showed more adventure and kept their promise to play attractive attacking rugby. For this we have to thank their captain, Brian James Lochore, who has led by tremendous example, and the management of Charlie Sexton and Fred Allen, great exponents of open rugby, who will tolerate no unnecessary use of boot and fist and who have made no bones about telling their players what is expected of them. Some of their best players have been categorically told that if they step out of line on this tour they will spend the rest of the visit on the sidelines.

During this tour, the legendary All Black second row, Colin Meads, was sent off against Scotland. Clem gave him the benefit of the doubt in direct conflict with most of the press:

Meads, no angel in the past, was sent off largely

because of... the different personal interpretations of New Zealanders and Britons in what is permitted in physical attitudes. Colin Meads is one of the greatest forwards I have ever seen and despite my being entirely on the side of the law, he retains a certain sympathy inasmuch as the final offence for which he was sent off was not as dastardly as it might have been... He only exposed the fallibility of even the greatest of players in a game whose very nature and charm is physical contact, and there, but for the grace of God might have gone many of us.

So I suppose old Brynamman attitudes can surface occasionally even in the pages of *The Observer*.

Before the Wales tour to New Zealand in 1969, Clem commented: "There is an intense rivalry. I well remember the famous full back Bob Scott saying to me in 1953 that it was Wales his team wanted to beat above all. And, when we got our decisive score against them in the last few minutes and led 13-8, I recall the tears in Scott's eyes." And so onto the 1978 match against Wales, which New Zealand won in the last minute 13-12 with a highly controversial penalty, kicked by the double All Black Brian McKechnie (he represented New Zealand in rugby and cricket). The following Sunday, *The Observer* featured a rugby article headlined: "CONSPIRATORS WHO CHEAT THE GAME". Clem blasted away:

The unacceptable face of rugby football during the last fortnight has drawn the considerable fire of the mass media... the line-out which won the match for New Zealand was one of the most blatant conspiracies to cheat that I have ever observed in almost twenty years of reporting rugby... Let me say at this point that I was not squealing as a Welshman in defeat. I am, I hope far too detached these days to care about such transient events. Neither am I trying to devalue the current All Blacks, who in every other sense on this tour have behaved impeccably on and around the field... I am merely reporting objectively on what occurred in that fateful line-out... I was concerned that these men (Haden and Oliver) provoked a situation which was an affront to the spirit and entirely against the ethics of the game. I would want to ask Haden, and the All Black forwards who instigated such thinking, if they want every kid, including the grown-ups to emulate such a ploy and turn the game into a farce. One can only hope that they now repent such foolishness.

Over the 36 years Clem spent as a chronicler of the game of rugby football, and having begun his career in that most cherished embodiment of the amateur tradition, Cambridge University, he was as well-placed as any commentator to follow the evolving drift towards professionalism. His position was unequivocal for most of this period in that he saw Rugby union football as the last great amateur game, that bestowed a universality and meritocracy over all participants, in that the game could reward the vanity and talents of great players through the opportunity to play international rugby on a Saturday in front of 70,000 people at Twickenham or Cardiff Arms Park, yet allow those exalted individuals go back to their workplace on a Monday and carry on living a normal life. Dad believed that there were other richer rewards in the game like the friendships and experiences shared at a particular time in a young man's life. He was however extremely practical and fully understood the commercial pressures that began to hit the amateur clubs from the late 1960s onwards, pressures that mounted as the pace of social and economic change soared to meet the expectations of the game.

In 1970, he wrote in *The Guardian*:

> Apart from being one of the great physical games of the world, rugby has always had as its main pride an immense social background. It has deliberately been a cult of manliness, cheeriness, beer and friendship... Rugby football is riddled with woolly thinking and hypocrisy. The best rugby in the world is currently played in France, the most efficient in South Africa and New Zealand. All these have highly competitive rugby. Every perceptive person in the rugby establishment knows that the French inimitably and deplorably bend the rules. Many players are paid in one way or another... How long can rugby afford to be as daft and hypocritical? It remains for a new generation of administrators to rationalise the huge benefits the game demands and to control the problems and abuses with strong and efficient management.

In *The Observer* also in 1970 Clem proposed:

> Is it not also time that we thought seriously in terms of a world cup? And how about a world seven-a-side tournament at Twickenham? Ye Gods, the mouth waters at the thought of such exhilarating happenings. I can see that the disastrously conservative and hidebound establishment which calls itself the International Board recoiling in horror at such developments. It is time to change this. Time for the game to have full-time business administrators. Rugby itself needs further attention. The try must be worth more than a penalty which must remain as a deterrent. I favour four points for a try, with the

penalty remaining at three points. The line-out must be rationalised. I preferred it when the jumper was protected by walling the line-outs. The rucking laws must be more clearly defined and the referees more insistent on the offside law.

Competitive rugby must be tried as a new challenge for the players. Whether or not it will bring higher standards is perhaps open to argument. I believe it will be enormous stimulant and again will help to revive the flagging fortunes of so many clubs who are close to going broke.

But by 1982, the focus had switched towards the players themselves. In September Clem tried to analyse a money-in-the-boot scandal that threatened the very fabric of the game:

> The cynical commercial disregard for the first law in the Rugby Union Handbook, that "the game shall be an amateur game," by sports goods manufacturers and certain leading players has thrown rugby into its greatest crisis since the schism over broken time, which led to professional rugby league in the north of England. Revelations that Adidas has divulged to the Inland Revenue details of cash payments made to amateur rugby players throughout the UK has sent waves of anxiety through the game...
>
> It is widely known that certain players are under verbal contract to other firms, such as Pony, Patrick, Gola and Puma... It may be remembered that the All Blacks painted out the stripes on their boots for the Welsh game a couple of years ago. It was being said at the time that the All Blacks were not happy with the payment. After the game, Mourie, the captain struck back when he said, tongue in cheek, that they painted out the stripes

because they did not want to advertise a boot of such poor quality.

The French are having a good laugh at our expense. It was known last season that the French players, of whom the home unions have always been wary in professional terms, knew that British rugby players were receiving under-cover payments from Adidas. They were annoyed with the French rugby administration, because the French Federation had defused the situation by signing official contracts with Adidas, both at national level and with certain clubs. The money in this case went to the French Federation and to the clubs.

Perhaps there will be a moratorium for the players to identify themselves by a certain date when they would be granted amnesty. For infringements after the deadline, players would be banned for life if found to be breaking their amateur status.

By 1990, the whole argument was beginning to move inexorably towards full professionalism, but this would not happen until August 1995. Clem wrote five years earlier:

The game is dizzy with unfolding developments. Its administrators continue to have to move swiftly, in matters of money at least, from a lofty plateau to the more accountable public domain. Their problems are both profound and extremely demanding, with calls for the relaxing of the amateur laws continuing to be the most bothersome.

Pressure from the southern hemisphere, Wales and even their own players and coaches saw England abandon their rigid stance on amateurism last week when RFU President Mike Pearey said they were prepared to be more flexible. So it can be expected that the International Rugby Board will have a sufficient majority in November to concede that players will now be allowed to earn money outside the game - through personal appearances, sponsorship and advertising...

Dad always had a soft spot for Romanian rugby from his early experience of captaining a Swansea RFC tour there in 1954, where he led his team out in front of a 90,000 crowd. In 1979, he wrote in *The Observer:*

The Romanians are only the spearhead of a determined advance by East European countries on the cosy domesticity of the five-nation championship. Following in their wake, in order of importance, are Russia, Poland, Czechoslovakia, East Germany and Bulgaria... it will probably take Russia only another five to ten years to become a major rugby force.

Discussing the state of the globalisation of the game in 1979 with Viorel Moraru - who Clem described as "the uncommonly pleasant and highly intelligent manager of the Romanian touring team," - Moraru thought the time was rapidly approaching for a massive expansion in the control of world rugby, as the International Board is too insular. Clem continued:

I share these views. For a long time the board has been too conservative. I can understand the necessity for retaining proper ideals, aims, objectives and a close control on conformity of law and its interpretation. But the explosive growth of rugby in the Americas, the East, the Pacific and Eastern Europe requires a new approach. It is surely time to merge FIRA and the various world congresses under the auspices of the founder body, the International Board, who for all their conservatism have done a marvellous job. We need emerging powers like Romania and Argentina as much as they need us. Not only to fill the financial void left by the absence of the Springboks, but to add new blood and colour to our game. The sooner the four Home unions embrace the fledglings who are already flying high, the better it will be for all of us...

This was prescient stuff, as by November 13, 1983, Clem reported the 24-6 crushing by Romania of Wales in Bucharest:

The air of pessimism which accompanied Wales to the first international behind the Iron Curtain by a Home union country was confirmed by a humiliating defeat by 24 to 6.

It brought great joy to Romania who, although astonished at the ease of their accomplishment, saw it as the final turn of the key to their acceptance as a full member of the European rugby community. The French, who have lost here seven times, have been telling us for years that they were worthy opponents. Not even the worst Welsh pessimist anticipated such a crushing defeat. It confirmed how deplorably Welsh rugby has declined from the beginning of this decade. Romania play Russia in Bucharest next weekend. They beat Russia by only 15-10 at Kiev last season.

But as Romanian rugby improved, with another win over Wales in 1988, the revolution took a terrible toll on Romanian rugby as Clem called for solidarity in *The Observer* on January 7, 1990. I can vividly remember visiting

Viorel Moraru, the Romanian touring manager and vice-President of the Romanian Federation, in his hotel room in Cardiff. Dad would always take him a goody bag full of quality men's clothing, Lambswool Sweaters, shirts, and stuff. The two men shared a long and deep friendship without ever really spending much time together. In a heartfelt article Clem wrote of his lifelong friend:

> Viorel Moraru is the brilliant designer of many of the magnificent new bridges over the Danube. He is also one of the great rugby leaders of our time, the man directly responsible for Romania's emergence as a force in the European game.
>
> But his pioneering work ended abruptly several years ago when his son defected. Moraru was deposed as vice-president of the Romanian rugby federation and relegated from his job as the director of the Romanian Railways Research Institute to teaching apprentices to fabricate concrete railway sleepers. Romanian rugby has mirrored his decline. My friendship with Moraru began in 1954 when I visited Bucharest with Swansea. Over the years we kept in touch and I was anxious to make sure he had not suffered during the revolution. I finally managed to speak with him last week.
>
> Often choking with emotion, he spoke of the deaths of three Romanian players, shot by the Securitate. Florica Murariu was an army captain and also captain of the team that beat Wales just over a year ago. Radu Durbae was a major in the army who played 30 times for his country in the Seventies. The third was a young man from a minor team in Bucharest who died fighting the old regime.
>
> "I went to Radu's funeral at a cemetery for 800 people killed in the fighting," Moraru said.

"Around me that day there was hundreds of funerals, all young people, mostly young men, aged 17 to 25, for it was a young people's revolution." Talking of the game he loves he said: "We have had sad rugby without imagination. Tell you how unhappy our players were to play in Western Europe, because we could see how good life could be. Any success we had was always taken by the party which we detested. Now I am sure we will have a new spirit in Romania, we will have a joie de vivre and a new approach and imagination," he said.

He also told me of the grave problems facing the game in Romania, "We are very poor, we have nothing, he said. "There is not a single scrummaging machine in the country and we have hardly any rugby balls."

Encouragingly, though, offers of help have come quickly. (Including an appeal launched by *The Observer* in conjunction with *Rugby World* magazine) The French were the first to get in touch. According to Moraru, Albert Ferrasse, the President of the French federation is considering donating a franc for every spectator in the French championship this season. Dudley Wood, the Secretary of the RFU, has said that England, mindful of the remarkable hospitality received in difficult conditions in Romania last May, will discuss an initiative at their next committee meeting. Scotland and Wales are also actively considering ways to help as are Bath. And I would hope that Swansea, with their long associations will also help…"

Clem was hugely fond of Vivian Jenkins, the rugby Correspondent for *The Sunday Times* from the early 1950s to 1976, who had a distinguished sporting career playing rugby for Wales at full-back (1932-39). Vivian was a fellow Welshman who could claim an All Black scalp as he was part of the team that beat New Zealand in 1935. He was also vice-captain of the 1938 British Lions tour to South Africa.

Vivian played first class cricket for Glamorgan (1931-37), and gained Blues from Oxford University for both cricket and rugby. I fondly remember him from the Press Box and he was a delightful, genial character who can legitimately claim to have been one of Wales' best all-round sportsmen. He was one of the very few invited to cover Clem's 1955 British Lions tour and wrote a cracking good book on the back of the tour, *Lions Rampant*.

Dad and Vivien once stopped off in Fiji (1969) on the return from New Zealand after Wales' disastrous, ill-fated tour. Dad said they were enjoying a few 'cold one's' in a beach bar near Suva, when a very drunk, foul-mouthed American smashed into the bar causing mayhem. The interloper aggressively demanded, "large bourbon on the rocks, pal." Clem said the American's behaviour deteriorated from this point onward as he threw back the bourbons at an alarming rate. The Yank had a rictus grin on his face as he slumped against the bar, burping and farting with complete abandon. Dad and Vivian did their best to ignore the interruption and continue their conversation, but the American had other ideas:

"You two limeys sound like you got something stuck up your ass!" snarled the Yank, whom Clem was beginning to recognise, but greatly dislike.

"Which of you guys has the balls to fight me," he snarled.

"Certainly not I old chap!" Viv Jenkins retorted, in his soft Welsh lilted Oxford accent. "But a word to the wise, take my advice and stand down before you get frightfully hurt." Viv had witnessed, first hand, the astonishing power of a Clem Thomas punch, when he was designated 'chief slotter' and enforcer with the Lions in South Africa in

1955. Clem was a trailblazer in this regard for Willie John McBride's 1974 tour and the infamous '99' call. Viv suspected that Clem, even at 40 years of age could, if pushed, wreak extreme damage on a vicious drunk looking for a fistfight.

The American propelled himself off the bar top, throwing an almighty 180-degree haymaker aimed firmly at Dad's chin. Clem stepped inside the punch and slapped him hard across the face, knocking him to the ground. Viv Jenkins hissed, "For God sakes Clem, don't hit him again. You'll kill the poor idiot!"

Dad and Clem both shared a moment - the penny had dropped. The drunk, fighting Yank was none other than Lee Marvin, the Hollywood film star, who a year earlier had shot *Hell in the Pacific* in Fiji, and had returned for a spot of Marlin fishing and publicity shots for the movie.

The bar owner had summoned the Fiji police who arrived en masse, demanding an accounting of preceding's. The peerless Viv Jenkins softly downplayed the altercation with an urbane calmness that soothed ruffled feathers, "a dreadful misunderstanding by like-minded troubled souls, cousins from Wales and the United States, a mere storm in a tea cup, it's all over now officer."

Lee Marvin pulled himself from the floor, nodded his agreement, and slapped a matey arm around Dad. "Bourbon's all round," he drawled, and they drank into the early hours.

Clem confided in Viv, when they finally staggered back to the hotel that, Lee Marvin had got away with it by being too drunk for a proper fight. He was, and always remained, one of Dad's very favourite actors.

Peter Stead, the historian and broadcaster confirms that he spoke at some length with Richard Burton's brother Philip, when writing his book *Richard Burton: So Much, So Little* (1991). A wonderful anecdote about Lee Marvin came to light. Phillip recalled receiving a phone call from his brother in Hollywood who forbade him from ever going to see his latest movie *The Klansman* (1974). Richard told him that he had embarked on such a mammoth drinking session with his co-star Lee Marvin that he had absolutely no recollection of shooting a single scene in the movie. The director, Terrence Young, was forced to shoot most of the scenes with Burton and Marvin seated or lying down due to their inability to stand on two feet.

Clem also had a lot of fun as a rugby correspondent, with friends and family in most of the established rugby venues of the world. Greg, my middle brother, today works as a media advisor and consultant to World Rugby and to SANZAAR in Sydney. Greg rescued the rugby reputation of the British Lions' press officers following Clive Woodward's daft decision to appoint the Blair-era spin doctor, Alastair Campbell. I have on my mind the scandalous exploitation of Gavin Henson over selection in particular - it was inexcusable. Campbell is undoubtedly a very accomplished PR executive, albeit not cut out for the freemasonry world of The British Lions - particularly when the lions are undertaking the ultimate challenge by touring New Zealand.

Greg was the media manager and press officer for the Lions in South Africa (2009) and Australia (2013). At that time, Stephen Jones, *The Sunday Times* doyen of today's press box, was heard to remark "How fantastic it is that the Lions have got a proper rugby bloke running the media…" Greg started his rugby media career with the Australian rugby union in the early 1990s, and early on found himself organising a press briefing at the Sydney football ground (1994), where Clem was in the assembled press audience. The rumours were flying that summer of the imminent first SANZAR deal with the Channel 9 TV organisation. At the start of the press conference attended by the Australian coach, Bob Dwyer, and the captain, Phil Kearns, Greg specifically instructed the press to confine questions to the Irish test series. When questions were asked for, Clem was first in like a kangaroo on speed: "What impact will the future enormous revenue streams from the TV deal have on Australian rugby?" Quick as a flash, Greg interjected and sternly instructed his errant father to focus his questioning on rugby matters… Chuckling as he left the press conference, Dad grabbed Greg by the arm and said, "Well done Greg, I was just testing you!!!"

Another game Clem was often up for, was to wager with friends he spent the Friday evening with on the eve of an international test match. He famously cleaned up following a soiree at one of his habitual Parisian restaurants, *La Gaulloise,* in the 15eme arrondissement run by his great friend Pierre Combin. The wager would invariably be the cost of lunch on the Sunday after the match, and would entail Clem being given a series of difficult, awkward words that he had to incorporate into his match report in *The Observer* on the Sunday. On this occasion he was given 'ping-pong ball' and 'goldfish'. On February 23, 1969, his match report on the France v England match carried the oblique sentence: "Puget, the French scrum-half, must at times have felt that he stood a better chance throwing a ping-pong ball into a goldfish bowl, for the English not only took eight heads to three but continually disrupted and slowed the French ball…"

This great tradition has been continued to this very day by the legendary Welsh wing Gerald Davies. I bumped into Gerald a few years ago after a Wales v France encounter in Cardiff after leaving the Cardiff and County Club on Westgate St. I was with my good friends Rob Davies and Geoff Bentley and after catching up a little with Gerald we all got to talking about Clem's tradition of inserting an odd word or two into his match reports as a wager. Gerald, quick as a shot, said he was game for picking up the mantle and Geoff suggested the word – marionettes. The following Monday in *The Times* he wrote "At times Wales played like marionettes…"

Gerald, that promised bottle of Bolly is in the post!

7

PLAYING POLITICS WITH THE LIBERALS

"It is not the critic who counts; not the man who points out how the strong man stumbles, or where the doer of deeds could have done them better. The credit belongs to the man who is actually in the arena, whose face is marred by dust and sweat and blood; who strives valiantly; who errs, who comes short again and again, because there is no effort without error and shortcoming; but who does actually strive to do the deeds; who knows great enthusiasm, the great devotions; who spends himself in a worthy cause; who at best knows in the end the triumph of high achievement, and who at the worst, if he fails, at least fails while daring greatly, so that his place shall never be with those cold and timid souls who neither know victory nor defeat." *Theodore Roosevelt*

When in January 1974 the Prime Minister Ted Heath announced a snap general election with the question, "Who governs Britain?", Clem decided that he did, and stood for Parliament for the Liberal party in the Gower constituency in which we lived. He ran a campaign of high energy, hectic commitment and low cunning, sending my fifteen-year-old sister out at night with our Mum to rip down opponents' posters and to replace them with mugshots of Dad, the Liberal candidate.

If you ask me what specific ideological compass drove Dad with sufficient motivation to want to go into politics, I would point to two principal factors.

Firstly, that he was forever concerned with the idea that the establishment, whatever that means, was unassailable, in that if you dared oppose it directly, you could never hope to win. He believed that the one way of generating fundamental, radical reform and change was to support the political party that best represented this aspiration. For Dad, that meant supporting the Liberal party, particularly the Welsh, Lloyd Georgian, strand of Liberalism. He believed that the most effective pathway for individuals seeking to become part of a new order or establishment required a meritocratic gateway to get in. He was deeply suspicious of both elites and closed-shop politics. Clem was highly supportive of the idea of joining what was then called the Common Market, and I certainly benefited personally by his determination to ensure that I became bilingual in French, hence my despatch during school holidays to stay with the Chatrier and Damitio families *en famille* in Paris and Epernon.

Secondly, Dad would often flippantly quip during conversation that he fancied joining the best club in the world, namely the House of Commons, with the facilities and kudos of being part of the Palace of Westminster. So, putting himself up as a candidate for the Liberals served to support a political philosophy that he genuinely believed in, but also served as a good wind-up for all his Labour and Tory friends in the rugby, butchery, and farming worlds.

Peter Stead in his insightful essay from *More Heart and Soul The Character of Welsh Rugby* (1999) noted, "I had first got to know Clem in 1979 when we were both prospective parliamentary candidates. He was once again preparing to fight Carmarthen for the Liberals, I was 'nursing' Barry for Labour, but in our home base of Swansea we were able to come together in the campaign for the Welsh Assembly... From his business base he wanted to establish links with academics and politicians in order to shape a new Wales. He wanted to learn, he wanted to note new names, book titles and ideas, but he was also conscious of the practical no-nonsense entrepreneurial dimension which he could almost uniquely bring to the world of Welsh radicalism."

Dad was a classic example of what I like to describe as a Lloyd George Liberal. Liberalism is often associated with free political institutions and religious tolerance, as well as support for a strong role of government in regulating capitalism and constructing the welfare state. At the beginning of the twentieth century, Lloyd George was the principal architect for the introduction of state financial support for the sick and infirm. This was referred to as "going on the Lloyd George" for decades afterwards, but - the legislation was commonly known as the Liberal Reforms. Under his leadership, Liberals extended the minimum wage to farm workers in 1909. When Clem was growing up in Brynamman during the 1930s and 1940s, Liberalism retained an appeal amongst the entrepreneurial small business class and in rural, non-industrial Wales it survived the Labour onslaught, by monolithic trade union movements that appealed to the industrialized working class, mostly due to a resolute social conscience within the Welsh nonconformist tradition.

Welsh nationalism never held any great appeal for Clem. He did not believe in an independent Wales, and despite being a fluent Welsh speaker (his first-language), he had no truck with the cultural radicalism that developed around the Welsh language in the 1960s. Dad's privileged, urbane upbringing at an English public school, followed by Cambridge University, educated him with a cosmopolitan worldview. Clem was influenced to look outside and beyond Wales, he hated parochialism. Touring countries like Romania and South Africa exposed him to two of the great global clashes in the later years of the twentieth century: racism and communism. First-hand experience shaped his outlook. Clem was a true internationalist to his very fibre.

Clem, for many years, consistently self-examined the Welsh condition, and often stated that in Wales we lack truly world class institutions, and we, as a people are far too parochial and insular in our attitudes. When posing the question. "What in Wales is genuinely world class?" there is not an awful lot to point to. Economically, we are over-dependent on the public sector, and we have lost the world-leading industries of the nineteenth century that we once excelled in: anthracite coal mining, steel, and copper production. The loss of these industries has left a huge hole in our economy that decades of inertia have exacerbated. Most of our accomplishments are cultural: in music, the Welsh National Opera, Bryn Terfel, Katherine Jenkins, Tom Jones and stadium rock bands like The Manic Street Preachers and the Stereophonics; in sport the Welsh rugby team and the wonderful Principality Stadium, and every 50 years the Welsh soccer team. Wales, for a country its size, always seems to produce an inordinate amount of talented individuals who perform on the world stage: Dylan Thomas, Roald Dahl, Richard Burton, Anthony Hopkins, Michael Sheen, Catherine Zeta-Jones, Rhys Ifans, Ralph Steadman, Shirley Bassey, the list is quite endless.

But sadly, none of our universities are truly world-class, and certainly none of our political institutions. There is no identifiable technological development, nor indeed architecture. Too much in Wales is of the lowest common denominator, a feature of the lazy, arrogant hegemony

Labour has strangled Welsh politics with over the past one hundred years or so. As Lloyd George once said, "A young man who isn't a socialist hasn't got a heart; an old man who is a socialist hasn't got a head."

Clem wanted to try and make a point, and by standing twice for Parliament he felt that by utilizing his rugby fame, he might provide the Liberals with an effective voice in Wales, extolling the virtues of raising standards across the board. Dad was always an advocate about the importance of education in establishing a doctrine of meritocracy, where all young people would feel they had an opportunity to succeed. He stood for Parliament in the 1974 February election (Gower constituency) and again in Carmarthen in 1979. Dad was also a candidate for Dyfed, West Wales for the European Parliament in 1978, his campaign pitch, "The only candidate, who was born, bred and who works in the constituency. If you believe in the European ideal then you must vote for the LIBERALS and CLEM THOMAS." Quite what he would have made of Brexit I don't hazard a guess. But I know that Clem would in no way be supportive of the Brexit foolishness driven by right wing Tory concerns. Dad would certainly question the validity of Britain's immigration policies over the past 20 years and he would have abhorred the lack of democratic validity inherent in the EU. I believe he would have been particularly incensed by European commissar style diktats issued by unelected, fifth-rate politicians from Luxemburg and Belgium that nobody has ever heard of.

The Liberal Council for Wales was founded by David Lloyd George in 1897. During this period the Welsh Liberals were a home for radical Welsh nationalism, but in Wales the nationalist passion never spilled over into violence as it did in Ireland. This was partly attributable to the strong English capitalist base present within the party. In 1906, the Welsh Liberals reached their peak when 35 out of 36 Welsh seats took the Liberal whip. But the party splintered after 1918, with the rise of Labour and the dominance of Lloyd George both contributing to the steady decline. Nevertheless, it was in Wales that the pre-war Liberals' support lasted the longest.

When Clem stood for Carmarthen (1979), it was more as a favour to friends like Geraint Howells, who had won Cardiganshire in 1974, and Emlyn Hooson, a barrister with a farming background who won the Montgomery seat in 1962. Clem knew Hooson from his time spent in Swansea as Recorder in 1971, whilst Hooson had contested the Liberal party leadership election in 1967, and was the Chairman of the Welsh Liberal party.

Dad was well acquainted with Geraint Howells, mainly through the cattle markets of west Wales. Howells was a hill farmer by trade in Glennydd, Ponterwyd near Devil's Bridge, where he had some 750 acres with over 3,000 sheep.

The Carmarthen constituency had been staunchly Liberal throughout the early 1900's up until 1929 when Labour finally broke through, only to lose it back to the Liberals who held the seat until 1957. Megan Lloyd George, daughter of the ex-Liberal leader and Prime Minister, David Lloyd George, changed parties and won as a Labour candidate in '57. This coincided with the gradual rise in the Plaid Cymru vote which itself eroded the old, established Liberal base which normally could be relied upon to deliver a minimum of at least 50 per cent of the poll. Megan held the seat until her death (1966) and the resulting by-election ushered in Gwynfor Evans of Plaid Cymru. The victory was regarded as a seminal moment - the first seat ever won in the House of Commons by a Plaid candidate. Labour finally regained it in 1970 and held on again in 1974 by the unbelievably slim margin of 3 votes. But Gwynfor Evans managed to prise it back for Plaid at the 1979 ballot, beating Dad in the process.

| Labour | Roger Thomas | 18,667 |
| Plaid Cymru | Gwynfor Evans | 16,689 |

Conservative	Nigel Thomas	12,272
Liberal	**Clem Thomas**	4,186
National Front	Charles Grice	149
New Britain	EJ Clarke	126

The turn-out was a healthy 84.4 per cent, but Clem won the smallest tally of Liberal votes in over a 100 years. He was squeezed by the Plaid Cymru resurgence, the Thatcher revolution and a stubborn Labour vote supported by the National Union of Miners along with other trade union movements who were angry at the deindustrialization policy that was increasingly becoming adopted even before Thatcher pushed it into turbo drive. The pit closures had actually begun under the Callaghan Labour government. To be fair to Dad, his heart wasn't really in it and he readily admitted that he had not fully engaged in the election, unlike 1974 when he was all blood and thunder. Dad felt obliged to stand under pressure from the party and to fulfil past promises. He could hardly refuse as he held a real genuine affection for the Liberals.

There is a rather sad and indeed sordid post note to that particular election. The winner, Roger Thomas (Labour), was convicted at Gowerton Magistrates Court in Swansea, of importuning for immoral purposes at a men's public lavatory and fined £75. He never stood for Carmarthen again.

Dad's commitment to the previous 1974 election had been a different kettle of fish entirely. Clem genuinely committed heart and soul to a venture he knew he had virtually no chance of winning. But being as competitive as he was, Dad threw the kitchen sink at it. He dared to dream the impossible by winning a seat that the Liberals had last won in 1906, and had last contested in 1931. The task facing Clem was psephologically impossible. The incumbent Labour MP, Ivor Davies, had won a staggering 77 per cent of the vote in 1966, and a solid 53 per cent in 1970. Dad's circle of friends thought he was crazy to even consider it. But they were all aware of his powerful personality and no-one could entirely discount a shock upset where Clem was concerned!

The highlight of Dad's campaign was a visit to our home in Southgate, Gower, by the leader of the Liberal party, Jeremy Thorpe. The political diarist Andrew Rawnsley described Thorpe as a "dandy, exhibitionist, superb showman, shallow thinker, wit and mimic, cunning opportunist, sinister intriguer, idealistic internationalist and a man with a clandestine homosexual life." It might be argued that these were the very attributes that made him the perfect Liberal leader for the 1970s. Thorpe provided a clear contrast with the pedestrian images of Harold Wilson and Edward Heath, being both younger and far more telegenic.

My sister Caroline clearly remembers the awe with which Thorpe was greeted by the Liberal faithful in Wales, who treated him like a superstar. They gathered in their thousands to shake his hand, hear stump speeches, and share a cup of tea with the great man. Expectations were sky high and a resurgence of the Liberal party was eagerly anticipated. The Liberal's fortunes were rising significantly midway through 1974. The public was equally disenchanted with both major political parties and community politics were proving extremely popular - the national electorate was receptive to the middle way like never before. Impressive local election results were followed by sensational by-election results. In October 1972, the Labour heartland of Rochdale was won, which sent shockwaves through parliament. The next year the Liberals racked up four more resounding victories against the Conservatives: Sutton, Isle of Ely, Rippon, and Berwick-upon-Tweed.

So when Heath, whose conservative government had been plagued by industrial unrest, called the general election, Liberal hopes were high, with senior Liberal strategists hoping for a significant number of seats, predicting around the 30 mark. In addition, they wanted to create a much larger population of solid liberal base voters from which the party could advance from in the future. During the election campaign there was evidence of disaffection with both Heath and Wilson, and all the pundits predicted a surge in Liberal support. Clem's commitment to the cause of liberalism in Wales was genuinely appreciated by the Liberal leaders in Westminster, and particularly by Thorpe, who knew they needed to recruit more candidates with instant name recognition if they were to succeed.

Clem did his job, and was regularly invited to the BBC Wales and Harlech TV studios in Cardiff to participate in a variety of debates and provide a Liberal viewpoint to political discussions. I remember asking Dad why he didn't sign up for the Labour Party so he could have a chance of actually winning a seat. He patiently explained his views on the need for radical, liberal change. This was totally anathema to the trade union-dominated Labour party, whose dogma and unworkable economics made it totally unappealing to self-employed, educated men like himself. He told me that he deeply mistrusted Labour because of the negative, sinister tone that certain politicians voiced around their Redistributionist Agenda. Clem always suspected that this had more to do with the politics of envy than genuine social justice and equal opportunity. He once told me that after a debate at a broadcast studio in Cardiff, Neil Kinnock approached him afterward and hissed, "When we get into power, we'll fucking have people like you..." Dad was naturally shocked but not surprised, and confided: "Kinnock is a typical Welsh Labour politician, full of piss and wind, but no delivery...ghastly little unattractive man."

Thorpe was confident that the party would make a significant breakthrough; on Election Day it secured its highest national vote to date - 6 million votes, and its highest share of the vote - 19.3 per cent - since 1929.

However, under the first-past-the-post voting system, these figures translated into just 14 seats.

This upturn in the Liberal vote helped Clem secure an honourable showing at the ballot box in his Gower constituency. The results were:

LABOUR	IFOR EVANS	23,850
CONSERVATIVE	DFR GEORGE	8,780
LIBERAL	**CLEM THOMAS**	8,737
PLAID CYMRU	JN HARRIS	3,741

The turnout was the second highest on record at 79.88 per cent, with Clem achieving the same percentage of Liberal votes as the national average. Dad was not disappointed to lose - he knew he was on a hiding to nothing when he stood - but it gave him a certain stature and even notoriety both locally, and amongst his *Observer* and business associates. He demonstrated that he was a man of principle who does not shirk a challenge, and he fully understood that the Liberal party needed supporters like him to selflessly put their heads above the parapet, so the party could progress as an electoral force.

After the election, the two-party system that had dominated British politics since 1945 began to crumble, and Clem was forever proud of the small contribution he made towards trying to make the United Kingdom more pluralist with representative democracy accurately mirroring the will of the people. Dad often reasoned that the major constitutional change required to effectively achieve true democracy was a form of proportional representation, which the Liberals have been attempting to introduce, unsuccessfully, to Westminster politics ever since that general election in 1974.

I recall that Dad took quite a bit of stick, especially from his English, conservative friends, most notably Peter Robbins, who said it wasn't his fault that he lost... it was the Liberal party election slogan, "Vote Liberal and Feel a

Man". This was a shot at the leader Thorpe, who within months was being exposed as a man with dark secrets, most notoriously, for that unenlightened era - he had previously had a sexual relationship with a would-be male model, Norman Scott, whom he had first met in 1961

By 1974 Thorpe, at the crest of the Liberal revival, was terrified of any exposure that might lose him the Liberal leadership. As Dominic Sandbrook, the entertaining political historian wrote, "The stakes had never been higher, silencing Scott never been more urgent."

There followed a bizarre period when several improbable characters became household names, as a convoluted and amateurish conspiracy to kill Scott was gradually revealed in the tabloid press. This included the allegation that Thorpe had hired a hitman to kill Scott but the would-be assassin, a pilot named Andrew Newton, succeeded in only shooting Scott's dog, a Great Dane called Rinka! Amidst a feeding frenzy in the tabloid and broadsheet newspapers, support and sympathy for Thorpe dwindled. There were four defendants brought to trial for the conspiracy and all were eventually acquitted of all charges. Thorpe, unlike his party, considered the decision to be "a complete vindication".

Most assessments of Thorpe's career emphasise his downfall rather than his political achievements, "a fall unparalleled in British political history", according to his *Daily Telegraph* obituarist. While Thorpe hoped that acquittal would ensure he would be remembered primarily for his revival of Liberal fortunes in the 1960s and 1970s, which Dad had contributed to in Wales, unfortunately the trial shattered his reputation beyond repair.

The prosecuting counsel at the Old Bailey likened the case to "a tragedy of truly Greek or Shakespearian proportions - the slow but inevitable destruction of a man by the stamp of one defect". However, to Thorpe's credit, before the scandal took him down, he promoted his brand of internationalism and social liberalism, highlighted his long involvement with the anti-apartheid movement, his denunciation of dictators, his opposition to the death penalty and his total rejection of racism. There is widespread agreement that the man Clem met that day in Gower was an outstanding political campaigner - persuasive, witty, and warm, "his astonishing memory for faces persuaded voters that they were intimate friends... his resourceful mind afforded quips and stunts for every occasion."

The recent crop of Liberal politicians, especially Nick Clegg, credit Thorpe with providing the "driving force that continued the Liberal revival that had begun under Jo Grimond (the previous leader)." Whilst David Dutton, in his *History of the Liberal Party* (2004) surmises, that in spite of Thorpe's bold style and charisma, "the party drifted without a sense of conviction and underlying purpose, dominated by tactics rather than ideas." Thorpe positioned the Liberal party firmly in the moderate centre, equidistant from Labour and the Conservatives, a strategy that was very successful in February 1974 when dissatisfaction with the two main parties was at its height, but which left the party's specific identity obscure, and its policies largely unknown to the electorate.

Douglas Murray, associate editor of *The Spectator*, in his review of Michael Bloch's 2014 biography of Thorpe wrote, "Jeremy Thorpe had hoped to be remembered as a great political leader. I suppose they all do. And perhaps he will be remembered longer than many other politicians of his age or ours. But it will always be for the same thing. Jeremy, Jeremy, bang, bang, woof, woof."

The Liberal party of the early 1970s that Dad joined was comprised of a bunch of colourful, almost psychedelic characters, one of whom was the writer, broadcaster, food critic, and professional gambler, Clement Freud. Clem knew him of old from their time at *The Observer* and by the mid-1960s he was one of the highest paid journalists in

England, writing humorous articles for the *News of the World*, cooking for *The Observer*, and sports for *The Sun*.

Freud, upon returning from the war, opened the Royal Court Club above the Chelsea Theatre, where for £10 per week he engaged then-unknown artists - such as, Rolf Harris, David Frost, Jonathan Miller and Dudley Moore - for cabaret shows. Within the world of arts and entertainment Freud was a playful, nonconformist, and contrary man who got an impish pleasure from confusing people with his sharp intellect. One evening in a Soho restaurant he asked for a bowl of chicken broth and stated, "I have washed up in better and hotter liquid."

In the early 1970s he was invited to Swansea as the guest speaker of the Liberal Party annual dinner, held at the Dragon Hotel. After his speech, he asked Dad if Swansea had a casino. Freud was a director of the Playboy Club in Mayfair, London, and a stalwart of the gambling scene of the late 1960s that involved John Aspinall, Jimmy Goldsmith, Lord Lucan, Peter Sellers, Ian Fleming, David Stirling, and Lord Derby, who was reputed to have lost £300,000 in a single night - the equivalent of almost £7.5 million today! Clem escorted Clement Freud across the square to the Society Club, a casino then owned by the Swansea entrepreneur Bernard George, and introduced him to the inner circle at the penthouse bar. Freud whispered in Clem's ear, "Do you think you could advance me £3,000 old boy?" Dad was slightly aghast at the request but nevertheless quietly asked Bernard if this could be transacted. Without any undue fuss, Freud promptly had his £3,000 and departed for the tables.

Dad told me that a good forty minutes later he was back; "I say old chap, any chance of another £3,000?" Clem duly obliged and enquired whether his credit was good enough with Bernard for him to stand as guarantor of Clement Freud. Once more, £3,000 was brought to Freud who promptly disappeared. Two hours later Freud re-emerged in the top bar, and suggested they should now leave for his hotel, as it was getting late, and he had an early morning train to catch. He proceeded to empty his jacket pockets, and plopped £6,000 onto the bar. "Thanks very much for the advance, Clem. I shall always remember my sterling night out in Swansea," he confided in Dad that he walked away from the roulette table with the best part of £20,000.

Clement Freud won a by-election for the Isle of Ely (1973), despite the Liberals not even fielding a candidate in 1970. He placed a £1,000 bet on himself at 33-1, and the winnings were the equivalent of two years' salary for a member of parliament at that time. Freud was renowned for his unorthodox behaviour. In 1980 he made a speech in the Commons calling for better wine to be served in the Houses of Parliament, and when the Northern Ireland Secretary, Jim Prior, ruled out the hanging of terrorists, Freud suggested that they be lynched instead.

Freud shared a very similar worldview to his first Editor at *The Observer*, David Astor, in that he once said, "Long live the amateur politician - amateur as in loving the work one does - who does what he thinks is right, what makes sense, and what will be to the general good of his constituents, to whom he will have made clear that he holds certain personal views on which he will not be moved: hanging, field sports, federalism and Sunday shopping."

Dad's favourite Clement Freud story involved the 1969 Great Transatlantic Air Race, sponsored by *The Daily Mail*. The race started at the Post Office Tower in London and finished on the 86th floor of The Empire State Building in New York. The race was held to commemorate the 50th anniversary of Alcock and Brown's first Atlantic Crossing by air (1919). "To broaden the appeal of the affair" recalled Freud in his 2001 autobiography, *Freud Ego*, "there was a passenger category, open to anyone making their way from London to New York using commercial airlines. Aer Lingus of Ireland sponsored the first prize of

£5,000 - and as their rules demanded a stopover at Shannon, where not too many non-Aer Lingus New York bound planes stopped, this was probably done to make the prize self-financing. It seemed my sort of contest. I sent off for the full rules".

The actual race was spread over eight days, from May 4th to the 11th, and Freud calculated that there were only two flights with fast connections from Shannon to New York. The plan was to leave the Post Office Tower to reach London airport by 3.50pm - and not a second later - to catch the 4.00pm departure to Shannon and thence New York.

Working backwards, Freud's time from the airport helicopter landing pad to the rendezvous was 90 seconds on a fast motor bike; the helicopter flight from a wheat barge moored in the Thames took 7 ½ minutes. Surrey Marine had a motorboat which made the trip from Cleopatra's Needle steps, on the Embankment, in 1 ¼ minutes, including getting into the chopper.

At New York, Freud had arranged a motor bike to take him from Customs to Kennedy Airport's Heliport, a helicopter to whisk him onto Manhattan, landing at 30th Street Heliport and an ambulance to beat the evening traffic to the Empire State Building on Fifth Avenue. That Wednesday, with everything working like a well-oiled machine, he achieved the fastest time. Freud won the passenger category £5,000 first prize in 8 hours, 4 minutes and 18 seconds.

The shortest time category, and *The Daily Mail* title with a prize of £6,000 was won by the Royal Air Force who decided to use the unique Vertical Take-Off and landing capability of the Hawker Siddeley Harrier. The Harrier used a coal yard next to St Pancras station to depart from and landed on the quayside of the Bristol Basin in New York.

Clem's interest in Liberal politics waned considerably after the 1979 election, as his energies were focused on his wholesale butchery business. Dad's rugby journalism was also keeping him very busy, especially with the increased number of summer tours, and there were always a range of entrepreneurial ventures on the go. But he never shed his liberalism, and defended radical, internationalist values throughout his life. Many of these values had been shaped back in South Africa in 1955. A pivotal moment was the three weeks he spent convalescing from his appendicitis at the farm owned by the renowned Battle of Britain fighter pilot ace, Sailor Malan, an extraordinary personality who sacrificed his personal popularity in South Africa for the benefit of liberal policies and the fight against apartheid and racism.

Dad, quite by accident, met Sailor Malan as an unfortunate and unscheduled appendicitis operation curtailed his participation in the first half of the British Lions tour. The acute need for an operation to remove the inflamed appendix was diagnosed the day of the match against Griqualand West in Kimberley.

During his stay in London after World War II, Sailor Malan befriended Sir Ernest Oppenheimer and his son Harry, head of the Diamond Trading Company which handled De Beer's diamond sales in London. When he returned to South Africa in 1946 he was offered a position with Anglo-American in Johannesburg. Sailor, Sir Ernest, and Harry Oppenheimer shared a common vision for the people of South Africa, and when the racist National Party took over (1948) with DF Malan as its leader proposing to introduce its vile apartheid policy, Sailor was aghast at the disgrace that would inevitably fall on South Africa.

"His country," he wrote to a former British pilot with whom he had once flown, was now in danger of "losing its ticket" to remain in "the company of the civilised nations of the world," the "humane world of decent values" that had prevailed in 1945 and defeated Nazism.

The lines were drawn. Sailor wholeheartedly engaged in opposition, and swore to fight for the same principles that took him into the service of the Royal Air Force in the mid-1930s. He brought the same grit to bear that he used when piloting the Vickers Supermarine Spitfire, a fast and agile, technologically advanced, fighter. Sailor was a true hero; in May 1940 his 74 Squadron 'Tiger' fought over Dunkirk, inflicting losses on the enemy for which Malan was awarded the Distinguished Flying Cross. In the lull between the Dunkirk evacuation and the Battle of Britain, he flew perilous night sorties attacking Heinkel bombers. In August he moved up to Squadron Leader and took full command of 74 Squadron. His tally of enemy aircraft continued to rise, and by March 1941 he had bagged an astonishing 15 enemy aircraft destroyed, 6 jointly destroyed, 2 presumed destroyed, and 7 damaged.

Earlier, before the Battle of Britain, he had already established a formidable reputation as a tactician of aerial combat. The more widely-spread flying formations practised by his Squadron came eventually to be adopted as standard tactics by most Fighter Command units during 1941. His staccato style, *10 Rules of Air Fighting,* was easily and readily digested by all pilots. With its classic injunctions never to "fly straight and level for more than 30 seconds in the combat area," and to "fire short bursts of one to two seconds only", this precursor to the *Idiot's Guide'* quickly achieved widespread fame across Fighter Command and saved many a combat fighter.

Sailor's incredibly long "hour" as a fighter ace eventually saw him appointed commander of Biggin Hill fighter wing in 1941, and his final score - to use the cosy sporting vocabulary of deadly aerial combat - was 27 aircraft destroyed, 7 jointly destroyed, 3 presumed destroyed, and 16 damaged, a total of 53 aircraft. If you ever care to know what sort of man Sailor Malan was, he was brilliantly portrayed by the actor Robert Shaw in the 1969 epic movie, *The Battle Of Britain,* where the character of Squadron Leader "Skipper" - his bearing and conviction fully realised - represented implicitly a leader hard on himself and hard on his pilots.

Like all the best fighter pilots, Malan was essentially a duelling 'industrial engine' - cool, precise, and detached, his overriding emotion that of satisfaction at a telling hit in which "everything I had learned had come right". That included getting in very close, to make sure of a kill. In Fighter Command, the recommended range for opening fire was 400 yards. For Malan, it was usually a more intense and lethal 250 yards. Incredibly it was sometimes even less, he would think nothing of closing to an edgy 150 or a sometimes suicidal 100 yards.

Sailor reported that, in May 1940, being "very short of fuel", he "couldn't afford a long chase," and therefore "closed rather rapidly," racing in head-on, opening his guns at a nerveless 50 yards. For the enemy, death at the hands of the "Springbok Spitfire Killer" was the total destruction of a plane, its occupants as incidental as they were inaudible. In the aftermath of a 'kill', "you knew Sailor would be rubbing his hands, a bloody hard and cold pilot. "He just hated the Germans, always wanted to make a mess of them," said Dad.

Clem remembers Sailor as being a very social, immensely kind, and fascinating host for the three weeks or so he spent with him (June/July 1955). In the diamond town of Kimberley, he was at the centre of all things, serving as an effective constituency political agent for his friend, Harry Oppenheimer. Sailor was a family man, a charming raconteur, and cut a handsome figure. He was a fair and liberal-minded personality who Dad remembered seemed to have the respect and affection of all around him. Clem put him amongst a small group of men with whom he had an affinity and utmost respect. He always stated that Sailor had God-given leadership qualities, just like Wayne Shelford, the All Black captain, or Tony O'Reilly, his good friend, teammate, and billionaire entrepreneur.

Malan loved to throw a party - a trait that started in

the early 1940s, when his Biggin Hill fighter sector was renowned for throwing the most boisterous parties in all the war. Hunt Balls and Cabarets were a regular occurrence in between scrambles. That included what the *Tatler and Bystander* (June edition 1943) called "the most wizard wartime party", the lavish 'Thousand' party ever held at the Grosvenor House Hotel. In gossip-column guise as "War Ace throws a Party", its genial host, Group Captain Malan, was shown "in his accustomed manner", namely, "glass in hand" and with " an alluring woman guest" dangling on his arm.

Dad enjoyed telling the story of Sailor Malan's visit to a posh, snooty Southern English girls' public school, Cheltenham Ladies. The ace fighter pilot began to describe a thrilling combat "show" over the English Channel:

"Really, there was simply no time even to feel scared. I had two of these fuckers coming up on my tail. One fucker was coming up at me from the left, and then I spotted two more fuckers a few hundred feet above me, just waiting for their chance..." At this moment, an increasingly agitated headmistress stood up and interrupted the guest speaker. "Girls, as some of you may not know this, Group Captain Malan is referring to a common type of German aeroplane called the Focker". To which a bemused Sailor Malan retorted: "Madam, I don't know anything about that. All I can tell you and your girls is that those bloody fuckers were flying Messerschmitts."

Clem told me how during his convalescence Sailor would sit with him in the evenings on the verandah of his splendid sheep farm, and the two of them would share an ice cold beer whilst Sailor patiently answered a whole range of questions that Dad hurled at him. Dad said that it was his first exposure to the unpleasant realities of apartheid, although by 1955, Sailor had decided to withdraw from direct action liberal politics in South Africa. But Clem said it was Sailor who educated him on the politics of South Africa, and made him realise that amongst the whites, there was an enormous philosophical divide, roughly split by the Anglo/Boer divisions. He admitted that until the late 1960's he had falsely assumed that the white liberals would win the political arguments in an increasingly technocratic world, but the opposite had happened. The liberal opposition fell away, just as it had in the early 1950's when Sailor was active.

In 1951, the Springbok Legion and the Action Committee for War Veterans founded the Torch Commando as a means to combat the Nationalist government's plans to withhold the vote from non-white South Africans. As a founding member, Sailor became deeply involved in a movement which would fight for basic human rights and oppose political oppression - something that Dad confirmed was very important to him and for which he risked his life during World War II. But when the Liberal Party offered him a place in their ranks, he let them know, in no uncertain terms, that this struggle was above and beyond the political arena. Solving the problems of the impoverished non-white communities, such as lack of food, housing, education, and utilities, was more important than promising to do so politically as a means of gaining and keeping control.

Sailor Malan and the Torch Commando fought against the nationalist government's racial policies for more than 5 years and, at their peak, had a following of 250,000 members. The government of DF Malan were so concerned with the influence the movement might have under the leadership of the war hero Sailor Malan, that it undertook an aggressive, negative propaganda war to discredit the Torch Commando and its leaders. For the rest of his life, Sailor was totally ignored by the South African government, who caricatured him as a "flying poodle" dressed in leathers and flying goggles, in the service of Jan Smuts and the Jewish mine-bosses who were labelled the "Hochenheimers".

After his first heart attack, Dad became more self-aware of his own mortality, and would reflect on the huge diversity of people and characters he had encountered during his life. Because of the high tempo of his life, he noted that many of his best encounters were necessarily fleeting but still profound. I believe that the time he spent with Sailor Malan was possibly the most instructive for him during that Lions tour. Dad consistently said that the tour changed his life and general welt-view, and the influence of Sailor Malan was powerful and lasting; it cast a long shadow over all that followed and helped shape his convictions.

Sadly, in 1963, Sailor Malan lost his fight with Parkinson's disease and died at the young age of 52. Writing of his funeral, Owen Coetzer, the esteemed journalist and writer, contemplated:

> It was the swallows. On that gloomy September 1963 day, they seemed like purposeful, miniature Spitfires of another fateful September 23 years earlier.
> The summer of 1940
> The Battle of Britain
> In the gathering dusk, the swallows whirled and wove complicated patterns against the cemetery's tall cypress trees, oblivious to the piper's lament. "Flowers of the Forest", skirled to the sky. Then the "Last Post".
> A fitful breeze tugged at the wreaths that enveloped the simple grave in Kimberley's West End cemetery. Finally, the last figure turned, snapped a salute, and walked slowly away. The swallows flew on.
> A.G. "Sailor" Malan - South Africa's RAF Battle of Britain air ace had gone home. A neat grave, his last resting place.
> The epitaph on the headstone reads: *In the shadow of Thy wings will I rejoice."*

Over the years, Clem met and knew many Welsh MPs

from all sides of the political spectrum. There was one amusing encounter he liked to recount that took place at his butcher's shop in Mumbles involving a much-maligned Tory. John Redwood, who was Secretary of State for Wales at the time, pitched up one sunny summer's day. He was on a walkabout in the company of one of the few Swansea conservative councilors, Bill Hughes. Bill was an old friend of Dad's and over the years they had shared some property dealings. Redwood was experiencing yet another bout of public opprobrium, with regular rumours about his precarious political future in Wales being punted on almost a daily basis in one form of media or another. Redwood is probably best remembered for his rather crass, pathetic attempt to mime his way through the Welsh national anthem - *Mae hen wlad fy nhadau yn annwyl i mi* - at a Welsh conservative conference (1993). It is, without doubt, one of the truly great butt-clenching moments in politics. Dafydd Wigley, the Plaid Cymru MP, said that Redwood "went down like a rat sandwich in Wales". Dad greeted his Tory visitors, and mischievously asked, in an innocent voice full of double entendre, "There's so much talk of chop in the news today, perhaps the Secretary of State might like to buy some from a real butcher shop?" Dad said Redwood didn't flinch nor indeed even blink, but morphed into his full on 'Vulcan' alter ego. Dad was taken aback as he quickly turned on his heels and fled for the safety of Mumbles seafront, his face frozen in the mask of the patrician Saxon Gauleiter.

Another prominent Tory who Dad knew quite well, through the various business clubs and networks of Swansea and Neath, was one of the apostles of the Thatcher revolution. Lord Cecil Parkinson went on to become Chairman of the Conservative Party. He had been to Cambridge where he won an athletics blue in the 200 and 400 yards, and that qualified him for the Hawke's Club of which Clem was also a member.

Parkinson recalls going out on the town in Swansea in

the late 1950s and early '60s with executives from Metal Box in Neath and other tinplate businesses, and meeting up with Clem. He was a chartered accountant by trade and had originally started his career with Metal Box. Dad always rated him as the sort of conservative that he could identify with, since he came from a solid working-class background in Lancashire, and had won a scholarship to Emmanuel College at Cambridge. Parkinson was the very epitome of meritocracy, yet ironically became identified with some of the worst consequences of right wing monetarist economics.

I remember, sometime in the late 1980s, returning to South Wales on the train from Paddington, and quite by chance, I had the pleasure of sharing a carriage with Viscount Tonypandy, George Thomas. He had recently retired as Speaker of the House of Commons. George kept me amused by telling the story of how you can identify a Welsh lobster pot, amongst a line consisting of English, Irish, French, and Welsh pots. Of course, it was all about Welsh parochialism, and the moral was the rather narrow view of the world my compatriots seek refuge in. He reasoned that you can easily identify the Welsh lobster pot as it's the only one where if any lobster has the gumption to escape, the others grab at him and prevent it, ultimately ensuring their collective demise. A kind of 'if I can't have it, then neither can you' existential condition.

I personally experienced this peculiarly Welsh phenomenon when working back in Wales in the late 1980s for the Welsh Development Agency (WDA). I was running the inward investment effort from Europe and the rest of the UK. The policy promoted by a Conservative Secretary of State for Wales proved so successful that it started to cause consternation in Labour ranks and there was a lot of ill-feeling directed at the WDA. I was part of the new team and obviously dedicated to promoting the new ambitious policy. I hadn't really considered the option that I would be a target of in-fighting from my own team.

Rhodri Morgan, in my experience a third-rate politician who epitomised a rather dull, prole-type approach to politics, foolishly wrote to the auditor general, Sir John Bourne, and accused me of abusing WDA expenses. It was all pretty petty stuff and the main accusation was that I dined every Friday in a Swansea restaurant with the chairman of the agency, Gwyn Jones.

Gwyn lived in Gower, and had appointed an executive assistant from Price Waterhouse Coopers, a very clever chartered accountant called Chris Richards. I knew Chris from way back, having trained with him and even shared a flat with him before he got married. I'd also played rugby with him for Swansea. Without exception, all of our mutual friends thought we were like identical twins. I guess we very much might have seemed that way, both being 6ft 4ins with rugby builds; although I did look like a second row, seasoned in the boiler house, whereas Chris played on the wing out of harm's way. He has me to thank for his rugby career, and for winning a 100m sprint and being acclaimed 'fastest wing in Wales'.

Rhodri Morgan, in his desperation to condemn Wales' record-breaking inward investment performance in 1992 - a case of pissing on your own parade - resorted to hiding behind parliamentary privilege. He made a series of erroneous accusations, directing them at several individuals from Swansea, me included.

The truth came out in the wash, as it usually does. The chairman, Gwyn Jones, had organised regular lunches in Swansea each Friday to fit his timetable around commitments - he was a part-time appointment after all, and he willingly gave the WDA over 60 hours per week. It turned out that I had been mistaken for Chris Richards, his executive assistant. My comrades in the scrum had a good giggle about that - imagine being mistaken for a winger! Chris was often confused with me when Clem was present because people just assumed he was his eldest son. I remember one occasion when Clem took Chris along to a

Swansea v Llanelli fixture at Stradey Park. Chris Richards sat next to Derek Quinnell and they talked all match winding each other up over the Jack v Turk rivalry and having a good old laugh. Derek didn't realise until the end of the match that Chris wasn't Clem's eldest son!

What's more, years later at a rugby function in Cardiff, Rhodri Morgan admitted that he had used the letter writing as a means of targeting the Conservatives. He confided that the others and I were all merely collateral damage in a political battle. Ever since that occasion I've always considered comrade Rhodri an appalling man. Clem encouraged me to seek legal advice because he was also cited in the scurrilous letter sent on House of Commons writing paper to Sir John Bourne, the auditor general. However, a prominent barrister advised me that the issue of shadow parliamentary privilege is so murky and imprecise that any legal action on mine or Clem's part to seek redress would only have served to satisfy an urge for revenge on the rogue Morgan. Quite frankly we weren't prepared to spend the money.

Peter Walker, the architect of the policy that ruffled Rhodri's feathers, had been appointed Secretary of State for Wales by Margaret Thatcher. Walker was probably the most gifted politician I ever worked with. He used the appointment to run Wales as if he were its prime minister, or at the very least, the executive mayor of a city with 2.9 million people. Peter was quite bold in his vision; he wanted to raise living standards, and decided that his focus should be on employment creation in a country that was being so rapidly deindustrialised. The closure and cutbacks in coal and steel production were really starting to bite. His policy was to regenerate the Welsh economy using two primary approaches: firstly ramping up inward investment to generate immediate short-to-medium term jobs, and secondly, to put in place conditions that would stimulate indigenous businesses in the SME sector, a proven way of providing both short-term and long-term employment growth.

I was working in Bahrain, conducting import substitution project ideas and feasibility studies for the Ministry of Industry in Qatar, when I saw a job advert in *The Sunday Times*, outlining the requirements for three deputy-directors for Welsh Development International (WDI). Being a proud Welshman I didn't hesitate, and applied for the post of the European and U.K. foreign direct investment markets. Then followed a series of grueling interviews until I finally took up the post in 1988, and for the next three years worked closely with two conservative Secretaries of State, firstly Peter Walker, and later David Hunt.

Peter Walker had real political ability, and I found him to be an accomplished, articulate, confident Minister who bore his office comfortably. In fact, so comfortably, that he began to run his own Welsh foreign policy, using the WDA as his policy instrument, often with myself as the tip of the spear. Within the European Union at that time there was a fashionable view that to make the whole concept of Europe mean something to ordinary people, it was necessary, if not essential, to generate close ties at regional levels, and not just government to government.

It was generally preferred that these ties had to be beyond the city council twinning schemes which contributed very little. The leader of the most economically dynamic region in West Germany at that time was the Minister-President of Baden-Wurttemberg, Lothar Spath, who espoused a theory he called the Four Motors of Europe, which were the 4 regions of Baden-Wurttemberg, Rhone-Alpes, Lombardy, and Catalonia, between which he wanted to form extremely close economic ties so that business, R&D, foreign direct investment, and trade would flow freely between the four regions, thereby ensuring growth and future prosperity across the continent.

Peter Walker met Lothar Spath at a foreign office

function in London, and decided that Wales should become the "fifth motor". Walker agreed with the Spath thesis that a policy of regionalism across Europe would be more relevant to the localities who could build long-term links with each other.

Walker had already established an advisory board of heavyweight Welsh businessmen to counsel and coach the directors of WDI on our strategies for securing foreign direct investment. I remember the first hastily arranged briefing lunch in the Welsh Office in Whitehall. The three newly appointed deputy-directors were summoned by our Chairman, the dynamic and effective Dr Gwyn Jones, to meet the other members of the Advisory Board, which included Sir John Harvey Jones, the charismatic British TV business icon, and Chairman of ICI no less. I had been in post for less than 3 days, and as we sat down to lunch expecting a general chit-chat on the subject of inward investment, I distinctly overheard Gwyn Jones say,

"Now Chris will give us a summary of the overall European strategy and prospects for the next three months".

I must have looked a little startled, as indeed I was, and happened to look Sir John Harvey-Jones in the eye at that very moment. He gave me an enormous and encouraging wink! He knew that I had been dropped in it from a colossal height. I bull-shitted my way through what I had picked up from briefing documents I had hastily read on the train to London, and all the while he kept giving me approving nods of his huge leonine head. This all served to keep Peter Walker at bay and thankfully, Wales was at that moment completing a major Bosch project, which deflected any further discussion.

Within six months of Walker meeting Spath, I had established an office in Das Haus der Wirtschaft, the economics ministry in Stuttgart. This was despite considerable effort from the Foreign Office to prevent us. Our principal road block to becoming the '5th Motor' was not, as you might imagine, other competing U.K. Regions, but the British Ambassador, Sir Christopher Mallaby. Mallaby kept writing letters of complaint and criticism about Welsh Development International's activities, arguing that the foreign office had laid the ground work for Birmingham to become the '5th Motor'. Wales was portrayed by Mallaby as a region in perpetual decline, a wasteland of deindustrializing old smoke stack industries. He argued the Midlands was better placed and already attracting new car plants and inward investment. These foreign office papers were fed back to us by Peter Walker who had been warned of the diplomats' shenanigans by Margaret Thatcher. Walker confided that she would simply shovel a bunch of papers onto his blotter in the Cabinet room and tip him the wink!

In my experience there was no sign of anyone from the Midlands, or indeed Birmingham, in Stuttgart - they were conspicuous by their absence. With an open field we signed an official, binding agreement with the government of Baden-Wurtenberg, the ceremony held in the economics ministry. Sir Christopher Mallaby was, of course present, and as Walker and Spath shook hands, he asked me how on earth we had managed to pull this off. I remember fixing the esteemed, famous British diplomat in the eyes, and saying: "It was very easy Ambassador. I simply turned up here and asked…"

The major attraction for the Baden-Wurtenberg firms was to provide a bridge into the logistics chain of the regenerated British automotive industry. One major investment made at that time was a brand new Bosch component plant just outside Cardiff, and other firms quickly followed.

After the success in Baden-Wurtenberg, we developed the programme and opened an office in the Chamber of Commerce in Milan, the capital of Lombardy, Italy's wealthiest region. Wales built links with Pirelli, Fiam, and Cogefar - the specialist tunnelling contractor

owned by the Fiat group. Cogefar went on to build the
tunnel system in Cardiff Bay, and entered a joint venture
to develop Cardiff Gate. At the signing dinner in Milan, I
remember the Italians being delighted with a small gift we
gave them from Wales: it was a CD recording of a 14-year-
old Pavarotti singing in his father's choir at the Llangollen
Eisteddfod in the early 1950s.

The most dramatic and memorable visit I can recall
was accompanying David Hunt, Secretary of State for
Wales after the 1992 election. We went to Lyon in Rhone-
Alpes to meet the mayor Michel Noir, Charles Millon the
President, and Alain Merieux the pharmaceutical tycoon.
Sadly, we had just arrived in Lyon when news came
through late that afternoon that David Hunt's father had
suddenly died; both Gwyn Jones and I were with David
when the sad news arrived. I remember instructing the
concierge of the hotel to investigate flights to the UK, and
he advised intelligently that he should fly from Geneva,
not Lyon. So we got David back to Manchester, and the
Wirral, where he was from, that same night. The outcome
was that the Secretary of State instructed Gwyn Jones, the
Chairman of the Welsh Development Agency, to carry on
the official visit, and that it should not be cancelled. We
embarked on a two-day series of visits, with Gwyn playing
the lead, and me backing him up. The fun part was being
driven around the great city of Lyon in a stretch,
ambassadorial limousine, accompanied by four motor-bike
gendarmes, who stopped the traffic at will as we sped from
appointment to appointment.

Clem used to love hearing about these adventures
across Europe, and took great pride in the fact that I was
able to operate on the European stage. He was ever the
pro-European, and always encouraged me to become
bilingual in French, and German.

The most memorable character I was fortunate to
meet and get to know during this period was Manfred
Rommel, who was the Mayor of Stuttgart (1974-96), the

only son of Field Marshall Erwin Rommel - the legendary 'Desert Fox' who fought a brilliant military campaign in North Africa during the war.

I dined with him privately on several occasions, where he always proved a positive and constructive force encouraging Stuttgart-based companies to expand operations in Wales, particularly in the automotive components sector. Stuttgart is the home of Porsche and Daimler. He was a very witty and funny man, always looking for a gag, like a benevolent, wise uncle, and at times seeming to behave in the opposite manner to that you would expect from the son of the German Reich's most famous Field Marshall. He was highly regarded across continents, and I was lucky to have met such an accomplished individual. He became a liberal voice in post-war West Germany, supporting the rights of immigrants, backing civil liberties, and strengthening Suttgart's Jewish population. His politics are described as tolerant, liberal, and internationalist. He became a good friend of David Montgomery, the son of his father Erwin Rommel's great adversary, Field Marshall Bernard Montgomery - a friendship viewed by some as a symbol of British-German reconciliation following the war and West Germany's admission into NATO.

His response to the Nazis' horror was to emphasise the unity of Europe rather than German patriotism: "German history is too much for us", he told *The Times*. "The shadow is too great...I belong to the generation of burned children, and I am not so sure about our capabilities. My father once said during the war, "The best thing would be to live as a British dominion now that we have shown we can't manage our own affairs..." He was being sarcastic, of course. When I asked him in conversation how difficult it was to bear such a distinctive surname in modern West Germany, he replied that it served as a warning to everyone to never again march so willingly into a dictatorship.

Playing politics was a small part of Clem's life, but an important cameo in the canvas that he was painting. He always joked about being a defender of lost causes, but the role of underdog never suited him fully. At his funeral in 1996 I was approached by Richard Livesey, later Baron Livesey of Talgarth, who had won the by-election for Brecon and Radnor in 1985, and became Chairman of the Welsh Liberal party. He quietly and graciously introduced himself to me and spoke glowingly for five or so minutes about his affection for Clem and the contribution that he felt Clem had made to the Liberal cause in Wales. I rather think Clem would have enjoyed those kind words.

8

THE JACQUES HERTET OLD BOYS

"A Vaincre Sans Peril, on Triomphe sans Gloire…To Win Without Risk is to Triumph Without Glory."
Pierre Corneille, Le Cid (1636)

"He was born in Paris in a big white house on a little square off Avenue Foch. Of a mother blonde and beautiful and a father quiet and rich."
J.P. Donleavy, The Beautiful Beatitudes of Balthazar B.

Clem's first visit to France was in 1947 to captain the Welsh Schoolboys against the French team at the Stade Colombes Olympic stadium in Paris. It was the beginning of a life-long love affair with a country whose pleasures and contradictions both delighted and enthralled Clem until his passing. The experience of that visit alone perfectly encapsulates the Hemingway quote: "if you are lucky enough to have lived in Paris as a young man, then wherever you go for the rest of your life, it stays with you, for Paris is a moveable feast."

For the next 50 years Clem tucked into his French feast, buying a property in Saint-Vivien in the Medoc, north of Lesparre, in the mid-1980s, where he spent as much time as he could afford, primarily in the summer months. Saint-Vivien was a perfectly self-contained and tranquil village with two charcuteries, two bakeries, a convenience store, and a bar/restaurant in the square; add a travelling market every Saturday morning and it was ideal. The village was rural, quiet, and authentic. Clem adored the simplicity, and its location provided fabulous access to the nearby beaches of Montalivet and Soulac, the great Medoc classifications and vineyards, and further south a gateway to the whole of sud'Ouest France which Clem had fallen in love with ever since his first rugby tour there in 1949. However, Clem's journalism commitments with *The Observer* and latterly the *Independent on Sunday,* meant he was called away to attend the first Rugby World Cup in New Zealand in 1987, the Lions tours to Australia in 1989, and again to New Zealand in 1993.

There was a certain symmetry to his career as a player; his first cap was won against France at Colombes in 1949, and his last cap won, as captain also at Colombes in 1959. Clem witnessed over this period the evolution and growth of French rugby from also-rans in the 1940s to arguably the best team in the world by the early 1960s. In Paris for his first cap, Clem played against the great Jean Prat from Lourdes - for many years leading cap holder for France with 51 caps - and affectionately known as 'Monsieur Rugby' in France after his exploit of dropping two goals against England in 1955. That year, when France played Wales in Paris for the Grand Slam, Wales won 16-11, giving them a share of the Championship. But such was the esteem for Jean Prat, playing his last game in Paris, that the Welsh players carried him off on their shoulders; a fitting tribute to a great player. When he died, Michel Crauste, who succeeded him as flanker and captain of Lourdes and France, said as an epitaph, "Jean could make his team-mates put their bodies on the line because he always did it himself. He had inside him all the rugby values".

This impressive improvement in French rugby tracks

the eleven years of Clem's playing career, with Wales winning 5 straight from 1952-57, followed by 4 French wins (1958-61).

During this period France shared the 5 Nations Championship in 1954 (with Wales and England) and in 1955 (with Wales). They won their first outright title in 1959, shared the title with England in 1960, and won again in 1961. During these years the French were successful against the Southern Hemisphere teams, beating the All Blacks - thanks to a match-winning try by Jean Prat - and the Australians in 1954 and 1958. Amazingly, they won a series in South Africa in 1958, in an epic two test battle, drawing the first test in Newlands, Cape Town, 3-3, followed by the 9-5 victory in Johannesburg. France produced another sterling performance, drawing with the Springboks in 1960.

At the end of the 1950s, the French team was captained by another giant of a man in terms of rugby skills, leadership, and tactical intelligence. Clem once described him as "this bulldozer of a man with brains". His name was Dr Lucien Mias from Mazamet and he won 29 caps (1951-59). Mias was an early proponent for concussion protocols in rugby and lobbied the federation for many years. France was a deep well of mercurial, prodigious talent during this era, producing great players like Alfred Roques of Cahors, Michel Crauste of Lourdes, Michel Vannier of Racing Club de France, Michel Celaya of Biarritz and *Le Duc*, Amédée Domenech of Brive. The one trait they all shared, in Dad's considered opinion, was outstanding athleticism and handling skills, and they loved to put the ball out wide to the wings, whilst their forward play was ferocious, and at times pretty wild.

Clem loved the unpredictability of the French, as he said you never quite knew what they would do next. Mias was a 'difference maker' for France because he imposed his personality on the whole group by insisting on better discipline – he added a back-bone of steel, preventing

French teams from unravelling if placed under heavy pressure. Clem said you knew you'd won when you heard the bickering begin, with certain French players screaming at others with the inevitable shoulder shrugging that followed.

Mias was a tactical thinker, and one of the first players to develop line-out concepts. He realised the benefits of the spinning, driving maul that required 120kg forwards to pirouette like ballet dancers and used it to great effect whilst playing for his club Mazamet. He played against an aging Jean Prat in the 1958 French Championship final, when the two men famously hurled insults at each other. "You are not Monsieur Rugby, you are Mr Anti-Rugby" shouted Mias. Prat replied, "And as for you, if you got rid of your mouth, there'd be nothing left of you".

The catalyst for Clem's love affair with France was ironically not through the contacts he had made whilst playing rugby for Wales, but through his ongoing involvement in the sport as a rugby journalist with *The Observer*, which necessitated his attendance at the 5 Nations Championship games in places like Paris, Twickenham, and all the home unions, and his subsequent relationship with tennis correspondent Paul Haedens, who introduced Clem to the French Davis Cup player Philippe Chatrier. The eternal bond with France was strengthened further by the sudden death in a car crash of a much loved Parisian sports journalist, Robert de Thomasson, who wrote under a pseudonym as Jacques Hertet.

Haedens and Chatrier decided to organise a rugby match to commemorate their great friend de Thomasson, and so the Jacques Hertet Old Boys were created. They soon became more commonly known as the Hertet Old Boys. The invitation side was a mix of journalists, along with a formidable smattering of ex-French internationals, including legends like Robert Soro, Bambi Moga, Jean Dauger, Jean Prat, and Alain Porthault. Other characters from many different corners of French life were also roped in.

There were tennis champions Marcel Bernard and Tony Trabert, Olympic athletes Georges Damitio and Marcel Hansenne, even a newspaper editor from Pau, Rene Hegoburu - whose wife Yvonne created the Jurancon vineyard, Domaine de Souch, in his memory - the writer Jean-Loup Dabadie, co-author with Serge Gainsbourg of the musical *Anna*, and most bizarrely of all, the veteran volcanologist Haroun Taziev. Over the years many others were invited to join.

Clem was originally involved in establishing the ex-Welsh international team that played the inaugural match against Jacques Hertet Old Boys in Paris (1961). This was the beginning of his long association of being one of the organisers of the British opposition to the Hertet Old Boys who were always represented by a bunch of ex-French internationals. By the mid-1960s Dad, along with Peter Robbins, the man with the Beaujolais belt, started travelling regularly to play in French Old Boy tournaments in a variety of collaborative matches that celebrated birthdays, anniversaries, or more often than not, just an excuse for a gargantuan piss-up in the provinces.

In 1967 Dad took Peter Robbins down to Bordeaux for the final of the French rugby Championship between Montauban and Begles, the club I played for in 1977. He described the occasion in *The Observer:*

> Self-acknowledged Francophiles, both in terms of rugby and 'degustation', we headed the car 401 miles to the south in high humour. It was raining but the horizons were bright. After a three-hour lunch at Tours, where the 82 year old 'patron' drank Chartreuse with us and informed us that his rude health was due to riding a bicycle and being faithful to his wife, we headed for Poitiers and ran into the red-roofed Midi and the sun.

Once passed Angouleme, we were into the Sud-Ouest, the deep heart of French rugby. In no time we were in Bordeaux, where by arrangement, we met up with the great Bambi Moga, the formidable French forward of the late 1940's, now 26 stone of gentle charm and the coach for Begles, one of the finalists.

Bambi revealed the impressive programme for the weekend, the intricacies of the French Championship, and the impression that French rugby has been betrayed this season by playing the Camberabero brothers, who stifled French style and attacking flair.

In a small backroom we met the new revolutionary council of French rugby: the new President, M. Marcel Batigne, and Jacques Chaban-Delmas, the President of the Assemblée nationale and also Mayor of Bordeaux. They were powerfully square, strong-eyed and affluently gold-toothed. You sensed they were men of purpose and perhaps that this was the leadership which is making rugby the most rapidly growing team game in France.

On Saturday we attended the ceremonial laying of the foundation stone for the new Begles Stadium. At five o'clock in the evening came our hour of truth. We had to play in a four team tournament. Peter Robbins, Andy Mulligan and I played for the Jacques Hertet Old Boys, a sort of veteran French Barbarians side, together with some great French veterans, Robert Soro the lion of Swansea, Alvarez Albaladejo known as Monsieur le drop, Jean Dauger and at prop forward, the 52 year old Haroun Tazieff.

To our astonishment we beat a young RTF side...

And so Clem and Robbins took themselves off to the bar to celebrate. As was their wont they did not partake lightly.

We were stuffing the booze down and were half cut when to our horror someone came in and told us we were playing again in an hour," said Clem. "We hadn't realised that we were taking part in a triangular tournament and we were now coming up for the big one. For the medal.

They got themselves quickly back onto the field and were winning right up until the end when the opposition, the Begles veterans, scored a try and went in front.

There was a minute to go," says Clem, "and I said to Robbins that I was going to get the ball from the kick-off, dummy, make ground, give the ball to Robbins who was to draw the full-back and send Mulligan between the posts for the winning try…

"Bollocks!" said Robbins, but we kicked off, I got the ball, dummied, made ground, waited for Robbins who drew the full-back and sent Mulligan in between the posts for the winning try. Robbins said, 'I've heard of Welsh wizardry but this is bloody ridiculous', with Clem adding that Robbins never got over the indignity of "my having to wait for him to give him the pass."

This weekend typified and best illustrates the enormous pleasure Dad took from his involvement with such a richly diversified group of French characters, and defines an ultimate version of entente cordiale, where cordiale was the voluminous quantity of French cuisine and fine wines consumed. The Old Boys set forth on a quest to celebrate deep, longstanding friendships within their unique freemasonry in an annual batch of legendary lost weekends in Paris and the Provinces.

The ritual was for the Hertet Old Boys to play their match in Paris on the Friday afternoon before either the France versus England or Wales matches, followed by a communal supper held in Haroun Tazieff's magnificent 14th century apartment on the Isle de la Cite. Haroun, whom I had the pleasure of meeting on many occasions - including the time we managed to polish off a 1964 Chateau Petrus - was a Polish born French volcano expert whose dramatic films of exploding volcanoes and fiery lava streams made him and volcanoes familiar to television viewers in France and beyond.

Haroun was to volcanology what Jacques Cousteau was to the deep sea. Indeed, they were very close friends and shared multiple expeditions together over the years. President Mitterrand appointed him Secretary of State for Natural and Technological Disasters, or "Minister for Mini-catastrophes" as Haroun liked to call himself. He once confidently predicted that Nice would be hit by a catastrophic earthquake, creating a mighty fuss in France. Thankfully it is yet to happen. He famously clashed, in 1976 with Claude Allègre, a scientist who wanted 75,000 villagers evacuated from the slopes of Soufriere volcano on the island of Guadeloupe. Tazieff argued that there was no risk and turned out to be right.

More controversially he cast doubts on global warming: "Global warming is an outright invention. It is absolutely unproved, and in my view it is a lie," he once said. He also argued that holes in the ozone layer, which have been blamed on chlorofluorocarbons were discovered as far back as 1926, long before chlorofluorocarbons were even invented.

Haroun was an extraordinary character; he didn't play his first game of rugby until the invite from the Hertet Old Boys in the early 1960's, when he was 50 years old. He played at prop, and was still playing on his 80th birthday party, which was celebrated with a game of touch rugby!

The Hertet Old Boys always got together on the

Friday evening for what the French call le troisième mi-temps, the third half for the after-match meal and festivities. Players came from all over the South of France, with most contributing something to the occasion. Bambi Moga was a charcutier in Bordeaux, and obviously brought the charcuterie; his brother Andre, vice President of the French Rugby Union was a cheese wholesaler, the Toulouse gang, led by the Haedens family, brought along the goose and duck cassoulet. There was always case upon case of wine brought from every region of France.

Clem, Peter Robbins, and Andy Mulligan would bring bottles of Glenfiddich Malt Whisky, much to the delight of Bambi and George Damitio who were thirsty disciples of the Scottish tipple. The meal would be put together by the wives and girlfriends, and the large reception gallery would be set up with trestle tables and benches to sit upon. In the high-ceilinged Gothic stone hall, I used to feel as if I was dining in some medieval Benedictine monastery, but those thoughts were quickly dispelled by the enormous quantities of vin rouge consumed.

Charles de Gaulle once asked, "How can you govern a country which has 246 varieties of cheese?" Clem used to say that Robbins would make the perfect President as he had eaten all 246 of them! The two friends were close buddies, but there was always a competitive edge or barb, no matter the joke or jape. That particular evening, as Haroun's feast climaxed with the Armagnac and Glenfiddich, Clem and Peter got into an argument over who was the better athlete. One jibe led to another, until Peter called Clem out, and suggested a 100-yard race downstairs in the street to decide matters.

Dad was never one to back down and instantly agreed. The 70 party guests, led by Haroun all trooped out and descended en masse onto the Quai des Fleurs. 100 yards was duly marked out and the two men sprinted the distance. Clem took the honours, surprising his younger friend. Peter Robbins was not assuaged by his loss, accusing Clem of a late elbow in the ribs that afforded him a good two-yard head start. After a spot of further bickering, Dad foolishly bragged that Robbins could choose any contest, even tiddlywinks, and Clem would always win.

Now Peter knew Clem very well indeed, and swimming was not a strong suit, so he challenged him to a race across the River Seine. Dad accepted, fuelled by both his sprint victory and a further shot of Armagnac that Robert Soro was liberally passing around to toast Clem's victory. At this point, Haroun Tazieff and George Damitio stepped forward to urge caution and restraint - qualities sadly lacking in Paris on the eve of a 5 nations fixture.

Georges informed them they would surely die if they jumped in the Seine at that late hour. Not only due to the arctic temperature but also because of the fierce currents and flow of the river. Dad and Peter were not to be dissuaded, and ignoring this sound French wisdom, they emptied their glasses of Armagnac and resolutely marched off to the banks of the Seine. They alighted at the Pont d'Arcole, both intending to best each other across that stretch of river. There were further wiser heads who tried to intercede and talk some sense into both men. But their words fell on deaf ears and without further ado, stripping to their boxer shorts, the two men dived into the inky blackness of the Seine.

Dad said, "As soon as I hit the water, I knew I was in trouble. We had agreed to stick together, but a current had hit me and whisked me 10 yards downstream at an incredible rate, plus it was fucking cold. At that moment and for the next 5 minutes or so I was fighting for my life."

The current swept the two men quickly downstream. The horrified Hertet Old Boys set out in hot pursuit, some on foot, some commandeered bicycles and the savvy by fast car. There was a mad scramble to keep sight of the hapless ex-international rugby players as the Seine swept them away, down the Quai de la Corse, onto the Quai de l'Horloge, and finally a rescue party managed to pluck them from the jaws of death by the Pont Neuf.

For years after Clem and Robbins dined out on what they called their "Call me to God" moment, with Robbins declaring it a "bloody miracle" that that the two of them had survived. He was amazed that Clem had - after all, he could barely swim in the first place. Dad was coughing and spluttering and complained of a bronchial virus for months afterwards, blaming the polluted waters of the Seine and of course, Peter Robbins' contribution to the virus pool - Vive l' Entente Cordiale.

Dad loved the very special freemasonry his participation in the Jacques Hertet Old Boys afforded him, and the breadth of friendships he developed as a result. The catalyst had been Philippe Chatrier, who Dad absolutely adored and was probably the world's leading tennis administrator over the past 50 years. He developed his original powerbase in 1953 by founding his magazine, Tennis de France, in which his editorials made clear his dissatisfaction with the way the game of tennis was being run, and his vision for the future.

Chatrier met Jack Kramer, the American promoter who kept the professional game alive in the 1950s by signing one Wimbledon champion after another. Kramer actually approached my aunt Elizabeth during Junior Wimbledon offering her the opportunity to turn pro in the late 1950's! At that time, top amateurs were paid under the table to stay amateur. Like many who wanted to see tennis flourish, Chatrier became frustrated when one attempt to create "open" tennis after the next was blocked by amateur federation officials who were scared stiff of losing their perks and privileges. French tennis consists of a collection of regions, each with its own powerbase, and nothing could be achieved without them onside. Philippe realised this and hatched a plot.

In 1968, he persuaded his friend, the amiable Marcel

Bernard who had won the French single title in 1946, to run for the Presidency of the French tennis federation when Jean Borotra, one of the original musketeers of the 1920s, retired. "You'll win easily and then you can keep the seat warm for me," said Chatrier. "It will give me time to travel around and try to educate the regional presidents." The plan worked perfectly, and he began a massive modernisation of tennis in France once he took over in 1973.

By 1977 he was also President of the International Tennis Federation, and in 1988 joined the International Olympic Committee, getting tennis back as a full-time medal sport in the Seoul Olympics. His major contribution was also in the way he managed the professionalisation of both men's and women's tennis, insisting that professional sport could not just become a question of playing for pots of money, but that any sport, in order to remain credible, had to rely on its roots and traditions.

Chatrier decided to follow the golf model, insisting that there be 4 Major Open tournaments: Australia, French, Wimbledon, and the USA Open. Plus, tennis would continue with a relaunched Davis Cup competition annually to allow players the privilege and challenge of representing their countries, albeit in an individual sport. It is for these achievements that the centre court at Roland-Garros in Paris, which Philippe dramatically developed in the 1970s, is called the Philippe Chatrier court.

Philippe was a good-looking man in the classic Alain Delon style, except most people thought him more handsome than Delon. He had a sharp intelligence and penetrating gaze. Philippe took no prisoners, and embodied the steel fist in a velvet glove approach to life. He adored Clem, and my first *en famille* experience in France was *chez* the Chatrier family, his first wife Suzanne and two sons, Jean-Philippe and William. But neither boy shared my tastes for playing sport, and the next year I was despatched to the Damitio family. In France, Philippe

Chatrier was treated like a demigod, and he became one of the world's most accomplished sports administrators.

The second actor who was responsible for cementing Clem's friendship with Philippe Chatrier and who also became a close friend of Peter Robbins, was Paul Haedens. Paul was quite simply a lovely man to spend time with. He was the editor of the *Tennis de France* magazine started by Chatrier, with whom he won the French tennis journalists men's doubles championship in 1957. He also became the chief sports correspondent for the *Journal du Dimanche,* and took a particular interest in covering rugby. For twenty years from 1956 to 1975 he anchored the famous Sunday Sport television programme which had a TV audience of over 10 million in France. Paul was a charming, softly-spoken, intuitive, ever-smiling character who could always improve your day by simply saying, "bonjour".

Paul Haedens absolutely doted on Dad. In his eyes Clem was a sporting giant, a true rugby icon, someone whose playing exploits and achievements he personally witnessed throughout the 1950s. Paul always told me how he thought Clem represented his chosen sport, country, and indeed mankind in general with such élan and graciousness, that he was the greatest ambassador that ever walked the earth. He was absolutely fascinated by Clem's background and back-story. The 'Welshness' was completely 'other' to him and cast a spell over the bourgeois, liberal, literary French classes, which included his famous novelist brother Kléber. Who Pierre Assouline, the acclaimed writer and journalist, described as "a right anarchist, a companion of Blondin, one of his best friends, a man who loved literature and sport, rugby in particular…" The simple fact of being Welsh elicited a very different reaction from Paul, Kléber, and all the other Hertet Old Boys. Dad always sensed that his 'Welshness' set him apart and gave him an aura that his English friends, like Peter Robbins could never hope to match; being Welsh meant mystery, dragon's breath, and Celtic

legends, whereas being English simply meant les rosbifs.
Clem felt that the French appreciated the Welsh for our
natural nonconformism, nationhood, and language,
perhaps epitomised by Wales's stature in the rugby world
as one of the top rugby playing nations.

Kléber was obviously inspired because he went on to
immortalise Clem in his famous novel *Adios*, published in
1974. He set the first chapter in Langland Bay and the
Gower, around a Wales v France 5 Nations match in
Cardiff. Kléber created a character, Gwynne Griffiths, who
he based totally on Clem, and dedicated the book to
'Caroline', ostensibly his wife, but he also told Clem it was
for his daughter who he found so captivating on his
regular visits to us in Wales. This extract is from early in
the novel:

> The following morning Gwynne Griffiths, driving
> his small red car had shown me around the Gower
> peninsula. It was quite cool, for it was only the
> second day of Spring. I remember that Gwynne
> had stopped for a piss in the grass on the side of
> the road, and had indicated with a slightly sad
> shrug of his shoulders the house where Dylan
> Thomas lived. Immediately I recalled his round
> head, the curly hair, the clear eyes of the Swansea
> poet now long dead, supposedly according to
> rumour, from having drunk too much. I wasn't
> sure if the house of which Dylan had spoken of in
> Under Milk Wood was near the shore of this
> peninsula leaning towards the sea, such a
> mysterious country dominated by the chimney
> stacks in places like Llanelli. At the same time I
> thought of this woman whom Dylan had married
> and loved through to the end, this Caitlin
> Macnamara who walked alongside him throughout
> his journey. I ask myself today if the passions of
> the rugby match, the excitement of the dinner on

the eve of the match in The Dragon Hotel, the appearance of the black ponies on the marshes, the memory of Dylan Thomas, now eloping under the ground, and the images of Caitlin Macnamara in my head hadn't prepared me in a special way for the fable of Caswell Bay.

Gwynne Griffiths looked a little like Dylan Thomas, since he had rounded cheeks and clear eyes. Ten years earlier he captained the Welsh team relying on a wise head and a ferocious punch. At that time he lived in Cambridge where he studied Greek. Since then he had become a livestock dealer in Swansea and he was writing a book on rugby in which he wanted to redefine the laws of the game. We were behind the pine trees in Langland, focused on devouring a Montmorency duck. Gwynne was 6 feet 2 inches tall and weighed 97 kg.

Adios, a novelistic autobiography, is a great novel of love, where we see the hero, Jérôme, going from failure to failure in love, *a la Truffaut*, until finally he knows how to love and be loved. The book begins with the description of a rugby match at the Five Nations, where Jérôme meets a strikingly beautiful young journalist and they fall into bed. A long string of affairs follow with many discussions about the meaning of love. The book is built on a back and forth, imperceptible narrative; a mixing of eras and judgement on how adolescent love is tempered by adult behaviour. Jérôme plays his first rugby game in Cherbourg and it's his escape from his strict colonial parents. He says, "I never heard my parents say anything other than: "Tomorrow is the end. The soup is not salty enough. Put your hands on the table. Do you think it will be fine on Sunday?" The reader is encouraged to support Jérôme in his quest for liberation. The book follows a predictably Gallic path and Jérôme (spoiler alert) suddenly and unexpectedly falls in love, only for tragedy to strike at the end. The book won Kléber the *Grand Prix du roman de l'Académie française,* and was considered his best novel.

Clem had also been involved in a previous book by Kléber, who in 1966, hosted Dad and Mum at his townhouse in Toulouse. One evening they were sitting in the garden discussing the new book, with Kléber voicing his frustration at not being able to find the right title for his new work. Mum pitched up during the conversation, saying how lovely it was to be sitting beneath such a pretty lime tree. Kléber practically jumped out of his chair and screamed, "That's it! That's it! 'L'été finit sous les tilleuls', (summer ends under the lime trees)!" And that was the chosen title for the book which went on to win the *Prix Interallié.* I can still to this day fondly recall a family holiday spent in Kléber's and Paul Hardens house on the lle d'Oléron. It was during this holiday that Dad started thinking seriously about buying a house in France and I remember him and my Mum going off to the Dordogne for two days to view potential properties.

The affection Clem had for his gang of Hertet Old Boys was reciprocated by his acquired French family. Unwittingly he had stumbled upon a unique group of men and women who were connected by sporting relationships, deep friendships, and shared values. It was the freemasonry of freemasonries, and at the heart of the hub was the Philippe Chatrier - Paul Haedens - Georges Damitio axis, in addition to original stalwarts like Robert Soro from Arreau, Bambi Moga from Bordeaux, Pierre Combin from Morocco, and Haroun Tazieff from the edge of a volcano! It was a pretty heady mix of bon viveurs and living legends.

In 1966 Philippe Chatrier fronted a consortium of wealthy Parisian businessmen and politicians who combined to build a magnificent private sports club in Lamorlaye, near Chantilly. Amazingly, when I went to work in France in 1995 I lived in Lamorlaye, a kind of

Newmarket of France with top horse racing trainers like the Aga Khan based there. The private sports venue was called Club de Lys, and had a 36 hole golf course that is still there today, an enormous aquatic centre with both indoor and outdoor swimming pools, 24 championship standard hard tennis courts, an athletics track, 2 rugby pitches, 2 soccer pitches, and a state-of-the art equestrian centre for show-jumping.

In 1968, on my first visit, I regarded the club with shock and awe. It was paradise for a sport-mad 11-year-old boy. The sports director who coached us in athletics was the great French athlete, Ignace Heinrich, who won a silver medal in the decathlon at the London Olympics (1948). Incredibly, because Ignace had been born in Alsace, he was called up and forced to serve in the German Army in World War II, in a SS Panzer Squadron.

Heinrich was part of a remarkable escape from the Eastern Front, masterminded by Jacques André, whose father 'Géo' had competed in the 1912 Olympics and played several times for France in rugby. Jacques was an original member of the Normandie-Niemen squadron that flew sorties on the Eastern Front, fighting with Russian forces; he had 16 kills to his name and completely by chance recognised Ignace in a prison detail in the Soviet Union. Ignace had served in the Balkans but was sent to fight on the Eastern Front in 1944, whereupon he promptly deserted and joined the partisans in the Ukraine. He was captured by the Russians in 1945, and along with other Alsatian conscripts, incarcerated at Tambov POW camp. The infamous camp south of Moscow was appallingly harsh with barracks dug deep into the ground to withstand the fierce Russian winter where temperatures dropped to under -40 degrees - one out of every two inmates died at Tambov before even four months of internment.   Jacques André assisted his release and he luckily returned home on 20th June 1945. Ignace became one of Georges Damitio's closest friends, one of France's greatest athletes, and a keen member of the Hertet Old Boys.

Club de Lys was situated in the forest of Lamorlaye, had hundreds of weekend apartments, and a magnificent 16th century themed clubhouse with a whole series of canteens and top restaurants. It was breathtaking at that time, and reflected the injection of confidence and wealth France was beginning to enjoy in those post-war years, with a burgeoning Parisian professional middle class eager to bring their families to such a positive sporting environment.

A great deal of attention had been paid to sports instruction, with top-class coaches engaged, all ex-champions in their disciplines. The rugby teams were coached by Jean Dauger, the Bayonne centre who invented French flair, and Robert Soro, one of the greatest second rows ever to play for France. All the great tennis players of the 1960s and 1970s played and practised there; I remember watching Pancho Gonzales, who won the US Pro Tennis Championship 8 times (1953-61) and is considered one of the greatest in the history of the sport. I also saw Tony Trabert - who won 10 major titles including Wimbledon in 1955 - play there. Clem is on record as saying that Tony Trabert, with whom he played with the Hertet Old Boys, was so good an athlete and so good at rugby football that he could have played for any country in the world.

In 1969 I found myself squeezed into the back of a Club de Lys mini-van with their returning youth team after a rugby tour to Swansea organised by Clem. I was twelve years old and supposedly escorted by Gabriel Damitio, a big teddy bear of a bloke who was given the job by his father, Georges Damitio, to bring me back *en famille chez* the Damitio family who had a twelve-year-old son called Jacques. Originally, I was supposed to go to the family home west of Paris, but things went awry. This was the start of my lifelong friendship with Jacques Damitio and his wonderful family, although my first trip should have warned me that this was no ordinary family.

The Club de Lys mini-van crossed the Channel at Newhaven, and we arrived in Paris mid-morning in bright sunlight. My distinct memory of Gabriel's flat near the Eiffel Tower was that there were Gauloises cigarettes and packets of unused condoms strewn absolutely everywhere. As a medical student Gabriel obviously wasn't taking any chances. He had a heck of a job trying to track down the elusive Jacques. His Mother Janine told him that Georges had had to fly to Corsica in his private plane where he had a holiday house near Isle Rousse, and had taken Jacques along with him. Gabriel's instructions were to bring me to Jacques' grandparents' house in Grasse to await his return. So that evening we flew from Orly to Nice, and I well remember wondering what the hell was going on. Gabriel did not speak much English, and my French did not extend much beyond my tailor is rich.

I remember landing at Nice where Janine, or Jan-Jan as she was called, picked us up from the airport. The next day came and went, with no sign of Jacques, nor any news. The following day was much the same, no sign of Jacques. I was beginning to wonder if he even existed at all. Jan-Jan went out of her way to amuse me with visits to the perfume factories of Grasse and a leisurely stroll along the Promenade des Anglais in Nice where I ate my first melon ice-cream.

It was the end of the second day when the elusive Georges and Jacques finally turned up. After a mammoth screaming match amongst the entire Damitio family, it was decided that we would leave early next morning for Paris. Except that meant me accompanying Jan-Jan and Gabriel in a tiny Peugeot 204 on a road trip to Paris, whilst Jacques flew up with his father in the two-seater plane. In 1969, travelling by car from Grasse to Epernon near Rambouillet, 30 miles west of Paris, was quite an adventure, as only half the distance was covered by motorways. The journey took over 17 hours. This was the fabulous dysfunctionality of the French, exemplified by the Damitio family, on full display, and I loved every minute of it.

My eternal friendship with Jacques and the subsequent adventures we shared together are for another day. I'd like to add that we enjoyed our own Hertet Old Boys experiences throughout the 1980s and '90s that included lots of entente cordiale rugby weekends, old boy matches, street fights in Paris, legendary drinking contests in Harry's Bar on 5 rue Daunou, bullfighting across the ferias in south-west France, even owning a vineyard together in the Languedoc, and taking over the Presidency of Paris University Rugby Club (PUC). I shared many various business ventures with Jacques, even up until 2015, with a new plot to start a beach restaurant near Cavalaire, where he owned a holiday home.

The story of our friendship ended tragically in August 2015. Jacques had a sudden and totally unexpected heart attack at his home in Cavalaire which killed him in his sleep. What made it unbearable was that only a week before Jacques had visited me in Singleton hospital, Swansea, where I was recovering from my cardiac arrest. He lectured me on a clean-living regime and he looked fit as a fiddle, as he was swimming a mile a day in the sea off Cavalaire. I still cannot believe he is no longer with us; he was my go-to phone call on any matter. His death leaves a massive void, not only for me, but especially for his two beautiful daughters, Stephanie and Ann-Sophie, and his three grand-children. I will always, forevermore, treasure our wonderful time spent in each other's company.

Jacques even came to Blundells School for the summer term in 1973. Apparently, Jan-Jan had been incredibly impressed by my manners, and Jacques had begun to become an impossible-to-manage French adolescent. So Georges packed Jacques and Jan-Jan into his plane, a recently acquired 4 seater, after his friend Alain

Porthault had crashed the previous airplane! They landed in Fairwood airport in Swansea, and the next day Georges made two trips across the Bristol Channel to Exeter airport, where we waited for his return. I remember being alarmed when the door of the plane wouldn't close properly, so Georges tied it up with string!

We finally made it to school in Tiverton by taxi, and Jacques spent the next 10 weeks playing tennis (we won the House cup), learning to play poker, and drinking cheap whisky. If I'm entirely honest, I don't think an English public school helped his manners.

The original link was of course Georges who had met Clem in the early 1960's during the Hertet Old Boys weekends, when he played on the wing. Georges was a slender but muscled athlete with aquiline features, a Roman nose, and a haughty bearing. Slightly balding, with a razed hair line, high cheek bones, his eyes were a brilliant turquoise blue colour. He possessed a deep authoritative voice, and he always spoke slowly, almost a drawl. Georges spent countless hours teaching me to correctly pronounce la rue and le roux.

Georges Damitio was one of France's best athletes in the late 1940s and early 1950s; he was six times the French high jump champion (1947-53), and also long jump champion in 1947. He was the first Frenchman to jump 2 metres, winning the Mediterranean Games in Alexandria (1951), although his best French record of 2.02 metres was set in 1949. Georges competed at the London Olympic Games (1948), coming 5th in the high jump, and 6th in the long jump. He also competed at the Helsinki Olympic Games in 1952.

Georges' profession was a legal notaire - a property lawyer - and he had many sporting interests, including being a very capable tennis player, and of course sharing a small airplane with Alain Porthault, an accomplished sprinter colleague who also competed in the same Olympics. Porthault became the French 100m champion in 1948 and was nicknamed "la gazelle". He also played several times for France on the right wing (1951-53) and scored two tries in the French Championship Final for his club Racing Club de France in 1950.

Georges had been brought up in Morocco after his parents, who were furriers in Metz, decided in the late 1930s to swap businesses with another furrier based in Casablanca. His father had sensed the oncoming rush to war and was alarmed by the aggression emanating from Nazi Germany. He decided it was a good time to move to a French department *outre-mer* and the family settled in Morocco.

The Damitio family was happy there, but the winds of change were also blowing from France in the late 1950s, and Georges moved back to Epernon in 1957 to take up his notariat practise. He wrote a novel called *Les Pieds Noirs* (1957) (trans. Black Feet), in which he described French nationals living in Algeria who considered French Algeria as their homeland: "They are the Pieds-Noirs. The Arabs call them that simply because they are of European stock and born in North Africa. They are caught up in an adventure in which they are like foreigners…"

Infamously, Georges' passion for private flying led him into one scrape after another. Alain Porthault was extremely lucky to walk away from a near fatal collision with electricity pylon cables. Whilst George, after passing a navigation exam to upgrade his flying license, celebrated by flying to Morocco. On arriving above Rabat, he unwittingly flew directly over the King's Royal Palace that abuts directly onto Rabat golf club. This was where George was heading, so he flew low over the club house a few times hoping to tip off his golfing buddies that he had made it. Unfortunately for Georges, this just compounded the breach of protocol and aviation law affecting the airspace around the Royal Palace. Upon landing at Rabat– Salé Airport an army of Moroccan Royal Gendarmerie was waiting to greet him. He was promptly arrested, jailed for a fortnight, and then sentenced to two years in prison.

The story of his release is still, even to this day, shrouded in mystery, with even Jacques not knowing the full story. His Dad was a national figure in France and through various shadowy networks - including the Hertet Old Boys that I know included several senior military officers, and of course Jacques Chaban-Delmas, the prime minister of France, whom Georges was very friendly with - he was miraculously released after serving only two weeks in prison.

The last part of the story is the saddest. After a summer holiday in Biarritz where Jacques sister Bernadette resides, and who used to tease me mercilessly for decades over my substandard French, Georges took off from Biarritz airport with his wife Jan-Jan, their Polish maid, and Georges's dog. The plane headed out to sea over St Jean de Luz, and was never seen again. Tragically, no remains were ever found. It was a devastating tragedy that is painful to recollect. A few weeks later, Clem, Rob Davies, and I travelled over for the memorial service held in the church at Epernon. All the Hertet Old Boys were there that sad autumn day, but there was little gaiety.

Two grand characters who Clem adored as comrades in arms were Robert Soro from Arreau in the Pyrenees and Bambi Moga from Bordeaux. They are considered French national treasures, and comprised the French second row in the 1948 and 1949 teams that played and beat Wales on both occasions. Robert won 21 caps (1945-49), including the match played at Swansea that France won 11-3 (1948).

France captained by Guy Basquet at No8 and Jean Prat at wing-forward had never beaten Wales in Wales since matches between both nations began in 1907. Robert Soro once told me over a cup of tea, the true story behind the legend bestowed on him after the match of being titled "the lion of Swansea". I visited him in his home in Arreau in the foothills of the Pyrenees in 2003, where he described the 1948 trip from his club team in Lourdes to play for the national side against Wales.

It took many hours and days to travel from Lourdes to Swansea in 1948. The French team assembled in two cities on the way, firstly Toulouse, then Paris. Soro left Lourdes on the Tuesday, reaching Paris on the Wednesday night. Some of the players based in the south-west of France met up in Toulouse, the rest in Paris, from which they departed for the channel ports, taking the night boat on Thursday, docking early at Dover and then onto London.

From London the French party departed from Paddington to Swansea, arriving on the Friday afternoon. This of course allowed many hours for the team to discuss the forthcoming match and put in place their tactics to win the game. Robert told me that some of them, including Guy Basquet, had played against Wales at Swansea in a Victory International match back in December 1945, when a Wales XV beat France 8-0. He had remembered that the wind blew strongly off the sea from the west, the Mumbles end, and that the Welsh team always slowed the game down when playing into the wind. The Welsh tactic was to try and run the clock down with injuries, collapsed scrums, and general slow play. Then when Wales had the wind behind their backs they would accelerate the tempo, ratcheting up the pace, and catching the French team off-guard and off the pace of the game.

So the French plan was simple. When in Wales do as the Welsh. Robert told me that certain players, especially forwards, were nominated to feign injury whenever possible when France were playing into the wind.

That Saturday afternoon at St Helen's a fair wind was blowing up from the west. France won the toss and opted to play into the wind first half. There ensued some brilliant theatricals from Soro who feigned injury at every opportunity and whenever he took contact. As a forward he would be prostrate at the bottom of every maul and scrum. This culminated with him lying spread-eagled in front of the main grandstand, on the half-way line, only yards from the touchline, for all intents and purposes quite dead to the world.

The French bucket and sponge-man rushed on yet again to groans from the crowd - he was becoming a permanent fixture. He told Robert to stay still... it was only five minutes to go until half-time. Eventually, four French teammates had had quite enough, each took a leg or arm and unceremoniously swung Soro off the field of play and over the touchline. He landed with a thud just in front of the press box. Quite suddenly, Lazarus-like, Soro jerked upright, beat his breast in Tarzan fashion and ran back onto the pitch. The Swansea crowd erupted, cheering this tough, hardened Pyrenean giant of a man. One of the pressmen shouted out in all the excitement, "He must be the lion of Swansea", and the moniker stuck with this French team making history by winning 11-3 - their first victory ever on Welsh soil. Up until his death in 2013, Robert Soro was always known throughout France and beyond as the lion of Swansea.

He was an enormous man, who was infamous amongst the Hertet Old Boys for destroying every dining chair he ever came in contact with, particularly the old, wooden, antique, very expensive rickety ones which were incapable of withstanding his 26 stone frame.

After a Wales v France match in the 1960's Clem was invited onto the Sunday Sport French television programme watched in those days by a weekly audience of over 10 million. Robert Soro was there to give a proper French perspective. The anchorman politely asked Clem to enunciate the name of the longest village in the world. Clem duly obliged, speaking his Welsh with 'Burtonesque' baritone gravity,

"Llanfairpwllgwyngyllgogerychwyrndrobwillantysiliog ogogoch".

Robert Soro fixed Clem with a twinkle in his eye.

"Huh, that's nothing! In the Pyrenees we have a village called Ô circumflex!" And he put his fingertips together in the shape of a circumflex. The anchorman practically fell off his chair with laughter.

Bambi Moga was another giant of a man, with the athleticism of a matador, such was the speed of his feet. He was an enormous man for his generation - 120kg and 1m 87 in height. But Clem said he was as quick as a snake, immensely strong and powerful. He played 22 times for France (1945-49), and with his brothers, Alphonse, known as Fon-Fon and Andre, they won the French Cup in 1949 playing together for Begles, a communist commune south-east of Bordeaux's city centre.

Clem always enjoyed going to Bordeaux. Their friendship began in 1949 at Stade Colombes but was forged through the Hertet Old Boys years, and a shared professional interest in their butchery and charcuterie professions. I can clearly remember Dad getting more excited over his annual Christmas present from Bambi than any other gift bestowed on him. Invariably the package from Bordeaux would arrive containing two enormous tins of foie gras truffe, which Dad would open on special occasions, handling the foie gras with all the pomp and reverence of a communion wine.

It is no word of a lie to say that in the 1960s and 1970s, the Moga family practically ran Bordeaux. By this time the family had more than made its mark on the city in sporting, business, and political fashion. Not a great many people today would recognise the name Heinz Stahlschmidt, or rather Henri Salmide, as he chose to be called after the German occupation. He was the German naval officer who, in August 1944, refused to blow up the port of Bordeaux. He was an acquaintance of Fon-Fon (Alphonse Moga), who worked in the port, and who was also a prominent member of the French Resistance in Bordeaux and persuaded Henri not to follow his Nazi master's orders.

Salmide said he followed his Christian conscience, stating "I could not accept that the port would be wantonly destroyed when the war was clearly lost". On 22nd August 1944, four days before the planned destruction of the port, he blew up the munitions depot where the Germans had stored 4,000 fuses to be used in destroying the port. Salmide laid strips of dynamite inside the supply bunker filled with demolition hardware and thousands of pounds of ordnance and watched as the city shook from the huge explosion. His actions killed 50 Germans but were credited with saving 3,500 lives.

After the detonation, Salmide presented himself to the French resistance, and Fon-Fon hid him from the German forces that had branded him a traitor and ordered that he be arrested or shot on sight. Salmide spent the last months of the war in hiding at the Moga family home at the Cours de l'Yser, looked after by Fon-Fon and his mother Marcelline. The other two brothers knew what was going on, and kept up pretenses by concentrating on the family-run charcuterie and cheese businesses. Both businesses operated from stalls in the Marché des Capucins, Bordeaux's large wholesale food market where I worked for Bambi in 1977. Andre became the largest cheese wholesaler in Bordeaux, a vice President of the French rugby union, and eventually deputy mayor of Bordeaux.

The Moga family developed close ties to the Gaullist party - the Rally of the French People (French Rassemblement du Peuple Français or RPF) - after the Second World War due to the close friendship all three brothers enjoyed with Jacques Chaban-Delmas, who would become major of Bordeaux from 1947 to 1995, and Prime Minister of France under President Pompidou (1969-72). During the war Delmas had been in the underground resistance where his nom de guerre was Chaban. As a general of brigade in the resistance, he took part in the Paris insurrection of August 1944, with General de Gaulle. He was the youngest French general since the first French Empire.

After the war, right wing politicians of all hues were tarnished by their collaboration with the Nazi's in forming the Vichy government, under Marshal Philippe Petain. Charles de Gaulle launched the RPF in 1947 after he had resigned as President of the provisional government, but De Gaulle started organising his political future earlier in 1945. De Gaulle had been alarmed at the outcome of that year's French Legislative election, where the parties from the left - the communists and socialists - polled over 61 per cent of the vote, a complete rout of the right-wing parties. He despatched Chaban-Delmas to Bordeaux in order to ensure political control over this important city in western France, and Chaban's first point of contact in Bordeaux was of course with the Moga family.

Chaban-Delmas spent three weeks lodging at the Moga household, looked after by Marcelline, Bambi's mother. The Mogas' helped Chaban elicit the support of the Marché des Capucins traders, and guaranteed that the populist vote was firmly in his favour. Chaban also played rugby for Begles, the club dominated by the three Moga brothers - a very canny move that won many friends and votes in the communist-controlled commune! The result was that Chaban was duly elected major in 1947, and from this power base went on to become one of the most powerful politicians in France over the following 40 years.

Chaban was also a very fine rugby player, and played on the wing for a single international test for France against the British Empire Forces team (1945). His centre that day was the legendary Jean Dauger, and the second row consisted of Bambi Moga and Robert Soro, with Jean Prat playing at wing-forward. It's worth noting again that all four men played for the Hertet Old Boys.

I was lucky enough to get to know the Moga family very well, and am still in touch with Alban Moga. Only last year I hosted a table at the Ospreys v Bordeaux-Begles

European Champions match at the Liberty Stadium, where Michel and Alban were continuing the Moga involvement in Bordeaux rugby under their excellent and charming President, Laurent Marty.

In 1977 when I lived in Bordeaux, the Moga family wielded massive influence, they were adored by the Bordelaise and are still loved to this day. The Marché des Capucins opens at 2.30 am every weekday. I would work with the brothers until around 10am, clean up, have an aperitif from the little café around the corner, then go back to the atelier in the Cours de l'Yser, Bambi's townhouse about 800 metres away.

The house was a series of connected internal courtyards where the old stables had been converted into a modern meat processing factory. Bambi also lived there, and every day an early lunch was prepared by his sister-in-law, Monique, the wife of Fon-Fon. It was an open house, open table, arrangement that seemed chaotic, but Monique always seemed to know how many would be eating. The meal always started with a Glenfiddich and soda for Bambi, as his aperitif, followed by a simple bowl of potage. What came next depended on Monique, but it was always delicious, mainly beef and fish and Bambi had a taste for Cahors wine as his daily shot of rouge.

Chaban was a frequent visitor when he was in Bordeaux, and he would joke with Bambi and Fon-Fon about their triumph in the French Cup. Friends would drop in to see the 'great man' Bambi from all over France, and I remember the occasion someone brought a case of oysters from Arcachon, which I was duly instructed to open, "Dépêche Chris, ces huîtres ne s'ouvriront pas," said Bambi. I consider myself extremely lucky to have had the opportunity to gain insight into such a special family and group of people. Of course, I have my Dad to thank, I was only there because of his reputation amongst such a remarkable group of men.

Clem's favourite restaurateur in Paris was Pierre

Cambin, a close confidant of Georges Damitio - the two of them grew up together in Casablanca. Just like Georges, Pierre was an international athlete, running the 400 metres, and holding the Moroccan and North African record in the late 1940s. He was also Jacques' godfather, and established a series of distinguished restaurants throughout Paris in the 1960s and '70s; the most famous were *Le Gaulloise, La Route de Beaujolais,* and finally, *Le St Vincent,* appropriately enough the patron saint of wine in France. Naturally, these became the happy watering holes of Hertet Old Boys for decades after and over time became the designated restaurants for generations of rugby supporters. Dad, Peter Robbins, and Andy Mulligan also marshalled countless journalists through Pierre's establishments, and they always received a very warm welcome indeed.

Pierre was a short, balding, intense character, who screamed orders at his kitchen team in a never-ending torrent of mixed expletives and jokes. He was very mischievous, forever winding up both his staff and customers - mostly his customers with whom he had the definitive love-hate relationship. As a patron he was unsurpassed, providing generous hospitality that inevitably came in the form of a magnum of slightly chilled Fleurie, the drink that became his signature over the years.

Pierre's food was the taste of rural France, nothing overtly pretentious, very much the flavour of yesteryear, old school cuisine, traditional beurre et plus de beurre (butter and then more butter), very Escoffier-like, tête de veau (poached calf's head), rognons a la moutarde, coq-au-vin, boeuf bourguignon, brandade de morue, cote-de-boeuf grille, escargots, huitres, saucisse de Toulouse, and of course, jambon en persille. Pierre was without doubt Paris' elected rugby restaurateur par excellence and also chef to PUC, Racing Club de France, and even Stade Français.

Pierre trained a generation of young French chefs,

many of whom went on to run gilded establishments of their own in France and London. The brilliant chef Pierre Koffmann learned his trade through Pierre and went on to achieve great fame in London with La Tante Claire in Chelsea. Marco Pierre White and Gordon Ramsay, my great friends Christian from L'Estaminet and Danielle of Loup Pescadou, and a host of other luminary French cuisiniers working in London were all keen students. I used to regularly run into most of them in the West Car Park at Twickenham, where they would host the best picnic in the world. You can still see Pierre's influence on Koffmann even today, as his signature dish is stuffed pig's trotter.

Quite incongruously, the person to be found forever in Pierre Combin's presence on any given rugby weekend was Sir Anthony Evans QC - the former Lord Justice of Appeal from Neath. They were best buddies and practically inseparable. Evans was an old friend of Dad's and a great supporter of both Swansea RFC and the Ospreys. Anthony and Pierre made the oddest couple you were ever likely to come across. The judge and chef out on manoeuvres, with Pierre always in charge of the ingredients!

A great deal of the bewitching allure of French rugby for us Anglo-Saxons and Celts is the absolute anarchy and madness that from time-to-time afflicts the game in France. Whilst the French could turn a game based on physical confrontation into a sublime, poetic art form through their graceful, balanced, athletic passing movements, they were also capable of appalling gratuitous violence. Indeed, you can hardly escape the fact that certain teams revelled in such a reputation. Most notably the great Beziers teams of the 1970s.

I have been to games where so many red cards were shown that it left me dizzy. I once watched a Dax v Mont-de-Marsan derby and the match finished with eleven against twelve - it was bonkers. The two teams, only 50 miles in separation, had not met in a competitive fixture for almost twenty years, and probably with good reason.

The match was scheduled to kick-off at 9pm during the Fete de Dax. In Dax the bullfighting arena is just over the road adjacent to the rugby stadium. The bullfight ended around 8.40pm, with a tour of triumph from the three toreros, Enrique Ponce (four ears and a tail), Morante de la Prebla (four ears), and Miguel Abelian (three ears). There was a dazzling display of what the French call *tauromarchie* - dispatching six fighting bulls from the Spanish ganadaria (stud) which was established in 1914 in Abacete. These were the bulls of Samuel and Manuela A. Lopez-Flores, one of the most famous breeders of fighting bulls - the magnificent beasts cost almost 12,000 euros each. Absolutely thousands of aficionados poured out of the bull-fight arena, crossed the road, and became Dax rugby supporters by switching stadiums.

Frankly I wasn't sure which occasion portrayed the actual blood sport. My doctor, Dave Hughes, was with me, and it takes quite a lot to shake an ex-Cardiff Meds rugby player from Aberystwyth. But Dave, and Rob Davies, who was also along for the spectacle, were flabbergasted at the violent antics that ensued. The ball became irrelevant for the full 80 minutes as both teams went head hunting. It was absolute visceral bedlam.

Clem always reminded me that he had been present at the infamous Neath versus Brive 'Super Championship' tournament played at Pompadour in the Dordogne in August 1989. The extraordinarily aggressive game was only 36 minutes old when Neath walked off en bloc, under the instructions of their coach, Ron Waldron. There was a particularly vicious punching session, that would not have looked out of place in *The Rumble in the Jungle,* and both of Neath's second row forwards were sent off, along with a Brive player. Absolute bedlam ensued as the players argued the decision, and the atmosphere became so hostile, unpleasant, and threatening that British holidaymakers in the crowd felt intimidated and feared for their lives.

The French can take the thuggery too far on occasions, although since the professional game arrived in 1995, these types of events are dying out at the top level of the sport. But not in junior or local rugby as a visit to YouTube can vouch. In the late 1970's when Jacques was playing for PUC, Toulon had a menacing reputation. As the train got to within thirty miles of Toulon, the banter in the carriage would die down as each player began to focus on the reality of the physical challenge to come.

When playing Toulon, the players enter a long, narrow tunnel that leads to the pitch; just before kick off the two team's line up in the tunnel, and traditionally the lights would go out, with each Toulon player simply delivering a heavy blow to each opponent opposite. Immediately, the lights flick back on and the Toulon players clattered out onto the pitch, as if nothing had happened, leaving a totally discombobulated opponent wondering what the hell had happened.

This was always part of a two-pronged sting. The second act was the kick-off. Toulon would always opt to kick, and the fly-half would belt the ball into the crowd, forcing a scrum on the half-way line. With the scrum formed up, as the front rows engaged, the Toulon trio would lift their knees and smash them into the faces of the engaging opposition, CRACK! The second rows would pick up the baton and calmly step forward, launching a vicious right hook at their opponent, CRACK! Game over. Not many teams beat Toulon in Toulon in those days!

Clem also witnessed one of the craziest French Championship Finals ever played, when Agen beat Dax 9-8 in Toulouse in 1966. The French rugby paper *Midi Olympique* labelled the match, "The Final of Shame". It is on record as being the most violent final ever played in the history of sport. Such was the ferocity and disgraceful violence as thirty players engaged in a free-for-all brawl, punch up, gouge and Kung Fu kick fest, that Roger

Couderc, the legendary rugby commentator on French TV instructed the cameras to focus on the spectators sitting in the grandstands. In the inquest that was conducted later by the French rugby union, three players were banned for life. Nevertheless, after a one-year ban, by some mysterious and nefarious politicking within the union, the players were allowed to play again.

Clem seldom saw me play due to his *Observer* responsibilities that took him into England most weekends, but in 1977 I played for Begles against Bristol in a game to celebrate the twinning of Bristol with Bordeaux. The game degenerated fast after we let Bristol score two early, soft tries. At lunchtime we had been hosted by the wine shippers Averys in their old cellars, and I think some of my colleagues struggled to get into the game. The Begles captain, Michel Geneste, screamed at our fly-half Pierre Pedetour, who won one cap for France in 1980, to kick-off directly into the crowd, a la Toulon.

The scrum was set but then erupted as our front row smashed into the tough West Country men. With players like Nigel Pomphrey in their ranks they were not going to take such treatment lying down. So a pitched battle ensued that flared up over the next twenty minutes at every contact. Eventually, after another punch up at a line-out, the referee blew a long, shrill blast on his whistle. "Come here!" he shouted at me. "I haven't done anything," I lied. "I know, but you speak French. Tell them the next player who kicks or punches a Bristol player will get sent off, and I won't stop at one!" So I communicated the ref's threat to Michel, and we stopped the fighting, and in the second half, played some fine champagne rugby with scintillating French flair and pace, although Bristol hung on to win. The headline in the following day's *Bristol Post* read, "PEACEMAKER HERO CHRIS!" Sadly, Dad didn't give me a mention in his *Guardian* match report.

One of the truly memorable characters in French rugby from the 1950s onwards was Gérard Krotoff, the immutable President of Paris University Club, for whom the word Corinthian could have been invented, as long as epicurean and comedian were also attached to the description. They broke the mould when they made Gérard.

Krotoff had met Peter Robbins in Grenoble in 1952 when they played against each other in a schoolboy international, and Gerard was a haute fonctionnaire working for the Mairie de Paris. Gérard actually managed to make Robbins a Hon. Citizen of the City of Paris for his services to sport, specifically rugby football. He was Monsieur Rugby in Paris, and established in the early 1970's The Rugby Club, a restaurant in La Place de la Madelaine, near the Opera. The restaurant was located on the first floor of a nineteenth century Haussman building, and catered to the rugby community in Paris, particularly friends and acquaintances from the southwest of France.

One legendary night Clem and Robbins were invited for dinner, and began their antics over aperitifs, performing their party piece which involved stripping naked and swopping clothes with each other. Peter had spotted the flambé trolley, and told Clem to hold back as the others in their party took their seats at the table. Robbins stripped bollock naked, Clem found a copy of l'Equipe, rolled the paper up and inserted it into the crack of Robbins' naked arse. Dad produced his lighter and set the paper on fire.

The restaurant was a splendid walnut panelled interior, with shiny, polished oak flooring, and was accessed by a narrow, long corridor along which Clem now pushed Peter with terrifying velocity. Robbins appeared head first on the trolley, arse ablaze terrifying the poor diners with this sacrificial fire god impression. Peter became an instant legend in his own bonfire. Happily, no one got hurt. But Peter suffered some pretty painful burns, a small price for such an extravagant pantomime.

Krotoff ran PUC with the philosophy that every

player had to play hard for 80 minutes, but in the *troisieme mi-temps* play even harder. The partying that accompanied away games was the stuff of legends, with hard-nosed clubs in the southwest and the Pyrenees eager to play PUC for their Harlem-globetrotting reputation. The promise of a mega-piss-up and sing-song after the game had every club queuing up for fixtures.

The PUC players were keen to play their part too. On one away trip to Albi, the team stayed overnight at the Hotel Le Vigan, which had a large red neon sign blinking on its roof. One of the electrical engineering students had taken his tool bag with him, and two weeks after the PUC team had returned to Paris, a local citizen walking his dog in the central square in Albi noticed that instead of the usual flashing "HOTEL LE VIGAN", the letters had been transposed so the red neon sign blinked, "HOTEL LE VAGIN ... HOTEL LE VAGIN ...!!!"

This was the clever humour, the play on words, and 'work-hard play-hard' philosophy that Clem so readily identified with. And he was so blessed to have found a group of French friends with whom he could enjoy his rugby freemasonry. Dad was so deeply ingrained in French culture, and so readily accepted by the French, that by 1985 he had decided that he wanted to buy a property in France. And after considering Brittany and the Dordogne, he finally settled on the Medoc: the pine tree forested peninsula north of Bordeaux, with its long golden beaches and access to the great Medoc vinyards only a few miles from St Vivien de Medoc.

A good few years later in 1996, both Dad and my step-Mum Joyce had decided to move on. They visited Vernet-les-Bains, north of Prades in the foothill of Mount Canigou, described by Rudyard Kipling, as "a magician among mountains". Kipling spent long periods there and was well known throughout France following the success of the French translation of *The Jungle Book*. Sadly, Dad never made it to Vernet-les-Bains, but Joyce did go there, bravely opting to move there from Swansea after Clem's passing. And it was entirely apt that at Dad's funeral I read his favourite poem, *If* by Rudyard Kipling.

9

LIFE AT 101 MILES PER HOUR

Clem's life was enriched by deep and lasting friendships. Dad simply enjoyed people and had a gift for being able to converse equally with high society and ordinary folk; he was a very engaging man. He took the words of his favourite poet, Rudyard Kipling, to heart:

> "If you can talk with crowds and keep your virtue,
> Or walk with Kings—nor lose the common touch,
> If neither foes nor loving friends can hurt you,
> If all men count with you, but none too much;
> If you can fill the unforgiving minute
> With sixty seconds' worth of distance run,
> Yours is the Earth and everything that's in it,
> And—which is more—you'll be a Man, my son!"

Throughout his life he encountered some remarkable people, and even though some of these encounters would be brief, even fleeting, he made every moment count. It's sometimes hard to envisage, but Dad crossed paths with Nelson Mandela, Idi Amin, Prince Charles, Mohammed Ali, King Gustav V of Sweden, Prince Albert of Monaco, Sailor Malan, Jacques Chaban-Delmas, Jackie Collins, Lee

Marvin, Peter Collins, Brigitte Bardot, Richard Burton, Kingsley Amis, Danie Craven, Elizabeth Taylor, and - for a period in the 1990s - every celebrity that passed through the Groucho Club in Soho. Clem was personally acquainted with nearly every major rugby union player of the second half of the twentieth century, and whilst paid to evaluate their performances on the field, off it he always extended a hand of friendship.

His friendships arose during very different periods of his life, some fleeting and some constant, lasting forty or fifty years or more. At Cambridge his closest friend was Geoff Vaughan, an athletic, powerful second-row forward who played in the 1949 Varsity match with Dad. Geoff was Clem's best man at his wedding in 1954 and is my godfather. He emigrated to New Zealand in 1968 and bought a GP practice in Auckland. Dad and Geoff were thrown together when going up to St John's College in Cambridge (1947). As freshers they were assigned to share rooms with another undergraduate, Paul Massey, who became an Olympic rower (1948), winning a silver medal in the eights. He was a victorious member of the Cambridge crew in both the 1949 and 1950 Boat Race. Quite bizarrely, Paul has a mountain named after him - Massey Heights - in Antarctica. This came about after his stint as the Falkland Islands Dependencies Survey medical officer at Hope Bay in 1955.

The three undergraduates developed quite a reputation at St John's for riotous parties and practical jokes. They also joined a special fraternity known as "The Night Climbers of Cambridge". One of the many feats undertaken by Clem and Geoff involved scaling a 100-foot façade to exhibit a canoe and oars, festooned with red and white drapes - the colours of St John's. The drapes were stolen sheets and blankets and the intrepid urban explorers managed to raise them above the top of the Wedding Cake Tower, situated above the cupola in New Court, following a May Ball.

New Court in St John's College is Gothic in style, a romantic version of a medieval building. Noël Howard Symington, in his book *The Night Climbers of Cambridge* wrote:

> As you pass round each pillar, the whole of your body except your hands and feet are over black emptiness. Your feet are on slabs of stone sloping downwards and outwards at an angle of about thirty-five degrees to the horizontal, your fingers and elbows making the most of a friction-hold against a vertical pillar, and the ground is precisely one hundred feet directly beneath you... If you slip, you will still have three seconds to live.

Clem crowned his climbing achievements by plonking a chamber pot on the top spire. Geoff accompanied him and told me his hands were shaking like leaves - three storeys up was a long way down, not being a skilled mountaineer and all! An anonymous night climber once wrote, "Only we of the brotherhood knew the joy of the cigarette that is lit as we lie full length on the leads, hands all atremble, every muscle tingling with the effort and excitement of the climb just accomplished. Truly it is a noble sport and worthy of man." It's quite remarkable that extreme urban sports, with the climbing of man-made structures, were invented way back in the 1930s at Cambridge University - and Dad and Geoff were amongst the pioneers!

The parties they threw were legendary. Clem had the college porters in his pocket, for whenever bottles and glasses came hurtling out of windows, smashing on the cobbles of Chapel Court, the debris would be quickly swept away to avoid the ignominy of sanctions from the University proctors. Clem had procured their loyalty both through his charm and the ability to provide regular fresh farm produce that my grandfather, DJ, brought regularly to Cambridge in those years of never-ending rationing. On one mad-cap evening, Tony Armstrong-Jones, who later married Princess Margaret, and who was the university cox in the eights, was stripped naked, showered in beer, and forced to preserve his manly dignity by crawling under the sedan sofa.

Dad and Geoff were extremely proud of their College St John's record in the spring "cuppers" rugby tournament which they won in each of the three years they competed together. After a narrow win in the final against St Catherine's, Geoff remembered Clem destroying an arrogant, tall, "totally up himself" St Cath's supporter who accused Clem of cheating. Geoff told me that Clem hit the bloke so hard in the Volunteer Pub that he landed outside in Trumpington Road. It was a case of Clem demonstrating his considerable punching abilities, and backed up his constant refrain that he would never start a fight, but was always prepared to finish one.

Geoff comes from an accomplished sporting family and played rugby for Harlequins, Combined Services, and North Midlands. He was also a founding member of Old Luctonians rugby club in Kingsland, Herefordshire, in 1948. Geoff captained North Midlands on a record 38 occasions, and played in several England trial matches. Dad kept in touch with him whenever he was in Auckland covering rugby. I remember Geoff visiting us in Swansea over the years, but his relationship with my Mum was tested to the limit after her marriage to Dad. For some reason, Clem had confided in Geoff that he had booked the honeymoon suite at the Imperial Hotel in Torquay. When Mum and Dad arrived at the hotel that night, to their horror they found that their room had been cancelled, and an ambulance was in attendance waiting to whisk Mum away to hospital. It transpired that Geoff, masquerading as a Dr Madonna from Exeter, had phoned the hotel to warn them of a medical emergency! My Dad remembers the hotel manager rushing down the steps to meet them, offering his condolences about his sick bride and attempting to frog march them into the back of the waiting ambulance.

Geoff's elder brother, Brian Vaughan, a Royal Navy Commander, won 8 caps for England (1948-50), but sadly never played against Clem in an international. Brian became an English selector and was the manager of the British Lions tour to South Africa in 1962. Geoff's son Justin picked up the baton for sporting prowess and played international cricket for New Zealand (1992-97); he went on to become the CEO of New Zealand Cricket (2007-2012).

From the mid-1950s onwards, Dad's most constant and reliable friend was my uncle, Ian Jones. He married my aunt - Elizabeth Barter - Mum's younger sister. Liz Barter was a strikingly beautiful, dark-haired, lithe, athletic woman who had been junior Welsh tennis champion. She played at junior Wimbledon, and had been offered a professional contract by the legendary sports promoter, Jack Kramer. But Liz decided on a break from tennis - she had fallen head over heels in love with Uncle Ian.

Ian Jones was an ex-Royal Marine who had been educated at Brecon public school. He played rugby for Swansea, Swansea Athletic, and Swansea Uplands. Ian went on to develop one of South Wales' largest scrap metal and recycling companies for over thirty years. Ian and his father, Reg Jones, operated the Neath Abbey Wharf, developing a rail-head for coal trans-shipments to coal-fired power stations like Aberthaw, near Barry. In 1978 their company scrapped HMS Eagle, a sister ship of HMS Ark Royal and one of the two largest Royal Navy aircraft carriers ever built. Ian's company, South Wales Steel Supply, managed the break-up at Cairnyran, near Stranraer in Scotland.

Ian and Clem shared a similar appreciation of good food and wine. In the late 1960s Swansea was a black hole for gastronomy, and still is today. Ian took matters into his own hands and backed a young Swansea chef, Colin Pressdee, who established the Oyster Perches and finally in the 1970s, the Drangway restaurant in Wind St, which became the focal point for business lunching for almost two decades. On a Friday afternoon I always knew where to find my father!

Colin left Swansea for London in the 1990s, and is a good family friend who has made a successful career as a writer, broadcaster, and 'foodie' journalist. He very kindly organised the drinks and food at Clem's memorial service in St Bride's church on Fleet St.

My uncle Ian had an absolute dossier of Clem stories. One of his favourites was the time he arrived at a nightclub in Swansea with Andrew Vicari. Ian told me that as they were handing over their coats to the cloakroom, a body came hurtling down the stairs from the bar above. Ten seconds later, a second body was flying down the stairs, closely followed by a third. Ian turned to Vicari and quipped, "I bet Clem's up there!" Which of course he was! Dad had the reputation of being a one-man vigilante militia in Swansea throughout the 1960s. It was a rough, tough old town back in those days. Clem was frequently admonished by a whole succession of chief Superintendents trying to maintain order, but they all turned a Nelsonian blind eye whenever some young thug mistakenly picked on Clem, only to regret it later.

On another occasion, Dad followed some aggressive thug who had spat at him, and literally threw him across The Kingsway, fracturing the thug's arm, as he smashed him into the side of a parked car. The police reluctantly gave Clem a dressing down for using excessive force, but he wasn't charged. Geoffrey Nicholson, of *The Observer,* often told the tale of how Clem once parked on a double yellow line on the busy Queensway roundabout in Swansea. A local policeman stepped forward to book the driver when, realising who it was, reputedly said, "Oh, it's you Clem. Don't be long, please - I'll keep an eye on the car for you". I guess this typified the standing with which he was held by the local community, even when he was stretching the law. Peter Stead captured it rather well when he wrote, "Clem was above all a Swansea man, as entitled as anybody to be called 'Lord Swansea' although a title was the last thing the person who rejected the opportunity to be High Sheriff would have wanted...Even thirty years after hanging up his boots he still brought to journalism, politics, business and social life all the enthusiasm, bravery, robustness, directness and flair that had characterized his back-row play."

Dad's routine was to complete his "colour" article for *The Observer* by lunch-time on the Friday, releasing him to be out and about for the rest of the day. Invariably he would lunch at the Drangway with Ian, and Gordon Harris, a stalwart Swansea Uplands player who developed early motor finance and owned firstly the Toyota dealership in Swansea, and later in the 1980s, the Mercedes Benz dealership in Haverfordwest.

Often in attendance would be characters like Bob Lloyd-Griffiths, another Swansea Uplands player from the 1950s, who became President of the club until his passing. Bob had a packaging business in Macclesfield, and his wife, Anne, was my Mum's best friend. When I was four years old we went to visit them in Macclesfield for a weekend. I disappeared for a couple of hours and when I was eventually located in their outside loo adjacent to the garage, I had opened every pot of paint their decorator had kindly left me, and daubed a rainbow of colours across all the walls, the garage door, and even the car.

Bob was a fabulously bubbly character always joking and laughing his way through life. The family owned a house in Port Eynon, at the tip of the Gower peninsula, where we enjoyed many crazy parties and barbeques in our youth. Bob and Anne's children, Nicholas and Elizabeth (affectionately known as "Buffy"), were amongst both mine and Caroline's best friends. Our families shared a fabulous summer holiday on the Île d'Oléron in western France. Paul Haedens had lent Dad their family holiday home for the occasion. They were very happy days.

Dad's true soulmate was Peter Robbins, his old English back-row adversary, rugby correspondent for *The Financial Times* and one of the greatest jokers to come out of the Midlands. Peter had the uncanny ability to catch Clem out on any number of occasions. There was always an almighty tussle to out-con each other and both men went to extraordinary lengths. Dad once said of him:

> Robbins was the funniest man I ever met in my life. He was exceptionally witty but somewhere in him there was also a lot of pathos. He could be full of remorse and there was a bit of the Pagliacci (a clown with a broken heart, laughing on the outside but crying on the inside) about him but having said that, he always took positive positions about life and about people. He was never negative and he couldn't suffer fools at all. When he turned on someone he could be savage but having met a great many men in rugby football he was, to me, the greatest of them all. He had high values of playing, of humour, of friendship and I will never forget him for the rest of my life. Peter Robbins epitomised the whole reason for playing rugby football.

A towering friendship developed between Clem and Robbins, with Peter, as he did with so many of his friends, making Clem the butt of his jokes. His impersonation of what passes for a Clem Thomas laugh was a knockout and his best cutting-line, bearing in mind that he was the younger of the two, was that Clem was his boyhood hero! Although, that could be interpreted quite literally as Robbins used to watch Coventry in the days when Clem disported himself in their back row (1952), but I'm sure he didn't mean it that way!

Robbins once wrote: "Thomas was one of the few people able to take his weekday work with him on to the rugby field at weekends". Clem entered the badinage with the riposte that although he had played international rugby against Robbins on countless occasions, he could never really remember him!

There are many funny stories associated with Peter. Whilst at Oxford University, he was in the team coach on the way to play Cardiff at the Arms Park. A South African, Dennis Bouwer, had been brought late into the team, and was casually asked by Robbins as the coach neared the Welsh border, if he had remembered to bring along his passport. Bouwer, of course, never having been to Wales, had not, and in mock consternation Robbins, professing a dread of facing one of the world's greatest club sides with only 14 men, persuaded Bouwer to outwit border control by hiding in the boot.

Bouwer readily agreed, and a passing Welshman was brought in on the jape, pretending to be a customs official when the coach stopped at the "frontier". After travelling a few miles down the road, Bouwer was finally let out. But the pretence was rather bizarrely and unexpectedly maintained throughout the rest of the journey and indeed the match against Cardiff! Sadly, Bouwer sustained a nasty shoulder injury during the game and was taken to hospital. The terrified South African fretted away, convinced he would be apprehended and deported as an illegal immigrant. Bouwer worked himself into such a heightened state of anxiety that he discharged himself from hospital in order to make the coach trip back to Oxford lest he be discovered by the Welsh immigration authorities.

Clem admitted to being totally hoodwinked by

Robbins' brilliant mimicry on the morning of the 1974 General Election when he was contesting the Gower constituency for the Liberals. At 7am his phone rang and in broadest Lancashire tones, a caller purporting to be Cyril Smith, the eminent Liberal MP for Rochdale, praised Clem's work and wished profusely that it would result in him winning the Gower seat. "We up here at Headquarters are very impressed with your efforts", purportedly said "Cyril", and Robbins said afterwards that he could hear his friend purr into the phone. "I was utterly fooled," confessed Clem, and it was many months before the cause of Robbins' incessant mirth became clear to him. "I called him a bastard and he fell about", said Clem.

Not that Clem was always the innocent party. In 1970 we went on a family holiday to Baltimore in southern Ireland with the Youngs from Dublin. Dad and Peter Young were determined to go shark fishing off Kinsale. They allowed Keith, Peter's son, and I to tag along. So we hired a boat for the day, filled the hold with "rubadubee", a stinking cocktail of rotting fish, blood from the abattoir and fish guts, and set out for the killing grounds. To while away the time, we put a few rods out, and caught large cod. After a few "bites" on the shark-line that proved phantom, it was getting rather late in the day. I was snoozing in the hot seat, the line shrieked, and our skipper, Pat, yanked the rod from the holder and placed it in my hands. Thirty minutes later I was the proud catcher of a 100 pound blue shark. On the way back into Kinsale, we manoeuvred Pat onto another boat, and he caught another, a 375 pound and then some porbeagle shark, a record for Kinsale at that time!

Clem insisted we take our shark back to Baltimore, "to eat at the hotel", although he had other plans too. The following day, Dad and Peter Young butchered the blue shark, cutting off the tail and putting it in a shoe box with a saucy seaside postcard, on which Dad wrote: "We always knew you liked a piece of tail", and addressed it to Peter

Robbins' home in Sutton Coldfield. This sounds quite funny, but as with many practical jokes, this is where it all started to go horribly wrong. Unfortunately for the poor post office workers in Sutton Coldfield that scorching hot August, Robbins had gone off to France on his summer holiday.

The result was that the parcel could not be signed for, and stayed rotting in the post room for over a month! When Robbins eventually returned home, all hell broke loose. Peter was forced to pay for the cleaning and redecoration of the post room, such was the ingrained stench from the rotting shark's tail.

One of Peter's most precious rituals was his hosting of a picnic in the press car park at Twickenham. He drove a large executive Jaguar, and its boot would be stuffed full of the finest Fortnum and Mason had to offer. He would assemble his group of friends and family from the Midlands, whilst all the rugby press would then combine in what was always a pretty serious piss-up, especially after the game, once copy had been filed. One year in the early 1970s, one of the tabloid writers had brought a string of pop music dancers along. By early evening, the drinking was reaching legendary levels. Clem collared one of the dancers, and brazenly asked her if he could "borrow" her knickers to play a jape on Peter. Off to the port-a-cabin loo she went, and returned sans undergarments. Clem had procured his (or rather her) precious knickers. He slid into the Jag, and, sitting in the driver's seat, slid the wispy garment down the side of the seat.

It took until the Tuesday before Dad got the phone-call. "You absolute bastard, you Welsh c***!" screamed Robbins at great volume down the phone. "She's going to divorce me you stupid Welsh prat!" beseechingly adding, after he had calmed down, "you've got to tell her it was you…which is right isn't it? Please, you've got to tell her Clem…"

"Sure thing cock," said Dad, eminently satisfied by

the level of distress he had caused. Later that evening, fortified by Mr Johnny Walker, he phoned the Robbins household in Sutton Coldfield. What the two men had not considered however was that for months after, Eileen, Peter's much put-upon and patient wife, simply didn't believe Clem, thinking Peter had coerced his Welsh buddy into fronting this outrageous alibi! She said of Peter, "you couldn't help loving him, however he behaved. Of course, he was outrageous and his humour continued to embarrass me, occasionally, right to the end. But it was his outrageousness that made him different and being married to him was a great pleasure, most of the time".

Retaliation didn't take long. In January 1971, an old acquaintance of Clem's who had been the kit man for the 1955 British Lions in Kenya, notably Idi Amin, launched a military coup in Uganda, and seized control of the country. One of his brutish decrees was the 1972 expulsion of the entrepreneurial Indian minority. The British Government was forced to assist the immigration of 27,200 citizens of the U.K. and Colonies. Amin set a deadline of November 8th .

That October, a letter arrived at our home in Southgate, on the Gower Peninsula. With a letterhead from the Foreign Office, it seemed a typical letter from the British Civil Service, but what it said caused my poor Mum to panic. Poor Mum was fretting on its contents all day, until she could discuss it with Clem who had gone down west via Brynamman. Basically the letter officially required the chosen household to lodge and support a family of Ugandan Asians who would be arriving within the next 5 working days, and that this was by decree, and not subject to any appeal.

When Dad got home, tired after a long day in the cattle markets of west Wales, he exploded, until it gradually dawned upon him that the letter was simply too outrageous to be true; so one phone call later to the Midlands confirmed his suspicions. It was a jape crafted by

Peter Robbins, and brilliantly executed. Apparently he had sent out dozens to all his friends, causing absolute mayhem.

Their swansong was a trip to the Hong-Kong Sevens in 1986. They travelled Cathay Pacific first class thanks to Clem's acquaintance with the wily, grandmaster of banking, Sir William Purves, the first Group Chairman of HSBC Holdings, and title sponsor of the world-renowned sevens event. Sipping an ice cold glass of Bollinger, Peter was asked by the stewardess whether he would prefer to have foie gras and champagne or the Beluga caviar with chilled vodka. Robbins' response was unequivocal, "We'll have both" he said. Later in the flight Peter turned to Clem who was gazing admiringly down upon the ocean, "You know Clem, if this airplane fell 35,000 feet out of the sky today, you and I couldn't complain. We've had more than our fair share."

Later in the trip the two men took a tourists' day out to The New Territories on mainland China, where they were bused to a model communist Chinese village. Thoroughly bored by substandard fish and flower markets, there were the usual trinkets and tat for sale of absolute zero interest, except for magnificent chains of proper, gunpowder-filled Chinese crackers. Simply put, Chinese crackers are a whole string of bangers, typically 500 or even 1,000 all connected by a single fuse. Clem and Robbins, giggling to each-other couldn't resist. They bought a shedload, and carried them back to their staging point to await the bus.

The coach pulled in, and the two capitalist journalists dived into the alley of an adjacent long, squat building decorated in red and gold, with wooden shutters over the windows. Robbin, peaking around the corner of the building to gauge the last moment they could delay the bus, finally gave the signal to Clem, who lit the fuse with his cigarette lighter.

The two men sprinted across the road, jumped onto

the bus and made a beeline for the back row, apologising to the guide for their tardiness. The bus pulled away and as it turned out of the village gates – BANG, BANG, BANG, BANG, BANG!!! The chain of Chinese crackers exploded like an almighty artillery barrage. Dad was aghast; it sounded like the Normandy Beach Landings.

The building behind which he had detonated the crackers, was lit up like a Christmas tree and swarms of Red Army troops poured out, guns in hand, ready to fight World War III. The guide looked terrified and barked an order to the driver who put his foot firmly to the floor, the bus careering all over the road. They drove at full pelt for an hour along the highway back to Hong-Kong Island. The two sports reporters cum terrorists giggled all the way home.

Sadly, Peter died of a stroke in March 1987 aged 53. As his biographer, Michael Blair wrote, "having tried to measure Robbins's build-up to life at 100 miles an hour, from which there was no deceleration, I am finally struck by Tony O'Reilly's remark when he read the title of this book, *Life at 100 Miles an Hour.*

"What a splendid man - but I think they underestimated the speed!"

Peter's epitaph belongs to O'Reilly who wrote:

> Peter Robbins, the man with the Beaujolais belt as he described it, patting his spreading waistline appreciatively, was one of the great wing-forwards in post-war rugby. Combine two things that one rarely sees in wing-forwards in the British Isles - great upper body strength and a constant loping quarter-mile pace, which got him first to the scene of almost every breakdown - and you had Robbins at his peak. In the England teams of 1956, 57, 58 he was absolutely outstanding. How sad it was that those were the lee years between the 1955 and 1959 British Lions tours. He would have been

titanic in Africa in '55 where the hard grounds would have favoured his style of play. He was a man of wit, charm, perception and affection and he caused funny things to happen to himself and to others.

At his funeral Clem simply added, "I think God will enjoy his company."

On January 10th 1970, Clem went to Dublin to report on the Ireland v Springboks match, and as he described in a famous article he wrote for *The Observer*, "Life is full of nasty little surprises...

> If anybody had told me that on the Sunday I would be mounted on an 18-hand hunter charging petrifyingly over ditch and fence with the Naas Harriers, I would have politely suggested that he saw a vet.
>
> It happened because I played in the Varsity match of 1949 with P.D. Young, later to become captain of England. He was then a blond 16-stone Saxon with, as I have now rediscovered, a warped sense of humour. After being put out to grass by England he went to live, work and play rugby for Lansdowne in Dublin. Now Dublin and horses are like children and measles. Peter rather unpredictably, became infected (after all he was now all of 17 stone).
>
> Like Mrs Flaherty, who got confused with a feather, it was the terrible cunning of the man that I object to. He asked Peter Robbins and myself to stay with him for the Springbok weekend and then prevailed on me to stay until Monday. Robbins wisely flew home on Sunday morning leaving me to my host's mercy. I have had all my meals standing up since that fateful weekend. Sunday

morning we set out to the meet at Bolton Hill, near what turned out to be the aptly named village of Moone. Inevitably the first halt was the bar of a typically Irish boozer - rather like a speakeasy, for it was fronted by a grocer's shop and festooned with signs for things like sow and weener meal and cattle nuts.

My troubles started when I innocently drank the three largest port and brandies you have ever seen. I doubt if you could have got them into a pint glass. This of course was connivance at its very worst, for when our shooting break caught up with the hunt, Shelagh Cassidy, Young's great friend pleaded that she was not recovered from the flu. She looked remarkably healthy to me. But Peter took over her grey and Ann Young said "Come on Clem. Up you go."

Before you could say brandy and port I was legged up, bowler and all. It was like sitting astride a double-decker bus. At this high point of enthusiasm I suddenly remembered I had not been nearer than the racecourse rails to a horse for some 15 years.

Port and brandy is a marvellous drink - but it completely warps your judgement. In no time I was in full flight for the first jump. I oozed alcoholic confidence, but that is not to say that there was not a slight tremor of doubt in my mind. However, Big John, and no horse was better named, took me over with the comfort of an armchair.

There was no holding up now and like Gilpin, I was away willy-nilly. Within 20 minutes I was elated with confidence, but as usual, it did not pay to be too cocky. The time had come for Big John to have his little joke. After all, his dignity had been ruffled by this appalling novice.

As we took one of the milder fences I noticed again a disconcerting inclination of his to run away after every jump. This time he plunged away on a left-hand turn. Incidentally, we should have gone to the right.

Suddenly it was a rodeo, not a chase, and inevitably Peter was near enough to tackle with the same sort of twisted laughter he used in 1949 when a French forward tried to damage my prospects in Clermont-Ferrand.

My other really bad moment came when I scrambled on to a 6ft bank, and saw the two riders before me produce graceful parabolas before touching down on the Emerald Isle like a Welsh forward hurled out of a line-out by Pinetree Meads.

Then I looked down and, ye gods! I discovered why the village was called Moone. Suddenly Borman and Armstrong were colleagues of mine. At the very least it was like looking down from Everest on quite the biggest ditch I had ever seen. However, desperation is a wonderful thing and Big John wasn't the type "to leave you dying". Together we spoilt Peter's day by remaining united and from there on nothing was impossible.

The Naas Harriers are not a posh hunt. They are one of those splendid democratic yeoman outfits where nobody gets his colours to sit aloof in pink. You ride with the local vet, doctor, farmer, grocer, butcher, a German or two and, of course, the local priest. The enthusiasm is immense.

The journey back to Dublin was rich with hostelries and after fillet steaks and red wine at home, Peter and Ann Young rang Robbins in Birmingham to tell him of my prowess. He refused to believe a word of it. But the next morning a telegram arrived - "Are you available,

Grand National, March. Signed the Aga Khan."

The artist, Andrew Vicari, was one of Dad's most colourful and endearing friends. Andrew's life is a truly remarkable tale, the Sunday Times Rich List (2006) estimated his wealth at a staggering £92 million. Born in Port Talbot to Italian parents from Salsamaggiore Terme in 1938, Andrew was educated at Neath Grammar and the Slade in London. He met Clem and Ian Jones quite by accident one summer's evening at The Mermaid, a fine old public house in the Mumbles that is sadly no longer in business. The incongruous trio became firm friends almost immediately. Dad used to tease Andrew by saying they only put up with him because he was useless at cards, and he became the mark for their poker nights.

But I know that Andrew awoke in Dad a lifelong love of art. He greatly enjoyed his collection of local, Swansea and Gower artists that he hung in his lounge and dining room in De La Beche House. Over the years, Dad attended a multitude of house auctions and gallery exhibitions, gradually putting together a small collection. Amongst his favourites were Jack Jones, Alfred Parkman, James Harris Senior, James Harris Junior, Valerie Ganz and of course, Andrew Vicari.

Andrew has always been possessed of a strong sense of purpose and destiny, and at times he behaved with Mussolini-style histrionics, waving his arms about wildly and screaming his frustrations of the day. Ian and Clem weren't entirely sure what to make of him, but he was a dynamic, colourful character, who used his humour, intense charm, and Napoleonic strutting presence to great effect. Vicari almost certainly merits a book all to himself. He went to live in London in the early 1960s after years of spendthrift living in Swansea and Llancarfan, where he lived in a disused chapel, and served coffee in used Maxwell house jars.

Andrew was without doubt the best salesman ever to

paint a canvas. He had an extraordinary ability, for most of his life to follow, to pursue and procure money. He held a number of exhibitions in the 1960s in London and South Wales, and he somehow managed to live the high life on pure fresh air.

Whenever his pals from Swansea came to London, Andrew would organise a sumptuous dinner in the lavish restaurants he frequented like San Frediano on Fulham Road, Fu Tong in Kensington - the best Chinese in London in the 1960's - or even Trader Vic's at the Hilton on Park Lane.

Clem, Ian and Andrew were practically permanent fixtures at Fu Tong, which meticulously engraved the names of its most regular clientele onto bespoke chopsticks, kept for their sole use. Vicari claimed he once used the chopsticks reserved for Richard Burton and Liz Taylor which were made out of ivory.

At the settling of the bill - which when Clem, Ian and company were in town was always inevitably a substantial sum - the party would split the damage and pay in cash. This tradition enabled Andrew to place his latest credit card and scoop up all of the cash, which would always keep him going for a while.

We used to live in a large house in Morriston in north Swansea, and as a young boy I remember Andrew living with us for several months. Eventually, my Mum got sick and tired of Dad using Andrew as a pretext for a spot of bachelor-like living! She delivered an ultimatum – "It's him or me!" So Andrew packed his bags and left, and went to live with Uncle Ian Jones and Liz.

In the early 1960s Andrew had a massive extended family which was comprised of all of Clem's and Ian's friends, like Colin Maggs, an accomplished dentist in Mumbles, Brian Rees, QC in Langland, and David Cole in Penarth, with whom he would swop accommodation for the inevitable charcoal sketch of however many children his friends had at that time. There's a Vicari hanging in almost every household in Langland!

Clem loved to tell the story about a party that Andrew was throwing when he lived in a large spacious flat in Chelsea. Dad was staying there, and the doorbell rang for a delivery of booze that took a good 40 minutes to be unloaded from the lorry and into the flat. The driver then proffered an invoice and asked Clem to sign it. Dad stared at the cases of champagne, wine, and spirits stacked to the roof, and balked. He phoned Andrew at his studio, and Vicari cheerily told him to sign, as *The Daily Mirror* was picking up the tab.

Andrew got his major financial break by holding an exhibition in Beirut in 1970. This was before the civil war wrecked the Riviera of the Middle East. By complete chance, an important oil conference was taking place in the same hotel as Andrew's exhibition. Ever the salesman, Andrew printed 100 special invitations for all the Saudi Arabian delegation. The Saudis duly attended the exhibition, and the oil minister asked Andrew if he could be in Paris in a few weeks' time, as he wanted to introduce him to Prince Khaled bin Sultan bin Abdelaziz, a senior Saudi prince who had an interest in art.

Andrew made sure he went to Paris and organised a sumptuous night on the town for his Saudi guests. When the bill came, the Saudis insisted on paying, much to Andrew's evident relief. The outcome was that in 1974 he secured a lucrative commission for a series of 60 large mural-size paintings - *The Triumph of the Bedouin* - which today hang in all their grandiose splendour at the King Faisal Islamic Foundation in Riyadh. Andrew was then appointed official painter to the King and government of Saudi Arabia, and he undoubtedly transformed Islamic art in the country, a huge achievement for the painter from Neath.

Andrew's great passion was for mixing with A-List Celebrities in the entertainment industry, and this undoubtedly gave him the idea for a wheeze that he hoped would generate instant publicity for himself and his paintings. Vicari decided to paint three enormous canvases that depicted his own unique version of *The Last Supper*. He rather bizarrely selected Clem as his Jesus Christ, which prompted all manner of endless jokes about Dad being the son of God! Andrew's depiction of the apostles prompted even more comment, alongside a cherubic looking Jesus (Clem) sat a rather jolly looking Matthew, portrayed by Sir Harry Secombe, a stern and serious Judas was portrayed by the actor Stanley Baker, and Doubting Thomas was illustrated by a guilty, hangdog, brooding Richard Harris, the legendary hell-raiser and Hollywood Star. Vicari had even managed to paint in Mel Charles, the Welsh international footballer, Lionel Bart, the composer of the musical *Oliver* and Lord Wyn Roberts, the MP for Conwy (1970-1997) as further apostles!

It was painted in 1959 and was, as you might imagine, considered a very controversial piece at the time. Vicari was quite brilliant at self-promotion. But back then, rather strangely, he had no populist fan base, or indeed the kind of elite support that contemporary artists like Damien Hirst and Tracy Emin enjoy in today's art world. Vicari once commented upon this situation:

> I do not know why they say I'm unknown. I'm very gregarious. I know everybody. When I was a student at the Slade (school of fine art in London), Francis Bacon was my mentor. He would try to seduce me because I was very handsome in those days. Every time I used to see him he couldn't resist a little touch on the knee. I used to laugh him off. I knew Stephen Spender and David Sylvester. I knew Sartre. Truman Capote lived next door to me in Rome. I went round to borrow some milk from him one day. He came to the door in a baby-doll nightie. He said, "I'll see." Jean Genet was behind him with an Irish setter. I knew

Orson Welles. Jonathan Aitken I've known since we were members of the squash club at the MCC in Lords decades ago. You could not meet a more honest man. I've known everybody and everybody knows me.

As a Slade student and Soho bohemian, or strictly speaking a Chelsea bohemian, Vicari established himself as a portraitist. He painted a host of celebrities as varied as Augustus John and Norman Wisdom. This might have given him the inspiration for *The Last Supper* which his nephew, also named Andrew (Jnr.), considers, "a modern interpretation of Da Vinci's classic. All of the characters depicted were friends of his... Knowing his work as I do, it could be described as his Opus Magnum."

Vicari's later subjects included, French Presidents Charles de Gaulle and Francois Mitterrand, Mao Tse-tung, Sophia Loren, and Princess Caroline of Monaco. He was by his own admission, "the last oil painter in the line of Goya, Rubens, Velazquez and Raphael." The critics generally disagreed but Vicari mostly put this down to envy and said, "As Toledo was to El Greco, as Arles was to Van Gogh, Riyadh is to me."

One of his favourite stories was about a letter that was simply addressed to him as, "The King of Painters, Monaco". Sent from Riyadh, it actually reached him. A few weeks previously he had collapsed drunk in the tunnels connecting Fontvieille with Monaco port and been found by a group of young Saudis, who kindly took him home and put him to bed. Andrew had given them a photocopy of a newspaper article, titled "The King of Painters", because he couldn't find a business card. The Saudis had written to him to primarily check upon his well-being but also to confirm they had visited the King Faisal Foundation to view his magnificent collection in Riyadh - *The Triumph of the Bedouin.*

Andrew always playfully said afterward, "I am the

king of painters, and ever since 1974, when I became the official painter to the Saudi court, I have been the painter of kings."

What is undeniable is that Vicari revolutionised painting in the Arab world.

"For 14 centuries portrait painting was prohibited in official Islamic art. I changed all that. I was encouraged to paint portraits of leading figures in the court. Initially, I was told that in Islam, if you paint a man's portrait, you take his soul. And that is what a lot of Shi'ite Moslems believe. They say they are following the teachings of the Koran. But the Saudis told me, "We will change that popular misconception". And for the first time since the era of the prophet Mohammed, there was figurative art being made officially in Arabia. By me."

Vicari's promotion and art also broke down barriers in the Far East. He was immensely proud of his reputation in China, as he declared, "Do you know I was only the fourth occidental artist to be exhibited in China? After Rodin, Miro and Chagall, there was Vicari. I am one of the great figurative artists, one of the best draughtsmen." Though his estimation of his own artistic worth knew few bounds, he professed not to mind his low profile in Britain, "Why should I give a toss about what they think of me in this insular country?" he once said. Andrew had a low opinion of British contemporary art and there were only two painters he really cared for – Stanley Spencer and Lowry. He really thought there was no craftsmanship anymore:

"The two devils who are responsible for this are Nicholas Serota (director of the Tate) and Charles Saatchi. They should be executed for what they have done to British art…"

He was more favourably disposed toward the Arab world and his relationship with the Saudis lasted a lifetime; he made many close friends, including Ghazi Algosaibi, the novelist, diplomat and Minister of Industry (1975-1982) and Nasser Ibrahim Al-Rashid, the billionaire Saudi Arabian businessman.

Andrew lived a great deal of his life in Monaco (1974-2015) but returned home to Wales eventually for health reasons. He told me a few years ago that Al-Rashid was his largest collector and indeed his most loyal. Al-Rashid was very kind to Andrew towards the end of his time in Monaco, where he spent a great deal of time at his yacht, the Lady Moura; one of the largest private yachts in the world, costing over $200 million, was permanently moored there.

His principal patron, Prince Khaled bin Sultan bin Abdelaziz, when the first Gulf War broke out following the Iraqi invasion of Kuwait (1991), was commander of the joint Arab forces and made Vicari the Saudis' official war artist. Andrew produced 225 oil paintings, some of them 35ft high, in a series he called *From War to Peace in the Gulf: The Liberation of Kuwait*.

There were battle scenes, depictions of military hardware, and portraits of the chief protagonists. "We had a fabulous time," Andrew recalled. "I met Norman Schwarzkopf and Peter de la Billière, who became friends." Vicari was very fond of posing in the camouflage cap given to him by "Stormin' Norman".

But the project was ill-fated. The prince lost interest, and Andrew received death threats from Iraqi sympathisers, as well an offer from Iran to buy the collection for £5m – in order to destroy it. Eventually the prince had a change of heart and bought 125 of the works for £17m and housed them in a museum commemorating the Gulf War.

Vicari achieved other notable commissions, from Interpol and the CRS in France, the state security police, his good friend Vladimir Putin and even the State Council, chief authority of the People's Republic of China.

I can assert with authority, having discussed the subject at length with Andrew in the year before his death, that he came to regret the grand deception entered into by allowing the Sunday Times Rich List to consistently claim his worth at around £90 million based solely on insurance valuation certificates. The reality was that over the last twenty years of his life, Andrew was always extremely short of money, primarily because of his voracious habits and lifestyle, but also due to his unbelievable generosity that frittered away countless millions. This sadly led to his bankruptcy proceedings, which at his age and with his complete lack of financial literacy, was a tragic ending for such a wonderful man. However, this is now part of the legend. In conversation with his nephew, Andrew Junior, I've learned there is already substantial interest in his legacy from dealers in America, particularly from Miami and New York.

Andrew was my youngest brother Mark's godfather and it is because of him that Mark today lives in Monaco, as I did for six years. Mark played for Wales at the inaugural Rugby World Cup Sevens tournament in Edinburgh in 1993, a tournament that was dominated on the first day by Samoa and Fiji.

Dad dutifully filed a report with *The Observer*: "White Men can't Play Sevens". The following day, England improved dramatically; with a team that included Laurence Dallaglio, Andrew Harriman, and Chris Sheasby, they promptly went on to win the trophy. Clem was quite chastened by this turn in events, and insisted we didn't dare dally at the Gullivers hospitality tent for fear of humiliation over the headline and the critical article.

Marks appearance at RWC 7's elicited an invitation from Jeff Tordo, the French captain, to play in a French Barbarians match later in June at Grenoble. My brother was subsequently offered an illicit under-the-table deal to play for Nice. This involved a mix of cash, accommodation, and a car. Mark was a trainee chartered surveyor with Richard Ellis in Berkeley Square at the time, and promptly decided that the London property scene was no longer for him.

Mark decamped to Nice and plugged into Andrew Vicari's contacts and lifestyle, and hasn't looked back since. What is extraordinary is that, it was in a bar in Monaco that he met the newly appointed, first ever Monaco bobsleigh coach, Malcolm "Gomer" Lloyd, a fellow-Welshman who persuaded Mark to have a go at the four-man bobsleigh as a brakeman. Mark, blessed with his fast, athletic, 6ft 4ins frame and natural competitiveness, took to the sport like a duck to water.

Today, as a result of competing in several world and European Championship events for the Monaco Bobsleigh Team, Mark can count Prince Albert - who started the team, and was the driver - as one of his closest friends. Indeed, Clem hosted Prince Albert at his home in Swansea in 1996 for the Wales v France international, only months before his sudden death in September.

Clem's primary source of earnings was his wholesale and retail butchery businesses, but he became involved in a myriad of entrepreneurial ventures over the years. The one constant throughout was his business partner and longtime associate, Percy Watts. Dad met Percy in the late 1950s when he was contemplating a new phase in his life, having decided to retire from playing rugby at the end of the 1959 season.

Percy had started a small butchery business in Swansea Market which had been rebuilt and relaunched in 1961. Other established butchers began operating from that central location, notably Billy Upton, Len Vaughan, Henry Hall, and Hugh Philips. Most of them are still operating in Swansea Market even today.

Clem and Percy embarked on a joint butchery venture in Mumbles and established Swansea Wholesale Meats in Hafod to focus on large, public sector contracts supplying frozen, packed meat from Argentina and New Zealand. Percy bought 12 Portland St, which over the decades became Swansea's most notable butcher's business. It was perfectly located for that era, directly next to Marks and Spencer, only 50 yards from the Kingsway, and right next door to the famous Kardomah Café.

Percy was a neat, fastidious, well-organised character who spoke with authority, intensity, and directness on almost every matter under the sun, as if his life depended upon it. Once Percy became engaged with you on a subject he would treat the exchange as a mano a mano fight to the death. He was forever trying to prove a point. I believe, this was partly the reason Clem and Percy became such firm friends – the two sparred continuously over every subject known to man, and even some not yet known! Dad admired Percy for his sharp, cunning intellect, and liked the fact that, "Percy takes no prisoners…"

Together they were lethal, combining Clem's salesmanship and willingness to smash down every door, whilst Percy focused on the planning and invariably handled the details and accounting. Other ventures they shared included opening a café in Swansea Market, building various housing projects, investing in the Swansea Nissan car dealership, and starting a sausage-making and burger business.

Percy was also a hugely knowledgeable and committed opera lover, who attended Bayreuth, Glyndebourne, and possessed an unrivalled collection of opera recordings, wall to wall. In fact, he was so knowledgeable that during the late 1960s Clem organised a dinner in London with Britain's leading opera critic who wrote for *The Guardian*, Philip Hope-Wallace. At the end of the evening, Dad said you couldn't be too sure which of the two men was the opera critic, such was Percy's command of his subject. I believe after this meeting the two became good friends over many years.

In the 1980s, as Clem wound down the wholesale, abattoir business, the two would meet almost daily at 11am in the Kardomah, which served as their public office. The café had been made famous by Dylan Thomas and his description of it as – "My home sweet home..." - and it was the venue in the 1930s for the "Kardomah boys", which included the likes of Dylan Thomas and fellow poet and painter Vernon Watkins, who was the only person from whom Dylan took advice when writing poetry. They were lifelong friends, despite Thomas's failure, in the capacity of best man, to turn up to his wedding. Dylan used to laugh affectionately at his friend's gossamer-like personality and extreme sensibility. A story is often told that one evening in Chelsea, during the war time blackout, they were walking along and Vernon tripped over something and fell to the ground. Dylan looked with a torch to see what the offending object was and to his delight all that they could find was a small, black feather. Others in the "Kardomah boys" were the composer Daniel Jenkyn Jones, who composed the song-settings for *Under Milk Wood,* the writers Charlie Fisher and John Pritchard and the artists Alfred Janes and Mervyn Levy. Dylan Thomas immortalized the Kardomah - Swansea's version of the Algonquin round table - when he wrote of it as the place to talk about "Einstein and Epstein, Stravinsky and Greta Garbo, death and religion, Picasso and girls.

In 1941, Swansea was heavily bombed by the Luftwaffe in a three-night blitz which destroyed the Kardomah Café, prompting Dylan to write about the devastation in his radio play, *Return Journey* in which he describes the café as being "Razed to the snow". Forty years later, a new Kardomah gang had emerged, with Clem, Percy, Bobby Sullivan, manager and husband of Bonnie Tyler, Charlie, who was Percy and Dad's fixer, and the owner, Pietro Luporini, all now discussing Brigitte Bardot, conservative economics, Labour party follies, the Common Market, Ronald Reagan, life, death, wives and the reasons for the decline of Welsh rugby, with Clem proffering his daily racing tip to anyone who cared to listen.

One fun but dangerous venture the two butchers embarked upon was to combine forces to buy a 22-foot Westerly sailing boat. The yacht was moored in Mumbles, just off the Bristol Channel Yacht Club, in those days an elite institution that would not have looked out of place in St James' clubland. They called the yacht *The Baa-Baa,* with the emblem of the Barbarians rugby club, a prancing lamb painted on the bow. Given that both Percy and Clem made a living slaughtering lambs and selling lamb chops, this was entirely appropriate. As the eldest son, I probably have more memories about *The Baa-Baa* than Caroline, Greg or Mark; I can still remember the sensation in my tummy when weighing anchor (always my job) from the mooring off Mumbles Pier, and we headed across the Cherrystones in front of the Lighthouse, it was like setting off for the New World, since in the hands of Clem and Percy, you never quite knew if you'd be coming back. They managed to almost kill themselves by shipwreck and drowning on several occasions, whether defying the weather forecast of a force 9 gale on their way to Ilfracombe, or simply naively believing the sun always shone over the Bristol Channel with a fair wind guaranteed. After another close shave off Tenby that shredded their sails, Clem started describing the Bristol Channel as the most lethal strip of water in the world, with its vagaries of wind, currents, and a 50-foot tidal drop - the second largest in the world. Finally they invested in a ship-to-shore radio and a sonic depth finder.

There were many other characters who worked alongside Clem and Percy. Len Roberts became Dad's lieutenant and right-hand man. Len opened and ran the new retail shops in Cardiff and Neath and became general manager of Swansea Wholesale Meats Ltd. He was a hard-working, fast-talking, brylcreme slick, jack-in-the-box character from Townhill, who had no time for fools, and who did everything at 101 miles per hour, such was his extreme work ethic and determination to get things done.

Whenever a refrigerated lorry arrived from Smithfields, London, or the cold stores in Cardiff docks, Len would scream at us to unload the boxes of frozen meat of whatever denomination. He would take position in the freezer, a huge voluminous room with a condenser that made the noise of a jet aircraft engine. And we would jog from the delivery bay to the freezer with our loads which Len would expertly stack from floor to ceiling. In the background the band saw would screech away, sawing through frozen flesh and animal bone. The meat business is not for the faint-hearted.

It was Len who carried out the logistics operations over Christmas week to process 5,000 turkeys, picked up from Pembrokeshire turkey farms by a fleet of five trucks, weighed in, bagged, invoiced, and delivered in the 3-4 days before Christmas to the retail butchers of South Wales. As a boy, it was a high adrenaline, intense 7 working days, when Clem and Percy would fret over the weather, Len didn't sleep, living on sugared Typhoo tea the colour of mahogany, and my job was to go to the Wimpey every evening to buy everyone cheeseburgers. I got all the best jobs as the most enthusiastic butcher's delivery boy in Swansea.

One evening, as we were loading up the freezer again, Len asked me what I was doing that night. I pleaded neutral, wondering why he had asked. "I'm wrestling down the Patti Pavilion later," he said, "Tell your old man you want to come along". Naively, I entered into a discussion on wrestling with Len, as he built himself a semi-credible back-story. Dad arrived to take me home, and I piped up asking if he wanted to come and watch Len wrestle later. Quick as a flash, Dad caught on to my schoolboy naivety, and burst out laughing. The result was that Len and Clem almost had a wrestle there and then, as Dad berated him mildly for making me look an absolute idiot. I still see Len in The Pilot in Mumbles, and he always starts rubbing his shoulder muttering that he's too stiff to go wrestling down the Patti tonight. He's a wonderful reminder of a wonderful time, now long past.

Clem's enthusiasm for sailing came during a decade when single-handed Transatlantic yacht races were the focus of populist wonder and accolade, with a friend of his from Saundersfoot, Val Howells, at the forefront of this brave troupe of adventurous sailors, who captured hearts and minds, culminating in Sir Francis Chichester's single-handed voyage around the world in 1966-67.

Val Howells was one of five competitors who competed for the first *Observer* Single-handed Transatlantic race in 1960. The course of the race is westward against the prevailing winds of the North Atlantic over a distance of 3,000 nautical miles. The first race was from Plymouth to New York City. From 1964 the race finished at Rhode Island. This ground-breaking race was won by Francis Chichester in his 40-foot *Gypsy Moth 111*, in 40 days. Val Howells finished fourth in the *Eira*, a 25-foot yacht in 62 days.

I remember going on holiday to Saundersfoot in the early 1960s - a popular location with Dad, who could install his young family in a rented cottage, allowing him to get to Brynamman and the west Wales cattle-markets during August week days, whilst giving my Mum a holiday on the Pembrokeshire sands. We used to eat most nights at the Captain's Table, a restaurant established by Val Howells on the harbour. He sailed us across to Lundy Island one day, and in the evening Mum and Dad gorged themselves on fresh Pembrokeshire lobster, cooked in huge vats of boiling water. Val took me into the kitchens and I distinctly recall the high-pitched whistling noise emitted by the lobsters as they entered the vats, to emerge minutes later gleaming pink.

In 1964, Val Howells sailed the 35-foot *Akka* in the second running of the Transatlantic race and came an impressive 3rd, behind Chichester and the legendary French sailor, Eric Tabarly. Val was a larger than life, bear-like character who looked like a sea-going captain should, with a huge, bushy, black beard, piercing, clear brown eyes and a huge laugh. He was the kind of man who filled a room.

Sports Illustrated, the number one American sports magazine, reported before the 1960 race, "Val Howells, a bearded Welshman, practiced for the race by sailing alone last summer from Wales to Corunna, Spain and back. -- "When you've never sailed single-handed," said Howells, "it's fear that is uppermost in the mind - the fear of being afraid. Now that I have conquered that, I can conquer the Atlantic". -- To be sure that he stays in a positive frame of mind he plans to sustain himself principally on home-cured Welsh ham and cans of beer."

Over the years, from the early 1960s to the day he died, Dad could not resist getting involved in all sorts of different ventures that for one reason or another had great appeal to him. He was an old-fashioned entrepreneur, who would rely on the emotional gut-feel of whatever idea germinated in his head. He was not a creature from the Dragons' Den, with every decision vindicated by financial numbers and detailed market research. He trusted his own instincts, and when it came to butchery and the slaughter business, he certainly knew what he was doing.

He invested in the new Llandeilo bridge mart, tried to build a new slaughter-house for Swansea in the late 1960s that the council backed out of, leased Southgate Farm for 15 years, established a chain of Clem Thomas butcher retail shops during the same period in Mumbles, Cardiff, Neath, and Pontypridd, and in the mid-1970s relocated the DJ Thomas slaughter business from Brynamman to Three Crosses. Here he operated the abattoir until its sale in 1984. The Three Crosses Farm was owned by two brothers, Howard and Dai Morgan. Howard became a prominent conservative councilor on Swansea City Council and Lord Mayor, whilst Dai amazingly bred the 1987 Grand National winner *Maori Venture*, so named because in his youth Dai had spent time playing rugby in New Zealand, home to the Maori. The horse amazingly won at odds of 28/1.

Other ventures supported by Clem included building the first commercial structure in Bracelet Bay, an ice-cream kiosk that he sold to Bill Hughes, who used that opportunity to become the leading nightclub owner in Swansea during the 1970s and '80s, owning The Surf House sited on the original ice-cream kiosk, The Townsman, which was rebranded as Barons, The Penthouse, and The Coach and Horses. In the mid-1960s Clem fronted a consortium to establish the new commercial radio station Swansea Sound, but the bid failed, and in the mid-1970s he set up the *Neath Independent* newspaper with Geoffrey and Mabel Nicholson, that included as editor Simon Kelner, the future executive editor of *The Independent*.

Clem infamously once tried to set up an export business selling Welsh lamb to German wholesalers based in Cologne. On his expeditionary visit to make contact with the new German customers, he decided to drive, taking my two younger brothers with him on a busman's holiday. Unfortunately, his car broke down in Bridgend, and my Stepmother Joyce had to swap cars, letting Dad speed off to catch his ferry in her Citroen, whilst she was left to sort out the breakdown.

In the 1960s he also set up a café in Swansea Market with Percy Watts, and followed that by investing in a new upmarket Chinese restaurant called The Lotus Garden in Castle Gardens, fronted by an inscrutable, mysterious Chinese businessman from Hong Kong known only as "James."

James mysteriously disappeared one day, and has never reappeared in Swansea. But Dad's most serious venture was to buy the No Sign Wine Bar in Wind St in 1985. The No Sign was an iconic Swansea watering hole, frequented by the bibulous Dylan Thomas who featured its famous fourteenth century wine cellar and used it as the prototype for the "Wine Vaults" in his short story *The Followers*. The building has a long history in the wine and spirits trade and was not required to display a sign, like ordinary public houses, when it was licensed as a wine bar, hence the moniker No Sign Bar. Other trades were practiced in the building. In 1908, George Ace & Co was granted a licence "to store carbide of calcium" at 56 Wind Street. Calcium carbide was used industrially and as lamp fuel in mines and on early cars.

As company secretary, I was involved in the project, and we invested a considerable sum into opening up these cellars, assisted by the local developers, BJ Group, a hugely successful property business owned by Terry Francis, Mike James, and Rob Davies. Terry was one of the original, notorious "Swansea Mafia", a group of go-getting, local, Swansea businessmen, who from the mid-1960s controlled most property planning and development schemes in Swansea in ways they do not teach you at Harvard Business School. They were high-profile, colourful, opportunist and more Swansea City than Swansea Rugby Club. Others included Malcolm Struel, Gerald Murphy, and Brian Cornelius. They all belonged to a drinking den in Northampton Lane, called The Regency Club, which served as a base of operations for them during the afternoon when the pubs were closed.

The Regency ran an annual trip to one of Wales' international away matches. On the following Tuesday after the match - a slow news day in Swansea in those days - a photo would dutifully appear, regular as clockwork, of the Regency members setting off for Dublin or Edinburgh in a happy group photo taken the previous week. What then actually happened was that, immediately after the photo was taken, some members of The Regency got on the bus, and some didn't. Armed with the perfect alibi, certain members would hop in a taxi to Swansea train station to depart and meet their various mistresses around the UK. They got away with it for years.

BJ Group completed a remarkable transformation of the old cellars to create a massive, vaulted underground space that comfortably accommodates 250 people. These days it's a thriving live music venue.

Peter Stead remembers organising an event with Dad:

Occasionally I had dealings with him and this was particularly the case during the years when, as seemed entirely appropriate , he was proprietor of Swansea's most distinguished, distinctive and famous watering hole, the No Sign Bar in Wind Street. The Luftwaffe had succeeded in destroying most of Swansea's Victorian and Edwardian distinction, but mercifully parts of Wind Street survived not only aerial bombardment but also the inanity of later planners...An exterior plaque somewhat arbitrarily identified this as 'the best pub north of Salzburg', but more accurately a visiting American was heard to declare that he felt exactly as if he was drinking in Cheers, Boston's most famous bar. It was a super bar, especially when Clem was there to enthral the lingering lawyers and estate agents who constituted the usual suspects. But even better than the booth-lined bar and dining area was the cellar below, still in those days referred to by its traditional name of 'Munday's wine cellar.' This was the genuine thing: a stone-walled cellar that looked a little as if it had once been used as a torture chamber but which now served as a jazz venue with a perfect acoustic, or as a very baronial dining room. It was the perfect place for me to take the quite demanding University Staff Dining Club of which I was secretary. I discussed the menu with Clem. 'It has to be my new season Welsh lamb,' he decided, and we proceeded to choose a date that would allow perfection. On the night I was acclaimed as never before by thirty totally contented diners and I rejoiced in the way in which my friendship with the proprietor had paid off.

My memories of the No Sign are the early 5am breakfasts during the very first Rugby World Cup, held in New Zealand in 1987. Hundreds of Swansea business executives, lawyers, accountants, insurance brokers and bankers came to watch the matches on our big screen. The problem arose when going to work at 9am, everyone was totally pissed on Buck's fizz and draught Bass.

We ran into a serious problem at the end of opening week. Dad had offered the resident, and perennial bar manager, known to all and sundry as "Dante", a partnership. Dante had run the establishment for the Munday family for decades, and came with the furniture, like an old barrel of port. He was Italian and spoke unintelligible English. A wizened, nervous character, constantly smoking a cigarette he kept a beady eye on all the comings and goings in the bar. But after the end of the first week he was jumpy and more nervy than ever. Dad accosted me and asked if I knew what was wrong with him, as he had become evasive and tight-lipped. So I asked Dante what the problem was, advising him that for the partnership to succeed he needed to be totally transparent with Clem.

Dante confessed that two young thugs had come into the bar during the week demanding £200 of protection money, or they would cause him harm, trash the bar, and even cause a fire that would destroy the business. I explained this to Dad who following another brief chat with Dante said suddenly, "Come with me." We jumped into his car 'Sweeny style' and screeched down the Mumbles Road to the Sandfields pub, The Robin Hood, which was the base for most of Swansea's criminal enterprise back in those days. We walked in looking like a CID investigation unit. Clem dressed in his ubiquitous sports jacket and Baa-Baas tie, and me in a suit and polka dots. Dad approached the bar and asked if Philly James was around.

Philly was a Swansea 'capo'. Someone who controlled various nefarious activities, including the nocturnal bouncers at all the major Swansea clubs, and apparently no criminal activity took place without Philly either initiating it, or giving it his blessing. Philly was always in the know. In the 1970s I actually worked with Philly James and his crew on the door of the Penthouse Nightclub. My task was to collect the entrance cash. I can vouch that nobody messed with Philly James.

"Who's asking?" hissed the barman, earrings and tattoos prominent in a now totally silent pub as the regulars stopped talking to eavesdrop on our conversation. It was like walking into the saloon bar in a spaghetti western.

"Tell him its Clem," said Dad authoritatively in his best baritone Cambridge and public school accent. The barman disappeared for a moment and then returned, indicating with a twitch of his head where Clem should go. I waited at the bar for a half hour, and on his reappearance, he simply said, "Let's go". We never heard another squeak from the two thugs. Philly James had put the word out.

Clem became very friendly with the trio from BJ Group, and in the early 1990s also invested, along with Percy Watts, in a new Nissan car dealership in Swansea, a project set up by them. Dad was still a huge supporter of Swansea rugby club, which in the 1980s was effectively run by Mike James, an ex-Swansea second-row, civil engineer, a massive bearded, not-to-be-messed with character; whilst

Rob Davies became a stalwart of the Swansea Patron's club, a kind of kitchen cabinet of supporters who sustained a bar under the grandstand on match days, with a culture of a gentlemanly drinking brotherhood, with the emphasis on drink, more drink…and of course, rugby. By the mid-1990s, as the sport of rugby football braced itself for the professional era, Swansea RFC was fortunate to have these two men as the principal financiers that eased Swansea's way into the professional age, investing their individual wealth confronting the massive acceleration in wage inflation caused by runaway opportunists like John Hall at Newcastle and Ashley Levett at Richmond.

They were subsequently joined by Roger Blyth, and these three became the driving force that firstly sustained the professional game in Swansea, and then set up The Ospreys, which has proven to be the most successful of the four Welsh pro regions. Whilst I am in no way impartial, I genuinely believe that these three benefactors have never received the appreciation they deserve in sustaining professional rugby in Swansea. Unlike other so-called benefactors in other regions, they have never sought to recover their funding by terming the funding as loans. Clem was a huge supporter of all three, frequently dispensing advice and council to Mike James on matters affecting Swansea RFC and, as a player particularly Roger Blyth whose father, Len had played with Clem both for Wales and Swansea in the 1950's. Roger won 6 caps for Wales in the 1970's, and was unfortunate to play in an era that included JPR Williams; Roger was as fine an attacking full-back as any player in the world at that time, blessed with a tall, athletic frame, immense pace, lovely soft hands, and a howitzer of a punt that could float a ball 70 yards at St Helen's.

Dad became great friends with Rob Davies who would become my brother-in-law, and in the 1980s and '90s we often travelled together to the 5 Nations capitals. One special memory I have is sitting together at 2am in the morning in La Rhumerie, at Saint Germain des Près, where we were laughing so hard that tears were rolling down the cheeks of both Clem and Rob as Bill Hughes recounted the story of Jacques Lafitte, the famous French fighter pilot.

It was during the late 1980s and early 1990s that Clem developed what would become a one man vendetta in his questioning and criticisms of the various corporate governance issues affecting the Welsh Rugby Union. In 1989, Dad wrote in *The Observer:*

> The affairs of the Welsh Rugby Union have now dropped to such an appalling level, with the resignation of its President, Clive Rowlands, and secretary of eight months, David East, that only a revolution led by the clubs can put the national game back on its feet.
>
> Matters have reached such depths of duplicity that if the union was a publicly-owned commercial concern, it would surely have been put into liquidation and a receiver appointed.

The following 5 Nations campaign was a shambolic travesty of Wales' stature in the rugby world prompting Clem to thunder again in *The Observer* on April 1 1990:

> Tony O'Reilly, the most perceptive Irishman I ever knew, used to say to me: rugby is simply not a game without the Welsh - but then he was largely associated with the decades from 1950-80, when Wales carried an aura of achievement and were probably among the most popular, dignified and sought-after teams in world rugby. I doubt if he would say the same today.
>
> ...In Dublin we watched the nadir of Welsh rugby, the first wooden spoon, not only of their lifetime but in the whole proud history of the

game in Wales. We watched the accompanying ineptness with horror, which might just be the catalyst to spark off a popular revolt against Welsh mismanagement.

Let us say it: Wales are now not only a laughing stock, but are deeply unpopular overseas, particularly in Canada, Australia and New Zealand. Crisis has followed crisis, but the Welsh Rugby Union members have remained masters of inactivity. Remember the Evans Report and the successive crippling defeats by New Zealand - whatever happened to this season's inquiry into the South African affair?... Wales do not now have anybody of any stature from within their own ranks to produce a new revolution... The WRU could do with opening the window and letting some fresh talent in. I would go further: in June the clubs should demand that the WRU be reconstituted and rebuilt from top to bottom.

Clem refused to go away, as he continued to excoriate the union for its mismanagement of the game in Wales, pointing to the dearth of sports management and rugby expertise within, and the passive acceptance of low standards that exposed the Welsh game to ridicule on the playing field. In March 1991 he again roared in frustration: "The accelerating decline of the past decade suggests that it is time for a revolution in Welsh rugby. There has been one humiliating defeat after another, bickering and hastily made decisions which have proved calamitous. Welsh rugby lies in ruins."

Yet the situation got worse that summer as Wales were destroyed in Australia, losing 63-6 in Brisbane, and 38-3 in Sydney. By now Clem's campaign for radical change in Welsh rugby was becoming repetitive and more desperate, as an August 4th review raised his criticism to new levels, whilst welcoming the appointment of Alan

Davies as the new coach and chairman of selectors:

> Davies now has the unenviable job of converting a rabble of a team into some semblance of respectability in the eight weeks left before the World Cup. It is a virtually impossible task but I believe that he is the only man in the four home unions capable of rescuing Wales from being a Third World rugby nation.
>
> After the Welsh debacle in Australia, this appointment comes not too soon. Smashed-flat chicken is not only a popular Australian dish but also a perfect description of what happened Down Under, where Welsh behaviour on and off the field was both bizarre and disgraceful.
>
> Apart from the well-chronicled and ill-disciplined events in Brisbane after the Test, there were other dreadful moments of misbehaviour. I can confirm that the Welsh Baptist Church, in their assertion that the team's poor form was due to heavy drinking, were closer to the truth than many suspected, as some players were on the beer and out late before the big matches. Furthermore the rift between Clive Rowlands, the manager, and Ron Waldron, the coach, became so marked, and the players' discipline so poor, that the tour disintegrated into near anarchy.
>
> This breakdown is only a culmination of years of neglect and poor leadership which have made Wales extremely unpopular tourists. The KGB-style attitudes of the WRU are now legendary. In the past 10 years they have shelved report after report which have been critical of them and have made bad decisions galore. Carelessly, they lost two secretaries in a year, were responsible for disastrous appointments and made fools of themselves over South Africa. Leadership has

been non-existent and Welsh rugby is now left only with its memories and history.

The rumblings continued over the next decade, but Alan Davies sparked a brief revival by winning the 5 Nations Championship in 1994 following the inevitable humiliation of losing to Western Samoa at the 1991 world cup. The corporate governance issues never went away despite the appointment of some quality people like Vernon Pugh QC and a living holder of the Victoria Cross, Sir Tasker Watkins. By 1994, Clem had become a powerful advocate of rebuilding the National Stadium on a greenfield site in Bridgend, on Island Farm, that had housed a prisoner of war camp in World War II. Unfortunately, this period also saw the rise to power of Glanmor Griffiths, who typically displayed the low cunning only a WRU committeeman can muster with the survival instincts of Tolkien's Gollum! Griffiths, a squat, white-haired, beetle-eye-browed man, in the view of many has done more to destroy Welsh rugby single-handed than any other appointee, in the history of the WRU.

Griffiths presided over the early years of chaos as the sport went professional in 1995, and took the union close to bankruptcy with the over-ambitious and expensive rebuilding of the Millenium Stadium, with Welsh rugby forced to play catch-up ever since. Welsh rugby has been starved of investment until recently as the stadium debts were paid off precipitately in order to conform with the onerous banking covenants signed off by Griffiths. He compounded the situation by refusing to consider an offer from the English clubs to allow 8 Welsh teams into the pro English league then being set up. Today, following a tempestuous period under Roger Lewis as CEO, and Warren Gatland as coach, Wales have regained some respect as a major rugby nation, although the record against the three major southern hemisphere teams remains disastrous. The hope is that the relatively new management team led by Gareth Davies the Chairman, Martin Philips the CEO, and Dennis Gethin the President can restore long term financial stability for both the professional and recreational games in Wales. The recent expansion of the Pro 14 league, that added two South African teams is a reflection of some new, brave, radical thinking by the WRU and other stakeholder unions, with a clear understanding of the need to grow the professional regional teams whilst preserving the interests of the existing WRU clubs, and new forces within the game like the accelerating growth of women's rugby. However, if Clem were alive today he would maintain the pressure to improve standards, but also applaud the massive improvements that have taken place under this new regime.

10

THE LEGACY, THE EULOGY AND THE EPILOGUE

Clem died on September 5th, 1996, succumbing to a second, massive heart-attack at his home in Swansea. It happened at around 8.30am in the morning and he had just completed his final broadcast on BBC Radio Wales earlier at the Swansea Studios.

His funeral was held at St Paul's and Holy Trinity Church, Sketty, only four hundred yards from his final Swansea residence in De La Beche Road. A crowd of mourners were unable to fit inside the church and a multitude were locked out as the International rugby world assembled to pay tribute to a man, who in the words of an emotional Stephen Jones, was "simply a great, great bloke". The pallbearers were from Swansea RFC - a mix of Welsh international stars, British Lions, and Swansea stalwarts, some of whom had played with myself, Greg, and Mark. Clem is buried in the churchyard overlooking Swansea Bay where he once sailed his beloved *Baa-Baa*, and St Helen's, whose turf he bestrode with such grace, aggression, and skill forty years earlier, and which was one of the greatest sporting arenas of the of the twentieth century.

> I had an inheritance from my father
> It was the moon and the sun.

> And though I roam all over the world,
> The spending of it's never done.
> *Ernest Hemingway, For Whom the Bells Toll*

Clem had four children from his first marriage to Ann Barter: myself, Caroline, Gregory, and Mark. Whilst I would never describe Dad as a homebuilder, he was committed to family, and insisted on traditional gatherings on occasions like Christmas and Easter. He always insisted that he treated the four of us in an equal fashion, and as the elder child I am not aware of any friction between us apart from what is normal between siblings. He put us all through university, and maintained his life philosophy of "work hard and play hard."

Caroline, my sister, the only girl of the family with three brothers all obsessed with rugby, turned out, maybe not surprisingly, to be the creative member of the Thomas clan. She played piano, violin, and guitar, and from an early age was wheeled out to perform at family parties. *Edelweiss* being her star turn. She was a founding cast member of the renowned West Glamorgan Youth Theatre and met many lifelong friends there including Kevin Allen, director of the infamous Twin Town who was also best friends with Roger Pomphrey, who she later married. She obtained a degree in Drama and History of Art from Kent University and went on to have a varied and flamboyant career. Never one to conform to a corporate career, her path was set when Dad gave her money to buy a Jaeger suit for interviews and she spent it on a Sony Walkman and a designer denim jacket!

After working for "Action Space" at Covent Garden organising all the street entertainment with "Alternative Arts", she progressed to a career in television production, working in live television on the BBC flagship programmes *The Late, Late Breakfast Show with Noel Edmonds* and *Top of the Pops* and worked with many of the burgeoning comic talents of the 80s including Ruby Wax and Helen Fielding, the writer of *Bridget Jones*. Caroline produced a number of music videos with her husband Roger in the early 90s, most notably UB40; and was snapped up by Channel 4 to become Editorial Associate for the Arts and Music department. She also produced two outstanding documentaries: *Jimi Hendrix's Electric Ladyland* (directed by Roger) and *The Band.*

Caroline's wedding to Roger - who by then had started working on the iconic Comic Strip films - was the wedding of the year in Swansea in 1993, with the picturesque church at Oxwich swamped by a host of London musicians, artists, actors and reprobates, with the reception at The Rhossili Hotel (then owned by Ian Jones) - the venue of a truly rock and roll reception party that went on for days. It ended up in Vincents, a pub owned by myself and friends with a Blues and Oyster lunch 'do' with Keith Allen singing a hysterical Blues ode to my father backed by Swansea guitarist Martin Ace and others. I seem to remember Kevin Allen also doing a startling rendition of 'Blue Suede Shoes' in Welsh!

Dad loved Caroline's colourful life in London and soon signed up to become a country member of the Groucho Club, spending many a showbiz night up there with her and Roger. Roger was one of those guys who knew everyone in Soho and West London and went on to a successful career of directing music and documentary films before his untimely death in 2014. Their son, Tom Pomphrey, is now working in camera departments in the film industry, successfully picking up the creative baton from his father and mother.

Caroline's wedding was the stage for a moment of rare embarrassment for Dad. The wedding ceremony was held at the picturesque Norman church on Oxwich Point, St Iltyd's, where reputedly, a Christian building has been present since the 6th century. The road stops 400 yards before the Church, and is situated adjacent to one of Gower's most popular tourist beaches. That July the place was jammed, broiling under a burning sun. I was given the job of guarding a precious strip of tarmac where the road ended.

As is the want of all brides, Caroline was late. Finally, the Roll-Royce came around the corner, and stopped abruptly a good 200 yards shy. What the hell is going on I thought, worried that Clem had maybe upset her en route. The car door swung open violently, and Caroline, hiking the white folds of her long wedding dress, dashed out as if shot from a canon, swept up the trailing folds of cloth, and sprinted up the path toward the Oxwich Bay Hotel. She had been caught short… leaving Clem alone in the back of the Rolls, twiddling his thumbs.

The Roller attracted the attention of dozens of holidaymakers. A German tourist, who was shooting reels of film, asked me excitedly who the gentleman in morning dress was. I told him it was the Grandee of Gower returning from his lunch! The German promptly ran over to the car and with the expertise of a paparazzi continued shooting photos of the astonished Clem, his face reddening, trapped in the back of the Rolls. At one point, Clem had over a dozen cameras trained on him, flashing away! After what must have seemed an eternity, Caroline reappeared, and the car finally parked up. It was a funny moment.

I asked Caroline for her best recollections of Dad, and she wrote:

> Dad was a great Dad, always on-the-go with some enthusiasm or other. I remember most his huge appetite for life, his curiosity and genuine engagement with people and of course his ever-naughty chuckle! He was a great leveller was Dad, never a snob, and walking with him was almost always an adventure and the best of fun. You never quite knew who you would meet or where you would end up. One thing Dad loved above all

else was a convivial and hearty environment. He joined the infamous Groucho Club in Soho after seeing what fun Roger and I had there and became one of the favourite country members. Dad fitted right in amongst the boho media crowd and they held him close and cherished his lust for life. I believe that the camaraderie Dad enjoyed there brought back memories of the smoky, wild West Wales pubs along the well-trodden routes to St Clears and all the other cattle marts and the wonderful colourful characters Dad found there.

Dad taught me to be brave, to be unafraid of trying new things. "You reap what you sow" I remember him instructing me driving along the Mumbles road in the 1980s. I treasure that.

I take pride in my Thomas go-getting and energetic genes. They say the apple doesn't fall far from the tree and in my case I have returned to Swansea after a rollercoaster time in London, to find that Swansea and South Wales continue to hold his memory dear. Dad continues to cast a very long shadow: he was and forever will be one of Swansea's greatest ambassadors to the world. I am proud to have him as my father.

My brother Gregory attended Swansea University, and after obtaining an oceanography degree, promptly married his childhood sweetheart, Karen Price, in 1985. Greg was a highly-rated centre and wing, possessing a turbo-like change of pace, with the ability to show and go, teasing defenders as he smoothly glided past, ball always in two hands. He won every schoolboy rugby honour including Welsh schoolboys (1984), followed by Swansea University, Welsh Universities, and Students. He played first team rugby football for Swansea RFC (1981-84), and London Welsh (1985-89).

In 1990 Greg and Karen opted to emigrate to

Australia, and whilst Greg scored hopelessly low in the immigration points system since oceanographers were two-a-penny in Australia, Karen was highly valued as an occupational therapist.

Greg's rugby career continued with Randwick Rugby for whom he became top points scorer in 1991, and he played for the famous Sydney club until 1998. Whilst in London, Greg had joined the Institute of Marine Engineers as a media publisher, educating himself in the developing technology of desktop publishing systems and academic journalism.

In 1995 he joined the Australian Rugby Union as their media and communications manager, attending the 1995 Rugby World Cup in South Africa. He moved on in 1997 to become the senior media advisor to the Sydney Organising Committee for the Olympic Games, managing the media operations in the aquatics centre. In 2004 he left Australia and "headed home" to Europe to become Head of Media and Communications for the International Rugby Board, today rebranded as World Rugby. He moved his family to Dublin where the IRB is based, and in 2007, established his blueprint for Rugby World Cup media operations. Returning to Sydney in 2009 as a media & communications consultant, Greg has continued to work for World Rugby at the 2011 and 2015 world cups in New Zealand and England. He is currently planning the rugby world cup media operations for Japan in 2019.

One of the conclusions drawn from the disastrous Clive Woodward-coached 2005 British and Irish Lions tour to New Zealand was a unanimity amongst players, rugby journalists, and administrators, that the media operation conducted by the political PR guru Alastair Campbell had been a total disaster.

The next tour to South Africa was to be managed by the ex-flying Welsh winger Gerald Davies who in conjunction with the coach, Ian McGeechan, was determined to appoint, what he described to me over lunch at the Cardiff and County Club as "a proper rugby bloke with media expertise". Greg fitted the bill precisely, and so became Head of Media for the 2009 and 2013 British and Irish Lions tours to South Africa and Australia.

In November 1996, only ten weeks after Dad's death, the publishing house Mainstream organised the launch of Clem's book, *The History of the British & Irish Lions*. The book was well received, and after every tour since has been updated with the addition of an extra chapter written by Greg. Before the 2017 tour to New Zealand Greg completely revamped the book's design and content, ably assisted by Rob Cole. They produced a beautifully crafted coffee table volume, containing photos, programme covers, original match reports and more comprehensive statistics.

Today Greg also performs some consulting on behalf of World Rugby to assist the Oceania countries in the Pacific, and is also the Head of Media and Communications for SANZAAR (Super Rugby and The Rugby Championship).

I called Greg in Australia and asked for his personal reflections on Dad, and he wrote:

> Living and growing up in Swansea as a young sportsman was difficult being the "Son of" a famous Welsh sports hero.
>
> The tag was a constant and whenever you turned up for a match or were in the company of others it was always this is Greg Thomas "son of Clem" as you were introduced.
>
> But one thing I always admired was that Dad never tried to influence anyone in terms of who I was and what I did as a sportsman. He believed that if I was good enough I would be selected on merit. Hence at the various rugby trials I attended - and there were many - he never came. He never stood on the touchline alongside all the other

famous grandfathers, uncles and fathers. Many might find this strange and unsupportive but when I was selected for teams it always felt good that it was because of my performance not because Dad was there influencing the decisions.

He also did not mind what sport you were playing. I was a pretty good soccer player when young and played for Swansea Schools Under 11s (1973-74). We were Welsh and British Champions that year beating all before us but Dad never pressured me into playing rugby and said I should play whatever sport I liked. Of course I moved onto Gowerton School in 1975 and it was a rugby school and I ended up playing rugby for the next 20 years!

Dad was always one to give advice and I can remember the tut-tut or words of disapproval during my informative years when searching for a career. I tried accountancy (the day I quit and told Dad was a difficult day to say the least), I tried scientific research (on the back of my oceanography degree) but eventually found publishing and the media. Many have asked if I naturally followed in the path of Dad who was an accomplished rugby writer following his playing days but it was more an accident than a choice. One thing Dad never really encouraged was to see any of his sons follow him into the butchery business. It was a hard life and living, and he always said he wanted better for us. That said he always press ganged us into working in the abattoir, his butcher shops or on the meat delivery wagons in the school holidays!

Dad was also brutally honest and when I announced in 1989 that Karen and I were heading to Australia to work for a few years he looked at me and with that characteristic twinkle in his eye he said, "You will never come back". I laughed at the time but he was dead right. He had travelled to Australia, New Zealand and South Africa as a player and journalist and loved the southern hemisphere... he knew what I would find there and almost 30 years later we are still in Sydney. Of course, he died too young in my book and unfortunately missed the opportunity of seeing his grandchildren grow up; they would have loved him and he would have loved them.

Despite being so far away from Swansea and not seeing Dad too often, our paths crossed many times thanks to rugby. We spent many years together attending and boozing at the Hong Kong Sevens and his advice was always welcome. In 1995 I was working as a magazine publisher in Sydney and was asked to become the first professional media manager for the Wallabies. I asked Dad about the move and he believed the new world of professional Rugby would have a lot to offer and it was an exciting time for the game. Indeed, Clem was a progressive thinker and would have loved Rugby Sevens' introduction to the Olympic Games. A realist, he was supportive of the move to professionalism (which had just eventuated before he passed); the World Cup excited him and I am sure he would be pleased with the recent progress of the Northern Hemisphere. One thing he would be disappointed about is Wales' inability to beat the All Blacks. He played in the last team to achieve that in 1953.

So I took up the role with the Australian Rugby Union and several months later I went to the Rugby World Cup with the Wallabies. Dad was there covering the tournament for *The Observer*. We had a great time.

He was right - Rugby has been exciting and has

provided me with a rewarding career over the last 20 years. As a journalist prior to joining the Wallabies, I was so proud to be published alongside Dad in *The Observer* on Sunday 28 July 1991. Wales and England were touring Australia, both were well beaten and our articles, critical of the state of northern hemisphere rugby, appeared side by side in the sports section. I have the articles framed in my study.

The other thing I reflect on proudly is following Dad into the fold of the British & Irish Lions. While I cannot claim it was due to my playing ability it is still one of the biggest thrills in my career. As Head of Media I did two tours - 2009 to South Africa and 2013 to Australia. One of my great disappointments is that Dad never got to see that but I take solace in the fact that I was also able to take over the reigns of his wonderfully written work, *The History of the British & Irish Lions*. The official history covers over 125 years of glorious rugby tradition including Dad's tour to South Africa in 1955.

I am 54 years old now and yes the old moniker is still there. Just the other day I was among a group of rugby fanatics in Johannesburg at the Ellis Park Museum and I was introduced as Greg Thomas, head of media of Super Rugby, "son of Clem Thomas"…You know what? I am proud to say I am!

My other brother Mark, also enjoyed a rich and colourful rugby and sporting career, including following in Clem's footsteps to spend three years at Cambridge University. I recently called Mark in Monaco and asked for his personal reflections on Dad, and he wrote:

Just like my grandfather, father and two brothers, Greg and Chris. I followed the family into senior first-class rugby, playing my first game for Swansea at 18 years of age. To run out at St Helen's was a dream come true. I watched my heroes play there, whilst my highlight was selection against Fiji in 1985 before heading up to Magdalene College, Cambridge University. I played in two Varsities, and have bragging rights over Dad by scoring the winning try in the 1987 match.

My first degree was at Loughborough University where I shared a house with future England internationals, Andy Robinson and John Wells. At Cambridge, where I studied Land Economy, my team-mates included some very good players, notably Gavin Hastings, Andy Harriman, Chris Oti, Mike Hall and Rob Wainwright who remain close friends to this very day. College days led to representing Wales at Students level, and then playing for London Welsh, Harlequins and finally settling at Rosslyn Park (1993). I then gained selection for Wales by Alan Davies and played in the Hong Kong 7's and the inaugural Rugby World Cup 7's in Edinburgh. Alan knew that I had already spent three years focused on what was then an unofficial world circuit, and that I was one of a handful of Welsh players with any real 7's expertise.

As a youngster I had been blessed with athleticism and pace, which is why a 6 foot 5 ins winger emerged, and combined with my footballing skills, I played in every position in the three-quarters. My athletics career certainly helped, and at Loughborough I ran in the 100m and 200m British Universities championships, clocking 11.22secs in the 100m and competing on the same team as Seb Coe! Not bad for a rugby player.

Dad had always encouraged me to travel with my sport, and during my university summers I trained at high altitude and played for Vail in Colorado, USA, and then spent a season in Durban, South Africa playing for DHS, with a brief appearance for Natal. I also played for a multitude of colourful 7's teams over the years, notably Bahrain Warblers, Crawshays, Penguins and Public School Wanderers. The cast of characters I played with and against is a rugby hall of fame in itself, and included my great pal, Gavin Hastings, Michael Lynagh, Eric Rush, Pat Lam, Andre Joubert and Troy Croker. I once got beaten black and blue at truncheon point by the Spanish police in Benidorm, and was lucky to play for the USA in the Bermuda Classic World Cup in 2002.

Following the RWC in 1993 I was invited to play for the Grenoble Presidents XV for their Centenary against the French Barbarians, it was a high scoring match 54-48 or something like that. I scored 2 tries and was invited to play for Racing Club Paris by Franc Mesnel and also for Racing Club Nice by Jeff Tordo, the French captain the following season. It was a pro contract and the chance to live in the south of France, learn a new language, and get involved in international business was very attractive. My godfather, the artist Andrew Vicari, lived in Monaco so I had a support system and having played for Crawshays in the Monte Carlo 7s in 1986 and 1987 I had met Prince Albert and we continued our friendship as the years progressed. I even ended up as his brakeman in the Monaco bobsled team for 6 years taking part in many world championships in both the 2 and 4 man competing in Nagano, Calgary, St

Moritz and many other tracks.

I remember Christmas at Dad's after my first race and I was black and blue from the bobsled crashing in St Moritz and hitting the walls. Dad just laughed, saying I should have played rugby for a few more years. Given my friendship with the Prince, it is no surprise that we visited Wales regularly for 6 Nations rugby matches over the past twenty years. My last memory of Dad and the last time I saw him was for the 1996 Wales v France international. I had brought Prince Albert over to Swansea for a long rugby weekend - Dad gave him a grand tour of the Gower and we had a lot of fun in the local bars around Cardiff before the match, which was, I believe, the last match before the Arms Park got demolished and rebuilt as the Millenium Stadium.

Having worked for Richard Ellis in commercial property in London after my Cambridge days I now live in Monaco. Dad was a Francophile and loved France and I know he was happy when I told him I was moving to live there. If he was here today I am sure he would have visited many more times and enjoyed the red wines, rosé and cheese he so loved.

Monaco has been one hell of an experience, my best friend is the Prince and all because I played 7's rugby here many moons ago! The Prince presented us the losers' medals back in 1987 with Dad in attendance. It's funny how life works out and how your journey develops. I have had an adventure living here and have been involved in several unique projects, from sapphire mining in Madagascar, to marine salvage, treasure hunting in Cuba, the Philippines and around the coast of Britain, where amongst other things we found the World War I wrecks, The SS Arabic, off Kinsale, a

White Star Line ocean liner sunk on 19th August 1915 by a German U Boat, and The SS Hesperaan, a British ocean liner of the Allan Line also sunk in 1915, 85 miles from the Fastnet by U20. This was the same U-Boat that sunk the RMS Lusitania which basically brought America into the war. Dad always said, "life is the sum of your experiences." Now I am vice chairman of a holding company that works in finance investing internationally with a syndicate of families including the Brunei Royal family. My journey continues, but if it were not for my rugby I would not be here now.

Dad was an adventurer and I believe I inherited this aspect of his personality. I know he enjoyed hearing my stories and was always supportive of my next project. One time when I was in Antananorivo, Madagascar, I got a call from him saying ITV wanted me for Gavin Hastings' - *This is Your Life* - TV programme (Dad wrote his biography, the book is called *High Balls & Happy Hours*). Gav and I are still great mates after our Cambridge years, so I flew to Glasgow from Africa with a pocket full of raw sapphires worth $50k and got there just in time to be the last guest introduced, it was a very amusing evening! Dad was thrilled when I scored the winning try in the varsity. I know that it gave him as much pleasure as myself, when the cameras panned to the press box he was jumping up and down!

Dad was always full of surprises, he ensured that whenever I was back from university, on my return to Cambridge or Loughborough, I could stop at the butcher's shop or the cold stores and fill the boot of the car to the brim with meat. I used to feed our rugby teams on fine welsh lamb and sirloin steaks for a week after and when he came to visit he always bough a side of beef with him; the boys in the team loved him.

Dad was always up for a challenge and the funniest memory I have is when he was on his second honeymoon and he took me along to Corfu with him and Joyce. He had organised to go parasailing – it was so much fun as a teenager and I was up in the air in a heartbeat being pulled behind a speed boat. However, when Dad gave it a go, it was priceless - I remember him telling the boat driver to give it everything...! What happened next was hilarious. Dad was preparing himself on the jetty, when the boat sped off, the parachute filled with air, but Dad being substantially heavier than me, got dragged along the top of the waves, just about managing to get his feet out of the water. I always suspected Dad walked on water and now I had first hand proof! It took forever for him to get into the air. I was in absolute tears, and he was laughing the whole time! That summed Dad up, even when the shit was hitting the fan he always saw a way to get through it.

If Dad was here today I'm sure he would be applauding the Lions in New Zealand this summer, as the last time they drew a series was when he played in the 1955 tour of South Africa. I know he would be impressed with the skill levels and fitness of today's players but would be bemoaning the scrum situation where we lose 5-10 minutes a game having to reset scrums. He would frown on the focus on defensive systems that are stifling the game and would applaud the Super 16 teams who play with such abandon, and the growth of Argentina as a world force. Dad would be full of joy for the Fijians in winning the Olympic gold, as Fiji was his favourite place to visit. He would applaud the resurgence of Welsh, Irish and Scottish rugby given our limited resources and would be envious of the English administrative organisation. He would be shocked at the politics and economics affecting the Australians and Springboks. And as for the All Blacks, I feel he would congratulate them on their ruthless efficiency and heads-up rugby and still be smiling knowing he was one of a few Welshmen who have experienced the joy of beating them.

At Clem's memorial service held in St Bride's church on Fleet Street, Cliff Morgan delivered a superbly crafted masterpiece of Welsh oratory, which sadly was never recorded. Clem's great Irish friend and playing colleague from the Lions tour, Tony O'Reilly, wrote in *The Independent*, which he owned, his own private tribute:

It was the laugh that distinguished Clem Thomas. Part upper-class, part working-class; a cross between a real chuckle and just the hint of a tease. It was the sort of laugh that made you think he doesn't give a damn, but then he just might.

I first met him as a very young 18-year old Lion at Eastbourne as we prepared for the 1955 tour of Africa, or South Africa and Rhodesia as it was then called. He was kind, generous and tough. And then I remembered that he had marked Paddy Kavanagh - one of the legendary brothers - out of the game against Wales a few weeks earlier. Every time Kavanagh ran at Cliff Morgan he either waltzed with Clem or had to run around an obstructing Thomas to get at the Welsh Wizard.

Need I say that Morgan had one of his greater games for Wales. Clem, Russ Robbins and Jimmy Greenwood of Scotland are among the great back-rows that ever played for the Lions, and, were it not for his appendicitis, we might well have gone one better than split 2-2, a historic series with Africa in that startling summer of 1955.

Since then, he had never aged; the same boyish enthusiasm, the same Socratic questioning spirit, the same toughness to ask the hard question as a journalist and often of a friend. The Welsh as always knew him better than anyone. Leighton Jenkins (who played 5 times in the back row for Wales 1954-56 and captained Newport to their win over Australia in 1957) said to me once, "Watch him" as the Barbarians played Swansea during the Easter tour, "Watch him" he said, "as he lets the opposing out-half go for the gap and then catches him by his collar as he goes through" And he said, "The out-half's legs do run up an imaginary wall."

He lived life to the full and he enjoyed every minute of it - and right, I'm sure, to the end. I will treasure him in my box of memories. A memory of a big, fast, tough, generous, rawboned Welsh flanker of the highest class. They don't come better." - *Tony O'Reilly, The Independent, September 1996.*

It is over twenty years since Clem passed away, and I often wonder what he would have made of the painful yet exciting transition away from amateurism to professionalism.

As a journalist and commentator on the game, Clem was unequivocal in insisting on the highest of standards both on the playing side and the administrative side of the game. His voice consistently defended the ethics of rugby, and he attempted to promote the highest of standards within the WRU, whose mismanagement and ongoing incompetence frustrated Clem enormously right until the very end. Dad defended the amateur principle up until he conceded that the southern hemisphere countries were already running rings around the amateur rule in the early 1990's. But in 1985 he wrote in his magazine, Rugby Wales a vigorous defence of the amateur principal, following the Australian Rugby Union's unilateral decision to pay a tax-free sum of £250 a week. At that time the IRB rules allowed a daily touring allowance of just £12 a day:

> It seems to me that these recent Wallabies have hounded rugby football down the road of professionalism at a pace which has led the IRB groping in their dust.
> It will require a remarkable piece of statesmanship by the governing body of the game if amateur principles are to be maintained, upheld and safeguarded. I continue to hold the view that rugby union football - one of the great team games of the world - should always be played for fun within the context of an ordinary working life. To professionalise it would be to spoil its ethics and objectives.
> It would benefit only a handful of top players at the high price of cheapening a game which gives so much pleasure as it stands and where rewards can never be measured in monetary terms.

Overall, Clem would have applauded the global explosion of interest in rugby football, an awareness and an increase in playing numbers since his death that he always thought possible with the correct strategies applied by the rugby authorities. The acceptance of rugby as an Olympic sport has transformed the smaller, novice rugby nations into focused contenders for medals through their access to governmental sports funds exclusive for Olympic sport.

This wave of enthusiasm for rugby has, at the same time been reinforced by the ongoing success of the four-yearly Rugby World Cup tournament, with viewing numbers on TV ranking the event as the 3rd most popular sport on the planet, after the Olympics and the soccer World Cup.

The growth in rugby union football's popularity is mirrored across a range of statistical indicators. It was estimated by research analysts that the Rugby World Cup of 2015 held in England achieved a total TV and digital audience of 1 billion people, with 120 million watching the final live from Twickenham. This growth was driven by a 221% increase in audiences from the Far East, with 25 million switching on to watch Japan play Samoa following the astonishing win over the Springboks. Japan's last-minute match-winning try against South Africa generated 1.3 million YouTube views alone!

Clem often joked that within twenty or thirty years, countries like the USA and Russia, with their large pools of excellent athletes would be contesting rugby world cup finals, and that small nations like Wales and New Zealand would have to rely on their unique passion for the sport along with centuries of sporting traditions that would translate into the genetic code of future All Blacks and Welsh internationals.

Clem would have welcomed this increase in global participation, having himself played a small role in the 1970s and 1980s encouraging the emergence of both Fiji and Samoa. He became somewhat of a mouthpiece for these two rugby-mad communities, by exhorting the WRU and others to take full tours from these developing nations. When Swansea RFC held their centenary in 1973, it was Clem who persuaded Bruce Barter and the Swansea committee to invite the Fijians to be the centerpiece of the season's celebration. And after the humiliating defeat to Western Samoa at the 1991 world cup, I was with Clem when he went over to the Samoan hotel after the match, and was warmly embraced by Tufuga Efi, who became Samoa's Head of State (2007-2017). He quietly said to

Clem how sorry he was that, of all the teams they could have beaten, it had to be Wales, the one country who had already treated Samoan rugby with respect by awarding them matches in the 1980's. Tufuga believed that positive commentary from Clem in *The Observer* afforded them a credibility and exposure that they had not had previously.

As Mark wrote, Clem would have been thrilled by Fiji's gold medal performances at the Rio Olympics, winning their first ever Olympic medal of any sport, and he would have strongly supported the huge improvements in women's rugby playing standards over the past twenty years.

I believe Clem would have been far more demanding of the rugby administrations, whether at World Rugby for the international game, or the WRU and RFU over their ability to manage the financial aspects of professionalising a sport like rugby. He would have demanded, indeed more likely bayed for, far greater financial transparency and better funding models for both the game in Wales, and the rest of the British Isles. He knew by the time he died that professionalism threatened to rip the heart out of the game he loved so much. As he wrote: "What people do for love, they seldom do for money. And in any case, where is the money suddenly going to come from?"

Dad had identified the Rugby World Cup as a major source of new revenue, and would have been thrilled to hear England's success in generating in excess of £250 million in revenues. Today, he would be highly critical of the inflation associated with player compensation, arguing that players take too much too soon, which keeps the sport permanently over-leveraged and unable to generate a sensible return. In countries like America, all sports are professional and intended to deliver serious returns to the equity holders. Unfortunately, in the UK, we have not followed this model, preferring to follow the old soccer model, where clubs are running at breakeven, at best. Rugby union is still massively undercapitalised, with dysfunctionality endemic in each country's financial model, where virtually all profits are generated through the international game.

Clem would be currently warning the wealthier unions of England, France, Ireland and Wales that they need to also foster the game at both the amateur recreational level and at the professional clubs/regions or franchises. Professional sport requires financial rewards to be shared amongst all the stakeholders. Players are the essential component, but so are the customers of the game, the fans, supporters, and essentially in the digital age, television and media.

During the 1970s and 1980s Clem consistently criticised the unions who control the game for their lack of management expertise. Matters have slightly improved, but General Committees still lack the intellect to properly strategise a future and demonstrate long term stability from proven business modelling. Marketing of the game is left to television companies like SKY, with only lip service marketing from the unions who operate a cartel that rakes in the cash from the traditional competitions they control, namely the 6 Nations and the now valued British Lions brand.

The more powerful and risk aware clubs from England are now questioning the British Lions contribution to their future, an example of the sport's dysfunctionality within the British Isles. The reality is that the RFU own 25% of the 4 Nations team, and take their fair share of the profits from the Lions brand, both directly from revenues generated, and by way of reciprocal tour arrangements which bring the All Blacks and Springboks to Twickenham.

Clem would endorse the requirement of World Rugby to provide strong inspirational leadership, and would applaud its position as a leader in sports education, sports medicine, player welfare and integrity, with World Rugby employees today perceived as best-in-class benchmarks for other sports administrations.

His one major criticism would be to level the charge at World Rugby that it remains still a closed shop at the top Tier One level, sustaining its financial cartel. The four Home Unions retain a natural risk-aversity to properly democratising the game, with the USA, Russia, Georgia, Japan, Romania, Canada, and Germany, plus the three Pacific Islands, Fiji, Samoa, and Tonga, all knocking on the door to Tier One status. Since Dad died, only Italy, who joined the 6 Nations in 2000, and Argentina in 2013, have been invited to join the old club. Rugby union football needs to establish a more meritocratic pathway that allows these aspiring countries access to regular Tier One competition outside of the 4-yearly world cup cycle.

The 6 Nations is consistently termed "unique" and "the best international rugby competition in the world", but times move on, and with today's vibrant and increasingly competitive Tier Two European Championship run by FIRA, World Rugby should intercede to provide some radical leadership. This would focus minds in the Celtic nations to manage their resources more efficiently to ensure that their place in the top European tier is maintained.

Clem quarreled with the WRU, or certain representatives of it, from the day of his first cap in Paris, when a blazered middle-aged WRU committeeman pinched his gifted bottle of Cognac at the post match dinner. Over the next decades, he would lead the inquisition into the various issues that cropped up, from South Africa and apartheid, to corporate governance to playing and coaching standards.

I genuinely feel that Clem today would be totally supportive of the relatively new current management team running the WRU. He would encourage them to find imaginative ways to counterbalance the small market that Wales, with only 3 million inhabitants, offers. He would point to Wales' rich, highly respected rugby legacy of

CLEM

almost 150 years. It is this legacy - to which he made his notable contribution, both as a player and as a correspondent - that will sustain Welsh rugby in the years to come.

Clem's family legacy has been further continued by his grandchildren who are a good mix of internationalists, accomplished athletes, creatives and university graduates. His nephew Tom went through the age groups playing scrum-half for Wasps, and today is making a career in film as a young cameraman and director. In the last twelve months he has worked on projects in the USA, London, Wales, and soon India.

Greg's daughters, Lauren and Brooke, both graduated from colleges in Sydney. Lauren followed Greg's career into media and communications, and Brooke is a professional make-up artist, as well as the centre-forward for her Sydney-based team, the Gymea Club, and leading goal scorer in the Sutherland Soccer Association league. Gymea won the under 15A grand final in 2010, and the U21b grand final in 2014. Lauren worked as a media liaison at the 2015 Rugby World Cup at Twickenham, and currently works for the event management company, Live Nation, in London.

Hywelis, my eldest daughter, had a highly accomplished career as a student athlete, representing Wales in four sports, athletics (1500m and 800m), cross-country, triathlon and swimming. She held both the under 16 800m and 1500m Welsh titles at both swimming and athletics simultaneously, and swam for Wales at senior level winning a full Welsh cap. She won gold in the UK School Games in the 800m, and also represented Great Britain juniors in open water championship events across Europe, swimming both 5,000m and 10,000m races in France, Italy, and the UK. She has just graduated from Bath University, and is pursuing a career in management,

CHRIS THOMAS

working under a graduate trainee management scheme with the Quarter Group in Bristol.

Hywelis has inherited the love of the countryside that Clem was always imbued with, and she shoots her own 20 bore under her personal gun license, and sits, plucking feathers from the pheasants she shot in the manner I remember my grandmother Edna doing in Brynamman over fifty years ago.

Siwan, my youngest daughter, lives in Bristol today, starting out as a professional singer-songwriter, and works for Amnesty International, perhaps inheriting some of her grandfather's radical liberalism. She was a hugely talented junior swimmer, winning the British Age group championships for 100m, 200m, and 400m free-style, plus a few butterfly events. She won the Welsh age group 800m and cross-country championships, and also won the under 15 British triathlon championships at Aldershot - the first ever Welsh girl to take gold at the annual inter-regional championships. Hywelis had won several silver and a bronze over the years, but the gold always eluded her. In 2012 Siwan won both the 100m and 200m freestyle golds at the UK School Games, opening the London Aquatics Centre for the Olympics before a crowd of 15,000. She then spent 6th form at The Bolles School in Jacksonville in Florida, winning a USA National Swimming Championship with her swim team, plus she won a bronze medal at the American Junior Swim Championships held at the University of Tennessee. Two years earlier she had won five medals at the Youth Olympics held in Trabzon, Turkey, and medaled at the junior Commonwealth Games.

All these sporting achievements would have thrilled Clem, but a huge debt is owed to the girls' Mum, Marcia Howells, herself an outstanding athlete having swum for Wales, and when selected for Welsh honours at rugby when playing for Swansea Uplands - the club founded by Hywelis' and Siwan's great-grandfather Bruce Barter - discovered that she was pregnant with Hywelis! Marcia selflessly devoted hours to both Hywelis and Siwan.

One of the proudest moments of my life as a father was watching both girls compete together in the same Senior Welsh swim team at the National Pool in Swansea in a Triple Crown International event against Ireland, Scotland, and England, where they both swam in the same 4 x 200m freestyle relay team. Clem would have loved it!

A MAN DIES
So suddenly
in an instant which begins and ends
before we grasp that it has been
a world is gone. Death beckons:
yearnings are ice. Life a wind-
blown ruin. Love, legends of a bygone time.
The voyage seems a route to nothing.
A man dies. Earth revolves
as usual. People gossip…
God bless his soul.
We read obituaries and we walk
on our own
graves.

Chris Thomas
Langland Bay, 2018

COMING SOON

SON OF CLEM

CHRIS THOMAS

It is the Monaco Grand Prix and we have partied ourselves to an aspirin-supported standstill. It is wet, and the palm trees along the Promenade des Anglais glisten with misty rain. At 8.30pm on a Sunday evening, the six of us approach check-in, bedraggled and hungover; there is nothing neither chic nor cool about this perspiring group of rugby-playing Grand Prix fans, invited to Monaco by Jacques Damitio, courtesy of a distant uncle with a luxury apartment in Le Schuykill overlooking the port and Grand Prix circuit.

As we arrive at the check-in to catch our Paris Orly flight, large crowds are ominously gathered outside the terminal. We fear the worst: another strike. And sure enough, this Sunday evening, the entire workforce of ground workers at Nice Airport have decided to abandon their posts on the busiest day of the year. Welcome to France and its bizarre Republic represented by the vague concepts of fraternity, liberty, and égalité. Throw in a bit of solidarity, too. It is total, Gallic chaos. Everyone is screaming at each other, sunglasses perched atop balding hairlines, the smell of stale Guerlain and Dior merging with the thick, Gaulloise-scented air.

"Quelle Bordelle!" (What a fuck up!) screamed Jacques, surveying the carnage inside the terminal as people continued to vent their frustrations at the sight of lines of vacant, unattended check-in desks. We smoke a cigarette by the Air France Paris check-in, and finally Jacques snaps, "Fuck this clusterfuck! I'm going to have a look around to see if I can find someone. They must have more staff coming to sort this chaos out." He promptly jumped over the luggage weighing scales, opened an office door, and disappeared. Five minutes later, a smart, Air France blazered airport worker took his seat at the check-in desk. There was the percussive sound of the rattle and click-clacking of a computer keyboard being vigorously engaged.

The rebellious, waiting crowd quietened instantly in a Pavlovian response to the rattling keyboard. "Form a neat, orderly line!" commanded the airport worker; then I recognised Jacques, peering out from under the peak of his Air France flight captain's cap. Amazingly, hundreds of people immediately formed a conga-like queue. Dominique and Ivan groaned in anticipation of the road-crash to come. Jacques kept theatrically smashing the keyboard, like Liberace playing a piano crescendo. He had found a bunch of manual boarding passes, and had started to check-in passengers, sending them through to the departure lounge. The fifth or sixth passenger was an enormous, buxom blonde woman in her late 50s, with bouffant hair and smothered in a bear-sized fur coat. "Name and passport please, Madam?" asked Jacques unctuously.

"Madam Walentyna Golbenklopf-SachsWasserstein," stated the women rather grandly. Jacques looked at her with raised eyebrows. "Your name is far too long. Wait over there in the queue for people with long, Swiss names!" The woman turned purple and started screaming in rage, but the waiting queue would have none of it, and jeered her out of the way; an Alain Prost fan club literally pushing the poor frau into a corner.

Jacques continued his pantomime for another 10

minutes or so, before the proper airport employees finally
returned to their check-ins. We went through to the
boarding lounge, but the airport was reduced to chaos, and
the hours dragged by with no plane to Paris evident. We
had set up near the bar, and by 11pm Jacques was in full
flow. He loved to strip naked ('a poil'); he had obtained a
tiny waitress' apron that barely covered his manhood, but
failed miserably to hide the cheeks of his arse. Jacques had
acquired a broom that he ostentatiously brushed the floor
with, whilst wiggling his buttocks with a coquettish
flourish. Everybody laughed, and so the next jape was to
introduce our fellow passengers to 'Blanc Neige', (Snow
White). 'Blanc Neige' was Jacques' regular party piece.

By regular I mean he would always pack her in his
bag for away games and trips, where she would inevitably
provide him with a foil to have a laugh over. So, in the
departure lounge, Jacques started blowing up a full-sized,
5ft or so, plastic, Snow White, sex doll he had procured by
fair means or foul. Once up and bouncing, he went
through his crazed comedy routine with her, culminating
when we were finally called to board our plane at 2am with
the six of us shuffling on our knees in a line - a la the
seven dwarves - through the boarding gate, with Jacques
leading at the front holding Snow White high above his
head, all of us singing along in French. *"Hi ho, hi ho, it's off
to work we go, with a shovel and pick and a walking stick, hi ho, hi
ho, hi ho, hi ho!"*

But it was on the plane that the real trouble started.
Jacques buckled Snow White into the seat next to him. He
started to lick the doll lasciviously. Unfortunately, the air-
hostess in our sector of the aircraft had a complete sense
of humour failure, and screamed at Jacques to stop his
nonsense, and take the blow-up doll out of the seat.
Jacques point-blank refused.

She screamed at him in frustration, warning that this
was his last chance.

Jacques again refused, and ignored her, continuing to lavish affection onto his doll. The stewardess ran to the front of the aircraft, and returned with the Air France flight captain, no less.

"Monsieur," the commandant said, "Please pack up the doll."

Jacques, still pretty pissed and full of Republican revolutionary bloody-mindedness, still refused.
"Then this plane will not depart for Paris with you onboard. You must leave the aircraft at once and take your disgusting doll with you."

Jacques simply crossed his arms, and refused to budge an inch. It was at this moment, a handsome, chic, middle-aged, beautifully coiffured gentleman with salt' and pepper hair and a deep, gravelly voice said with some authority:

"Monsieur le Commandant. With all respect, this crazy man has entertained us - the suffering public - for hours, as we waited for Air France and others to assume their responsibilities. It is 2am on a Monday morning, and we are still in Nice. If you insist on removing this man from the plane, then I too will leave the aircraft…" It was Jacques' Spartacus moment: spontaneously dozens of passengers who had heard the verbal exchanges all chanted in unison: "Let him stay! Let him stay!" And a slow hand-clapping chant spread throughout the aircraft. Wisely, the captain turned on his heels, and within 10 minutes we were airborne after yet another French adventure with the indomitable Jacques.

23157703R00208

Printed in Poland
by Amazon Fulfillment
Poland Sp. z o.o., Wrocław